JOURNAL

OF THE

WATERLOO CAMPAIGN

JOURNAL

OF THE

WATERLOO CAMPAIGN

KEPT THROUGHOUT THE CAMPAIGN OF 1815

BY THE LATE
GENERAL CAVALIÉ MERCER
COMMANDING THE 9TH BRIGADE ROYAL ARTILLERY

IN TWO VOLUMES

VOL. II.

WILLIAM BLACKWOOD AND SONS
EDINBURGH AND LONDON
MDCCCLXX

Printed & bound by Antony Rowe Ltd, Eastbourne

CONTENTS OF THE SECOND VOLUME.

CHAPTER XV.

Passage of the Army—The Road blocked up — Preparing to Bivouac—The Nassauers—The White Flag—Reception at Forêt — The Peasantry — Village of Montay—Ordered to Return—A Night Alarm—A Halt—Visit to Cateau—Our Allies Plundering—The German Bocks—Wretched Fare—Return to Forêt—Female Costumes—Louis XVIII.—Again on the Move—Difficulties of our March—Aspect of the Country—Lose our Way—Our Destination at Last—Rejoin the Main Army—Caulincourt's Country House—Comfortable Quarters—A Warm Welcome—Our Sleeping-Quarters—French Cultivateurs—Their Characteristics—Our Dinner,   1

CHAPTER XVI

Passage of the Somme—Indifference of the Natives—Our Quarters—French Deserters—A French Chaussée—Mortemer and its Miseries—Improved Aspect of the Country—First Traces of the Prussians—Prussian Revenge—A Deputation—Valley of the Oise—Its Scenery—Our March unopposed—Preparation to Bivouac—Again in Advance—Beauty of the Scenery at Verneuil — Our Bivouac—Plundering — Senlis — Feelings of the Population—Prussian Lancers—Devastation by the Prussians—Chenevière—Our Night-Quarters,   .   .   33

CHAPTER XVII.

The Cumberland Hussars—Warlike Rumours—Expectation and Excitement—A Quiet Morning—Orders to Advance—We come on the Enemy—Our Dilemma—In Sight of Montmartre—First Glimpse of Paris—Prussian Devastations again—Comfortless Bivouac—Progress of the Prussians—A Halt—Davoust's Country Seat—Devastation in it—Destruction of the Library—Churlishness of our Allies—Rumours of Peace—St Denis—An Excursion—Aspect of the Country—Revolting Destruction—The Destroyers at Work—Visitors for Paris—Inconstancy of the People—Aspect of the Crowd—At Arnouvilles—The Royal Cortège—Louis XVIII., . 60

CHAPTER XVIII.

On the March—The Seine—Beauty of the Country—Passage of the Seine—Colombes—Drawbacks—My Quarters—The Garden and Grounds—View from my Window—My Chateau—Its Furnishings—State of our Horses—An Excursion—The Country round Paris—View of Paris—A Wet Day—My Landlord—Country Pleasures—My Occupations—Our Fare—A Fracas—Our Brunswickers Mutinous—Their Complaints—My Answer to them—Harvesting—French Peasantry—The Women—Food of the Peasantry—Inn Signs—A Lady of the Old Régime—A Ride to Paris—The Seine and its Banks—First Visit to Paris—Aspect of the Streets—Parisian Equipages—The Champs Elysées—The Place Louis Quinze—The Austerlitz Column—London and Paris—The Streets of Paris—The Boulevard des Italiens, . 94

CHAPTER XIX.

Our Major Domo—Inspection of Troops—Prospect of Change—Prussian Bivouac—The Louvre—The Venus de Medici—The Laocoon and the Apollo—The Paintings—The Tuileries—The Gardens—The Palais Royal—Habitués of the Palais—Road to Malmaison—Malmaison—A Panic—A Farmhouse—Versailles—Sevres and St Cloud—Hôtel Dieu and Nôtre Dame—The Invalides—Models of Fortresses—A Sunday, 138

CONTENTS.

CHAPTER XX.

My New Quarters—Their Desolate Aspect—First Night in them—
Change of Abode—My New Residence—Ma'amselle Rose—
A She-Dragon—Our Fare—The Villagers—The Maire and
his Complaints—More Grievances—The Postmaster of St
Denis—Insolence of the Villagers—The Allied Sovereigns
—A Review — Difficulties — Order from Headquarters—A
Complaint—A Visitor—Rascalities — The French Police—
Pertinacity of my Persecutor—Church Reopened—Sunday
in France—Review of Prussians—A Scene—A Craven—Our
Artillery—Positions of Troops — Scenes of Battles—View
from Montmartre—The Works on Montmartre—Belleville
and Vincennes—Aspect of Country—Washerwomen—Village
Gossip, ... 166

CHAPTER XXI.

Sisters of Charity—New Messroom—A House-warming — The
Bond Street of Paris—The Boulevards—Their Frequenters—
Street-Beggars — Street-Vendors — Street-Scenes — News-
Rooms—Open-Air Loungers — An Exquisite — A Parisian
Restaurant—Waiters—Parisian Cookery—Paris by Night
—Torment of Flies—Amicable Relations—The Peasantry—
Again at Paris—A Russian Equipage—A Picturesque Coach-
man—A Russian Boy—Russian Soldiers—The Austrians, 206

CHAPTER XXII.

My First Ride to Paris—The Aristocratic Quarters—Different
Quarters of the City—Differences in these—The Boulevards
—The Quays—The Squares of London and Paris—An Ex-
cursion—Again in Paris—Numbering the Streets—The Jar-
din des Plantes—The Menagerie—The Hothouses—Released
from Arrest — An Unfortunate Accident — A Comrade's
Quarters — Cabriolet-Drivers — The Fountains — A Street-
Lecturer—Itinerant Violinist—A Suicide—The Change of
Dynasty—The Luxembourg—The Chamber of Peers—The
Poultry and Flower Markets—Marauding Neighbours—A
Capture—Bibliothèque Royale—Cabinet des Gravures—Shop-
Signs in Paris—The Palais Royal—Café Aux Milles Col-
onnes—A Shoeblack's Establishment—The Jardin du Prince
—The Place des Innocens—The Vegetable Markets—The
Louvre once more—The Statuary, . . . 233

CHAPTER XXIII.

Admiral Rosily's Villa—The Duke and the 5th Division—Views in the Neighbourhood—Our Patron Saint—Village Amusements—The Fauigny Affair—M. Fauigny and the Duke—Injustice of the Duke—Indifference as to Dress—A General Order—An Affray—Russian Review—The Allied Sovereigns—The Russian Artillery—The Artillery Horses—Leave of Absence at last—Regrets at Leaving—My Portmanteau—Departure—Our Journey—We take the Wrong Road—At Amiens—The Hôtel d'Angleterre—A Caravan Journey—A Cabriolet—A John Bull Astray—Montreuil—An English Party—A Misadventure—England once more, . . 273

CHAPTER XXIV.

Our Fellow-Passengers—From Dover to Calais—For Paris once more—Montreuil again—Abbeville and its Cathedral—A Bridal Party—Hotel at Breteuil—A Race—Arrival at Clermont—The Stables at Chantilly—Our Old Quarters at Stain—Attempts at Comfort—A Dreary Winter—Our Occupations—Outbreaks of Fire—Preparations for Departure—Preparations for a Start — Leave-Takings — Our Quarters at Beaumont—Noailles and Beauvais—A Scene with our Hostess—The Theatre at Beauvais—Major Dyas—A Cheerless Day's March—Grandvilliers—An Altercation with our Host—Quarters at Poix—The Village and its Scenery—A Proposal—Comfortless Quarters—Difficulties at Airaines—Our Amusements—The Town Shepherd—A Court-Martial—At Boulogne—At Guines—Kindness of Our Hosts—En Route for Calais—Our Stay there—Embarkation and its Evils—Our Difficulties—Embark at last—England once more, . 304

JOURNAL

OF THE

WATERLOO CAMPAIGN.

CHAPTER XV.

22*d*.—MORNING fine, and things look more cheerful. March, according to order, at four. Troop turned out of its wet bivouac; did not look very brilliant; moreover, there had been no time for cleaning. The village street such a perfect slough that even the riding-horses struggled through with difficulty, and our carriages stuck fast several times ere they could be brought to the hard ground beyond. Immediately on emerging from the orchards, we entered on the same cheerless uninteresting country as before: interminable fields of corn, without enclosures, only broken here and there by small patches of coppice or young timber. Through this sort of country marched to Bavay; and here we formed up in the fields by the roadside and dismounted, whilst an officer was sent to summon the garrison of Maubeuge—the first word of an enemy since quitting Waterloo. As the infantry continued moving on, we were somewhat at a loss to conjecture what was to be done should the answer to our summons be unfavourable. The whole army—cavalry, infantry, and artillery, English and allies, all appeared to be marching along this one line of road. We heard nothing of any columns moving parallel on our flanks, and for about three hours that we halted here this incessant passing afforded us some amusement. The crowd was endless, though varied—regiments of infantry or cavalry following each other in constant succession, intermingled with, and striving to pass, the as endless file of waggons, baggage-carts, baggage-animals, led horses, batteries of artillery, and convoys of stores. All struggled to get ahead to choose a bivouac, or get the first-fruits of any village or farm on or near the road, which was sure to be left quite bare the moment the first corps passed—I mean bare of provisions; for I believe our people did not otherwise plunder. It might truly be said that a torrent of men and animals rolled along the road. Even when we resumed our march there was no cessation, no diminution of the crowd. The numbers of servants, sutlers, stragglers, and women were incredible, and added not a little to the general confusion. As far back, too, as I could see, the same swarm covered the road—the troops seemed to form the smallest part of the crowd. What the answer was to our summons we have not yet heard, but suppose all went on smoothly; for, after a wait of three or four hours, we again got under way, and made an attempt to penetrate the throng, but in vain— we got jammed and stuck fast. Lord Edward, seeing our case hopeless, abandoned us as soon as he could get his dragoons disengaged from the crowd, and took across the fields, leaving me directions to make the best of my way to Cateau Cambresis, and bivouac there if I did not find him and the brigade. In this state we were obliged to give up all thoughts of pushing on, and rest contented to swim with the stream. This swept us in due time into one end of Bavay (pleasingly situated on a rising-ground) and out at the other, leaving just time to see that the place had a clean and cheerful appearance, and that the street we passed through was well built and had many genteel-looking houses in it. Quitting the town by a steepish hill, we entered the forest of Mormal; and the road was bordered on both sides by a thick coppice of hazel, young ash, &c., over which the larger timber-trees reared their heads. Many corps of infantry had drawn off the road, and were busy cutting down the coppice to prepare their bivouacs by constructing huts of leaves and branches. Fires were made, and cooking already going on. Officers, divested of swords and sashes, were strolling amongst the thickets, or listlessly lolling under their leafy bowers. All this would have been very pretty, but that a heavy shower, which fell as we struggled through Bavay, had left everything dripping, consequently deteriorated the scene much. Still the grouping of the figures round the fires, or interspersed among the thickets, was very good. Emerging from the woods, we again entered on the ocean of corn; but here the features of the ground were bolder, and the view more extensive, though not less cheerless.

At some distance ahead, in a deep valley, of which the heights all descended by fine bold slopes, stood the little town of Cateau amidst flat alluvial meadows, the lively verdure of which, and that of a few trees, contrasted strikingly with the golden hue of all the country around it. The road along the plateau on which we now travelled was hard and excellent, so that, by watching our opportunity and pushing in whenever an opening in the crowd permitted, we managed, with some considerable wrangling, to get ahead. This was rather a dangerous operation, for the Belgic, and particularly the Nassau troops, were so savage, and so constantly threatening us with their bayonets, that I feared every minute we should come to blows. In this manner we had struggled on to the crest of the hill descending toward Cateau, where, to lessen the descent, it had been cut down, consequently was confined between high banks. Now, as the devil would have it, we got into this gully at the same time with a battalion of Nassau, and as both parties pressed on to head the other, some jostling ensued. Our wheels were too formidable to be resisted when in motion; but at last we got completely entangled, and then they turned upon us, striking our horses, and even pricking them with their bayonets. Our men, of course, resented this, and a serious affray was likely to take place; but at last, assisted by their officers, we disengaged ourselves without any one being materially hurt, although many had bruises, scratches, and slight bayonet-stabs. In this affair one fellow was very deliberately going to give me a *coup de bayonette* in the side, but old Quartermaster Hall knocked up the point with his sabre, and could scarcely be prevented from splitting his skull. The English, with whom we also occasionally crossed and jostled, contented themselves with abusing us. For some days after, we were constantly falling in with these very people, and our so doing resembling the approach of two angry dogs. I was constantly alarmed lest some serious affray should take place. But they have led me ahead of my march. Somewhat more than a mile before we came to the descent above mentioned, we passed through Forêt, a pretty large village, surrounded as usual by orchards, with a few small woods scattered about the vicinity, which diversified agreeably the otherwise monotonous scenery. On approaching this village, a dirty sheet or table-cloth, attached to a pole, and projected from a window of the church-tower, attracted our attention. It was the first time we had seen the immaculate *pavillon blanc* since entering the French territory; and one could not but admire the wisdom and foresight which had established as a national standard what could be readily furnished at any moment by every, even the most humble, *ménage*. A tall, thin, venerable-looking old man in the clerical habit stood by the roadside amidst several peasants, male and female. His countenance was radiant with joy, and he appeared quite elated in contemplating the column as it passed along. Pinch after pinch he took from a little tortoise-shell snuff-box in his left hand, whilst with earnestness he pointed out to, or seemed describing, something in our column. As I came up, followed by my trumpeter, the old man, uncovering his white head, made me a profound obeisance. This opened the interview, and I was soon master of his history. He had been driven from his *cure* by the Revolution; returned on the abdication of Napoleon last year; but the return from Elba had again nearly caused a second flight. He had, however, ventured to remain, upon the affectionate assurances of his parishioners, and after suffering during the Hundred Days most horrid anxiety and even indignities, had at last been restored to security and tranquillity by the battle of Waterloo. He was now come out not only to witness the passage of the brave English, to whom his country and himself stood so much indebted, but also to meet and do homage to his beloved monarch, who he understood would pass through Forêt on his way to his capital. Nothing could exceed the good man's joy; his spirits quite ran away with him, and his tongue ran nineteen to the dozen. At parting we cordially shook hands, and he tendered me the little tortoise-shell box with the most amiable *bonhommie*. How the rustics gazed! They seem a very ignorant, simple people, the peasantry of this country. Hitherto, since passing the frontier, we have found them everywhere pursuing their rural labours with as much tranquillity as in the most profound state of peace: quite undisturbed by, and exhibiting very little curiosity about, the continued passage of foreign troops along their roads and through their villages. The village of Forêt presented a cheerful rustic aspect—such as a village should. Thatched barns and farmhouse in the usual style of such buildings in England, standing detached and retired from the broad street, if so it might be termed, embosomed in apple or cherry orchards;—quite unlike what one so often meets with in other parts of France, where the villages, of stone houses three or four storeys high, with large windows, &c., appear more like pieces of towns cut out and popped down here than what is consonant to our ideas of villages.

From the place where our scuffle with the Nassau men took place we descended into the valley by a long winding hill, at the bottom of which the little village of Montay lay like an oasis in the desert; verdant meadows overshadowed by numerous pine-trees, a pretty rivulet winding along amongst them, here passed by a narrow stone bridge; the place itself consisting of one large farm, several cottages, and a small church;—altogether offering a refreshing variety in this ocean of corn. The heights rising abruptly above it on either side make this a sort of pass, which, had the retiring French thought fit to defend, would have cost us some trouble and many lives, no doubt. As it was, although we understood their outposts were not far, not a man was in sight; and we were allowed to pass as quietly as our own internal dissensions would allow, for the narrowness of the bridge produced here a fearful struggle. The road along which the army was marching, passing through Montay, immediately ascended the opposite heights. A road branching from this led to Cateau along the foot of these heights and through the meadows about a mile or rather more higher up the stream. We took this road, and thus, for the first time since leaving Nivelles, enjoyed the indescribable pleasure of having the road to ourselves. From the heights on this side of Forêt, whence the view was very extensive, I could distinguish nothing of the brigade; and now, finding ourselves quite alone, and seeing no symptoms of troops about Cateau, I began to be rather uneasy. In this dilemma I was about to establish my bivouac on a piece of turf just without the town—for the evening was fast closing in—when our lieutenant-major-general of cavalry, Lord Greenock, rode hastily up, and demanded why we were here. "My orders were to march to Cateau, my lord, and bivouac, with which I am complying. I expect Lord Edward will join us here;" and I gave him an account of their taking to the fields, &c. "There is some mistake in this," replied Lord Greenock. "Your brigade has halted at Forêt, and you must return thither, for you are now in a very dangerous position, and at all events ought not to have crossed the river. The enemy's outposts are on the heights; and should they attempt anything during the night, which is probable, you could never recross the bridge. Return, therefore, without delay." This was comfortable, to have to grope our way to Forêt, and when there pick out a bivouac; and the alternative that of remaining and being caught in this *coupe gorge*. The idea was not a pleasant one. Disobeying orders, too! We countermarched, however; but on reaching Montay the stream of people and carriages sweeping over the narrow bridge made it evidently useless attempting to move in a contrary direction. I gave up the idea, and established my bivouac in the little churchyard close to the bridge. I felt less compunction at doing this, because several regiments of Hanoverian infantry had extended themselves in bivouac along the meadows, both up and down the stream, on the same side; and, moreover, I had learned from Lord Greenock that two or three troops of horse-artillery and a large corps of hussars were occupying the plateau in front, between us and the enemy. Under the impression of security, therefore, I laid myself down after our evening meal was finished, expecting a good sleep; but my eyes were scarcely closed ere the never-to-be-mistaken sound of a distant cannonade caused me to start up again. Everything around was perfectly still; the Hanoverians seemed to be all asleep; and no stir or bustle of any kind in our immediate neighbourhood indicated an alarm. The cannonade, too, though sometimes more distinctly heard than at others, did not, on the whole, seem to approach. After listening for a time, sleep got the better of me, and I sank down in spite of the distant cannonade and the more immediate concert of thousands of frogs in the adjoining ditch.

23d.—A fine day. Uneasy at hearing nothing of the brigade being in motion. The cannonade during the night proceeded from Sir Charles Colville and the 4th division attacking Cambray.

About noon Sir Augustus Frazer, with Sir Julius Hartman of the K. G. Legion horse artillery, paid us a visit. From them I learned that headquarters are established in Cateau, and that the Duke intends halting in our present position for a day or two to give time for the rear of the army to close up, since, from the rapidity of our march, and from the whole marching in a single column, many corps are still a long way in the rear. At the same time, Cambray on our right and Landrecy on our left are to be secured before we advance further. Moreover, we are likely, it seems, to have another battle immediately, for the French army has rallied in considerable force, and is in position not far in front of us. Upon this intelligence I decided on remaining at Montay until the brigade should come up; therefore, leaving my second captain to inspect ammunition, and forward cleaning, repairing, shoeing, &c., I set off with our two visitors on their return to Cateau. This place, which is very small, is situated in a rich alluvial bottom amongst fine, well-irrigated meadows. The only trees, however, in this bottom are at Montay. The town is surrounded by a simple wall, perhaps only for excise purposes; and I was at a loss to conjecture the use of a single battery of two or three pieces near the gate leading to Montay. On entering this gate I was struck by the dismal aspect of the street within—narrow, dirty, and composed of mean-looking houses built of sombre-coloured stone, and scarcely a human being visible; for although headquarters were here, none of the members of it were to be seen in the streets. Priests in their black cassocks and band strode solemnly along from time to time. The house in which the Duke lodged was the only decent-looking one in the place. It stood at the extremity of the street, crossing at right angles the one we entered by—large, and pierced with numerous windows, apparently new, and having the advantage of a row of three or four fine trees in front. Some pretensions there were, too, to architectural decorations in the façade, which was of stucco, painted buff. Cateau was soon seen, and I returned to Montay, where I found the poor farmer (the farm adjoined the church) in great distress. The Hanoverians were plundering barns, farmyard, and all. "Ah, monsieur, tout sera abimé!" cried the poor fellow, wringing his hands, and presenting the very picture of despair. Yesterday evening he complained to me, and I did what I could to prevent it, but without much effect. The bivouac of these marauders in the adjoining meadows was only separated from his garden by a sort of willow hedge; and although I planted sentries for the protection of it, everything disappeared. This morning, becoming bolder, they have plundered his barns, &c., and even threatened the house itself. As we draw our own supplies of eggs, milk, &c., from the farm, I did what I could to save him from further plunder, and sent Breton to remonstrate with their commanding officer, and give him to understand that, unless he kept his men under better discipline, I would report him to the Duke. Got nothing by this, for he persisted in not understanding English. Thus we have been obliged to be constantly on the alert, and to keep them out by main force. The poor farmer is very grateful, and loud in praise of *les bons Anglais*, whilst he *sacrés*, &c., their allies down to the bottomless pit—" aux enfers." He admits the truth of what I said about retaliation, and turned up his eyes in horror at the account I gave him of the ravages committed by French troops in other countries. "Mais, monsieur, je le crois bien, les soldats Français sout de vrais brigands; ils pillent partout même dans la patrie; oui, monsieur, ici même;" and he related how a detachment of cuirassiers had quartered on him for three days, having only departed the morning of that in which we arrived. They had treated him cruelly; and not content with living on him all that time, were on the point of destroying everything that was left and burning the premises, when the unexpected appearance of some of our advanced corps obliged them to make a precipitate retreat. In the evening, a general parade of the Germans. They have formed a sort of diminutive tents for the night by striking two ramrods into the ground, crossed, to form each end; I forget how they form the ridge. A blanket is laid over, and the other two serve to lie under and over the three men the tent just holds. The different bands, all good, continued playing until after dusk, which we enjoyed sitting in the willow hedge smoking our cigars. The scene was remarkably pretty. Groups of men scattered about amongst the little tents, some preparing supper, &c.; the bands, with officers in picturesque costumes hovering about them; the town of Cateau in the background; and on either hand the picture shut in by bold naked slopes of the neighbouring heights.

24*th*.—Fine warm morning, but day promises to be rather too hot. Not a gun to be heard to-day by the sharpest ear; the business at Cambray must be settled somehow or other. Getting accustomed to our churchyard. To be sure, none of the graves are recent; it seems long since any one has been buried here. Hitchins and I have decided on breakfasting together; and as he is more at leisure than I am, he has undertaken the foraging department. This morning our repast consisted of bread (sour as vinegar), cheesy butter, and hard eggs, washed down with weak grog (Hollands)—table a grave. Ever since we passed Mons good bread is not to be had—all is of this horrid sour description. To the eye it is well enough. The peasantry make their bread in large flat loaves, 2 or 2½ feet in diameter—no mistake!—nearly circular. Sometimes the loaves are annular, and of the above diameter. Enter Lieutenant and Adjutant Bell, R.H.A., and I can write no more, for he no doubt brings news.

9 P.M.—Here we are, then, back again in Forêt. Bell brought us the order to return forthwith, as the brigade was to march without delay on Land-

recy, the commandant of which place refuses to surrender. We lost no time in obeying the order, and the road being now quite clear—indeed solitary—marched here in a very short time; and instead of finding the brigade ready to move, were surprised on reaching the village at seeing the Life Guardsmen quietly grooming their horses in front of the barns and stables of their billets. The place being already full, we were directed to bivouac, and accordingly I pitched upon this orchard, which is high and dry; but the trees are too young and too far apart to afford us much shade, which we want just now. The arrival of strangers attracted a concourse of villagers to our bivouac, many old women and young girls bringing quantities of very fine cherries for sale. The former were remarkably coarse and ugly, the latter generally pretty, and all had sparkling, speaking eyes. These, of course, sold their cherries first; but the article was too grateful in such a roasting day as this has been not to insure the sale of all. The costume of these women—who, by the way, seemed quite at home with us—was rather picturesque. Lofty white caps, with long flaps hanging down to the shoulders, their naked stays sometimes not very closely laced, bosom covered with a coloured handkerchief put on with a degree of taste, coarse woollen petticoats of a blue stuff striped with white or pink and reaching only to the calf of the leg, coarse woollen stockings, and clumsy wooden shoes (*sabots*). Most of them wore large gold or silver rings in their ears, and many a little golden cross suspended from the neck by a black riband or a strip of black velvet. The Duke has published a manifesto from Cateau. Several copies are stuck up in the village, and the people here seem very much pleased with it; and well they may, for it assures them they shall be treated like gentlemen, and not get the punishment which France, as a nation, so richly deserves. It calls upon the people to remain quietly at home, as we make no war on them, but ought rather to be considered as their allies; further, it goes on to assure them that the strictest discipline will be maintained in the Allied army, and that everything required by the troops must be paid for at its full value. The Forêtiens, and particularly the Forêtiennes, actually express astonishment at our generosity.

Louis XVIII., &c., passed through the village this evening on his way to Cateau. Leathes and I rode a little way out to meet him, which we did about a quarter of a mile off. The cortège consisted of several Berlines, escorted by about two squadrons of the Royal Garde de Corps— fine young men (all gentlemen), dressed in a very becoming uniform, blue turned up with red, and silver lace tastefully disposed, with Grecian helmets, silver, with a golden sun on the front, the most elegant I ever saw. The king was in the last carriage, on each side of which rode the Duc de Berri and that General whose acquaintance I made on the drill-ground near Alost. We had drawn up on the roadside as the cortège passed. The moment the Duc de Berri and the General saw us, they came up, and, offering us their hands, poured forth such a torrent of compliments and congratulations as made even our horses blush. His Royal Highness could never sufficiently testify his gratitude to the English nation, &c. &c.; was impatient to see us in Paris, for then and there indeed, &c. &c. The General was equally profuse in compliments and promises, so that, forgetting the adage, "Put not your trust in princes," Leathes and I have ever since been feeling the Croix de St Louis dangling at our breasts—*nous verrons!* The monarch was detained from his dinner more than half an hour by my worthy friend Mons. le Curé, who, in full pontificals, and followed by his congregation *en habits de Dimanches*, met him at the entrance of the village, and, standing on a little bank at the coach-door, delivered a long harangue, set off by Mandarine-like bobs of the head at the end of every period, and a most profound bow at the conclusion, all which were received and returned by his Majesty with exemplary patience and punctuality. At length the cortège moved on, and we returned to our orchard.

25*th*.—Here we are, another day's march in advance, not only without the expected battle, but also without having either seen or heard of an enemy. Nor have we seen any traces of one, having found the peasantry everywhere as peaceably occupied as if no war existed. Nothing more have we heard of Landrecy, which, I suppose, must have surrendered, since Lord Edward sent us orders this morning to march on Sequehart, where the brigade halts to-night. Accordingly I marched immediately towards Montay in a thick drizzling rain, which made this dismal country appear ten times more dismal. The cavalry regiments marched at the same time (about five A.M. ?) and we kept company as far as Montay; but there they left us, for we found the road again so choked with baggage, &c., that although we succeeded in passing the bridge, yet the deep hollow road (*encaissé* between very high steep banks), ascending to the opposite heights, was so inextricably crammed with carriages, and the unctuous soil so slippery, that I feared we should bivouac in the churchyard again. We attempted the ascent, and being better horsed than the others, succeeded in getting ahead wherever an opening offered. Our column was broken into as many fractional parts as we had carriages. At length, after a most arduous struggle, we mustered our whole force on the plateau, and pushed forward in the old way—sometimes getting along pretty smoothly by keeping one side of the road; then a choke would stop us for a time, until, an opportunity offering, the head of our column would make a dash and break the file of waggons; but occasionally in doing this, if the rear carriages did not keep close up, the waggoners would dash in their turn, and cut them off. Then again we got foul of our Nassau friends, and the old quarrel was revived; cursing, swearing, and bayoneting followed as matter of course. The road itself was execrable, and in places a complete slough. It appears that our march has been so conducted as to avoid the main avenues, and thus turn the fortresses; consequently, with the exception of some little bits of chaussée, we have been travelling on the cross-roads—in France always execrable. On gaining the plateau we saw everywhere around us again those interminable fields of wheat—not a hedge nor a dividing wall; the only relief a few small woods here and there. A hamlet we occasionally met with, and sometimes a solitary cabaret of the meanest appearance— "Ici on loge à pied et à cheval," scrawled on a board in black letters, on a dirty-white ground, invited the traveller to enter. Sometimes a longer inscription set forth other inducements. I pity the luckless wight who trusts to their hospitality. A remarkable feature in the cheerless scenery of these oceans of corn is the row of apple-trees so frequently seen skirting the horizon. The byroads here are frequently bordered by apple or pear trees, which accounts for this. As we advanced on the plateau, and still found no concentration of troops, or other indication of the neighbourhood of the enemy, our expectation of another battle vanished. Insensibly we had deviated from the general route, and found ourselves only accompanied by Major Bull's troop of horse-artillery. Bull had got the same discretionary orders from his general as myself, and was also making his way to Sequehart, where his brigade was to halt. The country had become prettier and more interesting, and the rain had ceased. Woods were more frequent and larger, and at last we marched through what might strictly be termed a wooded country. The ground, too, became more undulating, and pastures of green meadows occurred to relieve most agreeably the tiresome sameness of the corn crops. Occasionally, also, openings between the woods would give us glimpses of distant and pretty country. But where dwell the husbandmen who cultivate those lands? In this district we saw not a single habitation, and only here and there met a solitary peasant—not working, but in the road—moving from one place to another. Of these we incessantly demanded " Où se trouve Sequehart ? " and the response was invariably " *N'sais paw, Monsire*," or a shake of the head. Bull and I began to be uneasy as the evening drew on, whilst we were surrounded by woods, and not the slightest appearance of a village to be seen. Our own people were now the only troops visible, and we began to suspect what proved to be true—we had lost ourselves!

We were so enclosed by woods that it was impossible to see to any distance; and cross-roads branching off right and left became very frequent, so that we were puzzled how to proceed. Every peasant we met persisted in knowing nothing of Sequehart, nor had met any other troops. We were evidently astray. At last an old man, to whom the usual questions were put, after puzzling over it for a few minutes, begged we would repeat the name. "Sequehart!—Sequehart!" said he, two or three times. "*Monsire, n'le connois paw; mais, ma foi, ce sera sans doute Escars que vous cherchez.*" We stared in our turn, but the old man was positive, and insisted that we were leaving it behind us. After some little irresolution, Bull and I made up our minds to follow his directions; and accordingly, after a few miles threading our way between woods, arrived here a little before sunset. The village is already full of Life Guards, and therefore we are obliged to bivouac again; but that is of little moment, for we have an excellent spot on a rising-ground, covered with short velvety turf, close to the chaussée leading to St Quentin, on the other side of which, about two or three hundred yards distant, is the village of Sequehart, or Escars, so buried in the foliage of fine walnut-trees, and of the hedges enclosing the gardens and some fields, that scarcely a roof is to be seen; and it is only through the ascending columns of blue smoke from amongst the trees that the site of the village is to be detected. From the swelling hills up which the St Quentin road runs in front of us, the short clean turf, and the chalk (or gypsum) that appears in patches where this has been removed, we might fancy ourselves on the South Downs, in Sussex. It is a sweet rural spot, and, what is better, we see few signs of war about us; for except Walcott's troop (rocket), which has just come up, no other soldiers whatever are to be seen. Bull left us at the other side of the village, and our cavalry are, like it, buried in the foliage and invisible to us. We understand headquarters are at Joncour, a village not far off, and that Lord Hill's division is at Belleglise, somewhere in front, so that we may sleep securely to-night. Lovely evening.

26*th*.—Fine morning. Marched early, and, crossing the downs, traversed beyond them a pretty well-wooded country, diversified very agreeably by several large sheets of water, formed by embankments, and regained the route of our army, which we had deviated from yesterday at Belleglise, just as the bustle commenced. Plunged once more into the torrent, with all its *désagrémens* and vexations, and swam along with it as before. The wooded country gave place to the dismal sea of corn a little beyond Belleglise; but after travelling about four or five miles through this tiresome region, we once more came amongst trees, and crossed a deep ravine, or rather wooded valley, in which was situated a most respectable-looking country-house, brick, with stone angles, window-cases, &c., standing upon a terrace, with an old-fashioned garden divided into rectangular beds, with stone vases, &c., sheltered in the rear by the woods, and to the south looking upon a fine sheet of water—artificial, no doubt—most probably formed by damming up the stream which we crossed in the bottom. The country people told us this place belongs to Caulaincourt, Duc de Vicenza, which is no doubt the truth, since in my map I find it called Caulaincourt. The hanging woods and shady winding paths of this ravine appeared to us heavenly when contrasted with the dreary exposed plain above; and this, if possible, was more hideous than ever when we again debouched upon it—a dead flat, unrelieved by the slightest undulation—a sea of wheat extending to the horizon, with here and there a few clumps of beggarly pines, and the usual straggling lines of apple-trees fringing the horizon. I forget where, but it must have been just before crossing the valley at Caulaincourt that we left the direct route, together with Bull's and Whinyate's troops, as we were directed to halt for the night at Etreillers.

COMFORTABLE QUARTERS.

After marching two or three miles more over this uninteresting plain, on passing one of these circular pine clumps we suddenly came in sight of fine trees bounding the horizon, intermixed with buildings, which, on approaching it, proved to be Etreillers. The village is a very large one, composed principally of large farms, with a few dwellings of an inferior description, all, however, standing back in gardens, or in their large straw-yards, which are separated from the broad avenues constituting the village street by high walls, with a great gateway of entrance, and generally surrounded on three sides by orchards. Such quarters are quite a luxury; for although we are three troops in the village, yet all get under cover, man and horse, in houses, barns, stables, &c. The appearance of the place is not gay, and may truly be said to harmonise in tone with the dreary but fruitful plain around. The buildings are generally of a dark stone, with enormous thatched roofs, which, if not lively, has at least an air of substantial comfort that makes ample amends for everything else.

I have established myself in a most comfortable farmhouse of the first class, and, to complete my good fortune, have an exceedingly pretty and most obliging hostess. Instead of the black looks an intruder like myself might have expected, I was received with smiles, and a welcome which sounded sincere. I was shown into their best room (the one which I now write in), my horses into the best stable, and everything done to make me most comfortable. My fair friend has let out one reason for all this, although I still believe genuine hospitality has a great share in it—she is delighted at having English instead of Prussians quartered on her; all the country are in dread of the latter. As may be supposed, we were soon quite at home—I say we, for my second captain (Newland) was with me. In the stable, men and boys have been at work helping our men to clean their horses, whilst in the house the women busied themselves in arranging our room, cooking dinner, and even asking for our dirty linen, which they are in the act of washing for us, so that to-day I can afford a clean shirt and still start to-morrow with a clean kit. The room we occupy is large and rather dark, for there are only two small windows looking out to the farmyard, and these rather obscured with the white draperies with which they are ornamented. The furniture is coarse and clumsy, made of walnut, and is as black as ebony. One side of the room is occupied by two sleeping-places, let into the wall, exactly like the berths on shipboard. The bedding in these, though coarse also, is very good, and, like everything else, scrupulously clean; the sheets have just been put in. Our servants have comfortable beds allotted to them, and have become as much at home in the kitchen as if they were old acquaintances. Whilst dinner was preparing, I sallied forth to see how my people were put up, and had scarcely left the yard when I encountered an old peasant wearing an enormous cocked-hat, and having a drum suspended from his neck by a broad band, on which he occasionally gave a sort of roll or flourish. His grotesque figure, as well as his employment, attracted my attention, and I was somewhat mystified on observing that every flourish on the drum was responded to by an opening of doors and the sallying out of old ladies, each bearing under her arm one of those enormous loaves already mentioned. What can all this mean, thought I? Is it possible that in this most military of all nations even women are subject to regulations, and obliged to conduct the *ménage* by tap of drum or sound of bugle? One old lady, with a huge annular loaf, whom I questioned, soon solved the query. The commissary had ordered the inhabitants to feed the troops, and this drumming hero was the crier, who gave notice to that effect, and was likewise collecting all the ready-baked bread at the church for distribution. The thing seemed perfectly well understood, each roll of the drum producing precisely the same effect as the crier moved along the great rambling street. The old women, as they trotted towards the church, made a clatter with their *sabots* like so many horses. Many of the people I found had, on our first arrival, concealed everything; but the dread of being plundered was soon removed, and all is now confidence. As far as I can judge, these people seem to live well enough in their own way; and in every house one is sure to find good beds, very high, being raised upon an enormous palliasse. There is no want of silver spoons, and even forks, in many of them; and their stock of household linen (good) is really astonishing, many small *cultivateurs* possessing as much as would set up two or three of our middling farmers. I use the term "*cultivateur*" to designate a class quite common in France, but scarcely known in England. They are proprietors of small estates (perhaps only a few acres), fractions of large ones sold in lots during the Revolution. These, of course, they cultivate themselves, with the assist-

ance of their families, and are thence styled
"*cultivateurs*" by the Government, and are
obliged to put this, coupled with their number
(they are all numbered), upon their carts, &c.—
for example, " Joachim Laroque, cultivateur, No.
3755 ;" or " Jean Baptiste Amand," &c. &c. &c.

We find them a simple, obliging, but very ignorant race; and their *patois* is to me almost
unintelligible. Some with whom I conversed
this evening either were, or pretended to be, quite
ignorant of what has been taking place in the
great world. They had heard that France was
at war with England, Russia, and Prussia, but
that was all. They had never heard of Wellington, nor of Nelson, nor even Louis XVIII.
They had, however, heard enough to inspire them
with some dread of the Cossacks and Prussians.
I asked them if they knew Buonaparte?
" Non, monsieur—non y pas!" " Napoleon ?—
aw mais oui, monsieur, c'est l'Empereur que
ça—n'est ce paw vrai, monsieur?" They had
heard of him because he made them pay taxes;
but of his wars they were as ignorant as all the
rest, and did not speculate the least in the world
as to how and why we are here.

Returned *home* (conceive being *at home* in a
French farmhouse!) just as the good woman was

placing a most inviting fricasseed fowl and *omelette aux herbes*, smoking hot, upon our table, to which, with a good bottle of *vin du pays*, we lost no time in doing justice. We have passed a most comfortable evening; and if we may judge by the laughing and chattering in the kitchen, our servants and the rustics have not passed it badly. As their door is opposite to ours, we have occasionally peeped in upon them, and been much amused at seeing the ploughmen equipped in our men's helmets, belts, &c. ; but their chief source of amusement appeared to be reciprocally teaching each other English and French words—the attempt at pronouncing which causes infinite fun.

CHAPTER XVI.

27*th.*—Fine warm morning. Started early after an excellent breakfast of coffee and *et ceteras*. Our orders were to rejoin the grand column at Ugny l'Equippée; but we had not gone far from Etreillers when two roads, branching off in different directions, brought us to a halt. Lord Greenock came up just at the moment, and blamed me for not bringing a guide from the village— " Better late than never." I took the hint, and sent Trumpeter Brown back with orders to bring the first person he could lay hands on, *nolens volens*. He went his way and brought back *a tailor*, escorting him like a prisoner with his drawn sabre. Not knowing why he was thus forcibly taken from his home, the poor tailor appeared terribly alarmed — imploring mercy even with tears. When told, however, what was expected of him, he soon became tranquil; so, sticking him at the head of the column, we jogged on again. At Ugny l'Equippée we rejoined the column and dismissed our tailor, slipping into the main stream as heretofore. We now learned that the army was about to cross the Somme, and soon felt that it was actually engaged in so doing from our long and tedious halts—there being but one ford, which made the operation a very slow one. As we drew near the river the country improved somewhat, became more undulating and more wooded, consequently prettier.

The Somme here is but a small stream; flat meadows extend some little way on each side, and are bordered by moderate hills, running out here and there into knolls. The point chosen for our passage was a ford just above a mill on the road to Nesle. Peronne having been taken yesterday by General Maitland's brigade of Guards, the only enemy we heard of in our vicinity was the garrison of Ham, and they could scarcely have opposed our passage even had they not been shut up by a brigade of light infantry and a troop of horse-artillery (Ross's), which had been sent to summon them. The different divisions of cavalry, infantry, and artillery, winding down the swelling knolls, some of which were prettily wooded, and the picturesque groups of staff and other officers on the points of these knolls, superintending the passage of their respective brigades, &c., formed altogether an animated and pleasing picture, although not much could be said for the beauty of the country on the opposite side of the river, which looked cheerless enough. It was in one of those groups, and the most picturesque of them— for they were German hussars—that I recognised and shook hands with my friend General Victor Alten, whom I had not seen for more than three years. An interesting meeting, for he was surrounded by a number of other old acquaintances of the 2d Hussars.

A foot-bridge at the mill enabled the infantry to file over; but we had to ford, and got a tolerable wetting, for the water was up to our saddle-skirts. On the other side, about a mile from the river, we reached Nesle, the intervening country enclosed but not wooded, consequently much more ugly and uninteresting than if it had been open. Nesle is a dismal, dirty town, situated on an eminence of no great elevation, and perfectly in character with the melancholy country around it.

This is the first town we have marched through in France. I think it must have been market-day, from the number of people in the streets; yet not the slightest apprehension or agitation appeared; and, as we passed along, the market-people merely turned up their heads, and the shopkeepers came to their doors to gaze on us, much as if we had been marching through Exeter, or any other English town accustomed to see troops.

Since crossing the Somme, the army has marched more cautiously than hitherto, consequently we have been all day with our brigade. At Nesle we got on a chaussée, bordered on each side by large elms, consequently forming a fine avenue; the country on either side without enclosures and not interesting, although better wooded than immediately about that town. Roye was ahead of us, but when within a few miles of it the head of our column led off the chaussée, crossing the fields by a by-road, and then another chaussée, Péronne to Paris, until we gained the village of Goyencour, situated in a pretty, because well-wooded, country. This village, like most of those we have hitherto passed through, is composed of a number of farmhouses scattered over a large space, and embowered amongst orchards and some of the finest linden-trees I ever saw.

The Life Guards and my troop are all housed, so that we are fortunate again. For my part, I am quartered on a small shop, which, however, is very clean; and we have excellent beds, Newland and I. In front of the house an open space affords good room to draw up our guns, &c., adjoining which are the very pretty pleasure-grounds of a handsome villa, seen through a stately avenue of lindens. This place belongs to some lady, who it seems has taken to flight on hearing of our approach, leaving, however, her butler and some other servants behind; so that Lord Edward, who has taken up his quarters there, is as comfortable as he could wish to be. I have just returned from dining with him, and a better dinner, dessert, and wines,* it is impossible to have enjoyed. What a treat in the midst of a campaign to enjoy such a party. Besides his lordship's personal staff, there were the two colonels of the Life Guards. The front of the house, having part of the pleasure-ground (it might almost be called a park) in the fore, has the town of Roye in the distance; a pretty terrace with aloes in vases and other choice shrubs occupies the space immediately under the windows, which, opening to the ground, admit one

* There was a species of Malmsey Madeira, the most delicious wine imaginable. The cellar seemed well stocked, and our table consequently was well supplied.

into a suite of elegantly-furnished rooms. Lord Edward was perfectly at home, and did the honours as if the house were his, and so did the butler and other servants. A quieter, better-ordered dinner, and more excellent, I repeat, could not be.

Lord Edward had heard that, after a little show of resistance, Ham had surrendered this morning; and we were speculating over our first glass of wine on the probability of reaching Paris without resistance, when an officer of the Life Guards came in to report that a strong corps of cavalry had been seen amongst the woods about a mile from the village. As his lordship knew positively that the main body of the French force was retreating before the Prussians, who had got a march ahead of us, he contented himself with ordering out a strong detachment to reconnoitre, and we continued at table. In the course of the evening the detachment returned, and a report was brought in that they had ascertained that the cavalry seen was a corps of about 600 men, composed of deserters from the French army; and these people, taking advantage of the present state of affairs, have been plundering and levying contributions in all the villages, and even towns, throughout this country — that the inhabitants of Amiens itself are greatly alarmed, and have been anxiously expecting our arrival as their only protection against these brigands — a French population actually hailing the arrival of their English invaders with joy! Not knowing what these desperadoes may attempt, we have doubled our guards. The division is ordered to be on the alert, and patrols are established for the night. I shall undress and enjoy my nice clean bed, nevertheless.

28*th.*—A fine morning, after a quiet night, notwithstanding the banditti. Marched early to Roye by a cross road bordered by apple-trees. Here we rejoined the main column, and got upon the chaussée to Paris by Pont St Maxence, &c., a fine broad road as usual, the middle paved (rather roughly) with a summer or unpaved road on each side, the whole bordered by noble elms, and generally a perfectly straight direction: tiresome this from the long vistas which open on one from the summit of every elevation. The country on either hand flat and covered with corn as usual, but had nothing of the wearying sameness of that I so much complained of a day or two ago; for here it was prettily broken by woods and villages, and the distance, instead of terminating with the fringe of apple-trees, presents an interesting range of blue hills. This day's march, however, has not been marked by any occurrence, either of scenery or adventure, worthy of notice. Towards evening, when Lord Edward was about to establish his night-quarters, he directed me to leave the chaussée to take possession of a little place about a quarter of a mile off; and here I am in Mortemer, perhaps one of the most miserable hamlets in all the country. Its short straggling street of poor cottages we found quite deserted, and they have taken away everything that could be useful to us, leaving only the walls and roofs. These cottages are built of rough limestone, and the interiors we have found so filthy and full of vermin, that, one and all, we have preferred to bivouac in the orchards ourselves, and have put our horses into the houses; straw spread under guns and ammunition waggons, with the painted covers closing them in to windward, forms no despicable sleeping-place. One of my drivers, rummaging about, has discovered a vast quantity of excellent household linen buried under the floor. Several other discoveries of this sort have been made; but I have strictly forbidden anything being touched, only leaving these *caches* open that the natives may know they have not deceived us, but are beholden to us for our moderation. Had we depended on Mortemer, we should have gone supperless to bed; but Mr Coates has been so successful in foraging the neighbourhood, that both man and horse have fared sumptuously.

29th.—Since yesterday the character of the country has been insensibly changing: country-houses with extensive gardens and pleasure-grounds, and a more careful style of architecture, seem to indicate an approach to the capital. The villages, too, alas! in my estimation, are changed for the worse—the large thatched farmhouses, barns, &c., and rural cottages, scattered amongst orchards and verdure, have given place to regular streets of three-storey houses. Pieces of towns —surely not villages—these! Mortemer was an exception. The scenery, too, has improved: features more bold and varied, better wooded, and habitations more numerous. The chain of blue hills seen yesterday continues to bound the southern horizon. The first village we passed after leaving Mortemer was almost entirely composed of respectable houses standing in gardens, and having lofty iron railings *(grilles)* to the street. I think this was Cuvilly. Hitchins and I breakfasted as usual, *en chemin*. We find this a good plan, marching as we do so early. Each of us has his cold salt-beef and biscuit in his havresack, and weak grog in his canteen. The troop fairly started, we drop astern a little, the Doctor produces the profits of his evening's forage in the shape of hard-boiled eggs, &c. I have seldom enjoyed anything more than these ambulatory breakfasts in the cool refreshing air of a calm morning. A cigar always concludes my repast, and prolongs the pleasure of it.

After travelling some distance through the sort of country just spoken of, we again emerged upon a high and open tract of corn, and in a hollow some way in front saw the neat village of Gournay, forming a broad street of clean-looking buff cottages, all, I think, slated. Here we stumbled upon the first traces of our allies the Prussians, who bivouacked (at least some of their corps) last night upon these heights. Of all disgusting objects in the world, there is perhaps none more so than the deserted bivouac—the ground everywhere covered with half-extinguished fires, broken jugs, &c., bits of rags, shreds of uniforms, straw trampled in the miry soil, remnants of food of all sorts, &c. In histories of war and warlike operations, the pomp and glitter and excitement are all that present themselves to our mind's eye, whilst the bivouac, the battle-field encumbered with carnage and misery, the hospital with its heartrending scenes, the plundered cottage, the brutal outrage, and a thousand other disgusting and harrowing episodes, are carefully slurred over if touched upon, but more generally never produced. Up to this moment I have actually not known with what part of the army we have been marching. As far as I could see, we have had an apparently interminable column ahead and astern of us; now, however, I find we are with the advance.

A few paces from the highroad, and in the midst of the bivouac (at the point from whence we obtain sight of Gournay) stood a monument of Republican and Prussian revenge — pitiful revenge!—such as, having enacted, a schoolboy would blush at—the mausoleum of some illustrious lady, whom a long inscription, in the true French style of mawkish sentiment, told us " had been lovely in person and elegant in mind—that, soaring above superstition, she eschewed the folly of laying her bones in *consecrated* ground, choosing rather to lie overshadowed in death by those trees of which she had been so enamoured (*passionné*) whilst living," &c. The monument was a stone pyramid, standing in a small square space enclosed by an embankment, and planted round with acacias. The Prussians had cut down the trees, nearly levelled the embankment, and made a fruitless attempt at destroying the pyramid itself. Descending from this eminence by a long but gradual slope, we entered Gournay after crossing a little stream tumbling from the heights. This certainly is the neatest and cleanest place we have seen in France; pity it is, however, that it stands so bare—scarcely a bush to be seen. I don't know how it happened, but when we reached Gournay we were ahead of almost everybody. About the middle of the long village several well-dressed persons were standing at the door of an auberge, attentively watching our advance. As we approached they hurried forward to meet us, eagerly demanding when the Duke of Wellington would come up. Now I suspected the report which we heard yesterday—of Paris having surrendered to the Prussians, and that Buonaparte had fled—might be true, and that these people were deputies sent to avert the wrath of the conqueror; so, addressing myself to the principal person, a short, square-built, rather pursy man, wearing some decoration, I asked if it were so, and when we might arrive there. My friend, drawing himself up, and affecting an air of contempt, exclaimed aloud, "*Paris se rendre?*—non, monsieur, n'y contez pas! il faut passer sur les corps de 200,000 hommes, avant d'y arriver," at

VALLEY OF THE OISE.

the same time coming close up, and tapping me on the knee, he whispered, "*Mais si votre Duc de Vellintone traitera, il tient la bonté à ses pieds, et fera tout ce qui lui plaira.*" I thanked him for the confidence, told him I knew nothing about the Duke, which made him stare, and rode on.*

Leaving Gournay, the country became more pleasing, because more wooded, and the fields generally enclosed by hedges. This style of scenery continued until it brought us to the valley of the Oise, by far the most interesting part of France we had yet seen. How can I describe my feelings when it first opened out before me? How, alas! can I describe the scene itself? But to see and feel it aright one must first have passed over the monotonous melancholy country extending almost uninterruptedly from Nivelles to the Oise —must have had the retina so imbued with the eternal brown and yellow of that ocean of corn as to see everything of a yellow or jaundiced hue —then he may imagine somewhat of the pleasurable relief with which the eye rested for the first time on the lovely scenery and refreshing verdure

---

* These people were deputies sent from the Provisional Government to treat with the Duke, but I have never made out yet who he of the decoration might have been.

of this charming valley. The ground, descending by a gradual slope on our side, ran into a vast succession of most beautiful green meadows, everywhere adorned with magnificent elms, either standing detached, or in groups, or in rows. Beyond these, at about a mile from us, ran the Oise—a broad stream, sometimes exhibiting its sparkling surface nearly on a level with the meadows, at others encased between steep banks of some height. Immediately above the river rose a bold range of hills, thickly wooded from the river-banks to their summit. To the right and left this sort of scenery continued until further view was shut out by the overlapping hills. The road by which we travelled ran straight as a line across the meadows; and at the point where it appeared to cross the river was a pretty-looking little town, Pont St Maxence, partly on one bank, partly on the other. If we were to be opposed, there I thought is the position in which the French await us, and tough work we shall have of it. These ideas occurred to me as we descended toward the meadows; and as the corps in advance of us approached the town, I momentarily expected to see flashes and smoke issuing from masked batteries in the opposite woods; and it now struck me for the first time as a singular circumstance that cavalry should be

allowed to advance alone in the face of such a
position, for we had considerably outmarched the
infantry. Of course the Duke knew there would
be no opposition; and yet it was difficult to imagine what then had become of the French force,
which we knew was retiring before us—of the
200,000 men our friend at Gournay had spoken
of. No opposition was there. Instead of finding the banks of the Oise garnished with cannon
and bristling with bayonets—instead of broken-
up roads and inundated fields, woods full of riflemen and the town of grenadiers—instead of all
this, we found a peaceable population in a lovely
country, labourers in their fields and fishermen
on the rivers, whilst flocks and herds pastured in
quiet security on the verdant carpet which over-
spread the plain. The little town of Pont St
Maxence looked cheerful and pretty as we approached it, lying partly on one side of the river,
partly on the other. The wooded hills rose
abruptly over it, the lower part of their slopes
interspersed with pretty villas, standing amongst
vineyards and in gardens, with terraced walks
overhanging the scenery below. After marching
all day in a hot sun, what a feeling of coolness
and enjoyment was conveyed in the appearance
of the large open windows and shady balconies,

draperied with clematis and other elegant creepers, of these sylvan villas! It appears that the bridge had been broken down last year, and never repaired. To do this a detachment of the staff corps was pushed forward either yesterday or early this morning; but when we reached the end of the town they had not yet rendered it passable, and we were ordered to take post in the neighbouring splendid meadows, where, expecting to remain all night, we commenced at once establishing ourselves. Several troops of horse-artillery and some regiments of cavalry were already up, and others of all arms were continually arriving. The horses, unharnessed and watered, were already feeding, fires were lighted, kettles on, and every one was congratulating himself on having halted on so charming a spot. Thus settled, I strayed into the garden of a neighbouring mill, full of fine currants and cherries, to which the pretty *meunière* not only bade me welcome, but even herself helped me to the best fruit. I was just in the height of enjoyment of the delicious coolness of the fruit, and the piquant badinage of my companion, when suddenly the "boot-and-saddle" re-echoed through the valley, and a confused hum of voices arose simultaneously from every bivouac. With hurried thanks I took leave of my "Maid of the Mill," and hastened back to my people, expecting every moment a fire would open upon us from the opposite woods, having no idea that so sudden an alert could proceed from any other cause than the approach of the enemy.

In a moment our horses were reharnessed, the nose-bags with the unconsumed part of their feed attached again to the saddles, officers' baggage replaced on the mules, the kettles, with the half-cooked messes in them, suspended under the carriages, and all was ready to move. Corps after corps filed out of the meadows and took the road to the town; we followed the general movement, which we now learned was occasioned by the coming up of the infantry, who were to occupy the ground we left, whilst the cavalry was to push on beyond the river as long as daylight lasted. Still no word of an enemy.

The broken bridge had been repaired by the staff corps in so temporary a manner, that the very first detachment of hussars who passed deranged it so much as to render it quite unsafe, and we had to dismount at the entrance of the town and wait a full hour ere it was again rendered passable. This bridge, with its right-lined top, was to me an extraordinarily beautiful piece of architecture; and there is a charm in this right-line which I could not have imagined. The little town was all bustle, every auberge crammed with officers enjoying the luxuries of the French cuisine and vintage. At last the bridge was reported safe, and we recommenced our march, regretting the necessity which prevented our seeing more of this lovely place. Immediately on crossing, we turned to the right and pursued a tolerably good road winding about the foot of the wooded heights, which on the one hand rose immediately above us, whilst the silver Oise glided tranquilly along its course on the other. About a mile, or perhaps more, from Pont St Maxence, we quitted the river, and turning up a beautiful ravine, the slopes of which were partly covered with wood, partly with the rich foliage of the vineyards, we pushed into the bosom of the hills, quitting with regret this sweet river. It is impossible to imagine anything more beautiful than this evening's march. The picturesque scenery of the ravine; the clearness and serenity of the sky; the warm colouring hrown over the one side of the ravine by the declining sun opposed to the deep purply tones of the other; the various and varied picturesque military groups reposing on the turf by the wayside, or winding along amongst the vineyards, altogether formed a picture, or rather a succession of pictures, perfectly ravishing. Never shall I forget this evening!

The sun had set some time when we reached the village of Verneuil, which was to be the termination of this day's journey. Seated in the bosom of the hills, now veiled in a purply obscurity, intermingled with that yellowish hazy light always succeeding a warm sunset, the place looked beautiful. Several corps had already halted—some had taken possession of the houses, barns, &c., others bivouacked amongst the vineyards. Immediately about the village were large gardens enclosed by stone walls, and it was some time before I could make up my mind to invade these. There was no alternative, however. We could not remain in the road; the only fields I saw were covered with rich crops of wheat ready for the sickle, and even these could not be approached but through the gardens. The great gates of one of these were immediately forced open, and, trampling under foot artichokes, asparagus, &c., and flowers, we reached the field after a struggle through the *eschalots* of an intervening vineyard, which, with the vines and their fruit, were miserably crushed beneath our gun-wheels and horses' feet. I could not but regret this devastation, though it could not be avoided. The wheat shared the fate of the artichokes, and we soon established ourselves on it, surrounded as with a wood by the tall stalks of what was still standing.

What a splendid Rembrandt-like picture presented itself from this spot: the valley buried in hazy obscurity; the whitened dwellings, just made out, scattered over the slopes of the hills, whose bold outlines, one of them crowned by a ruined castle, cut strongly against the glowing but gradually fading tints of the clearest sky. In the farm just by we have found stabling for our own horses and lodging for some of our people. But the evening is so fine that I infinitely prefer the field. Seated on the ground with a lantern by my side, I scribble my notes in comfort; but an attempt has just been made to turn us out even from this humble abode—an officer of hussars with an order from General Grant to quit the ground immediately, as he wants it for his hussars. Good man! he thinks a 9-pounder or its ammunition waggon as easily moved as a hussar and his horse. It proved, however, a mere bugbear—he wanted the house and stables; and his emissary having full power to treat, the affair is amicably arranged by our giving up the stable.

30*th*.—Fine morning again. Quitted with regret this lovely country, and climbing the hills by a steep gravelly road, gained the plateau—covered with corn as usual, but here diversified by a pretty sprinkling of trees. Lieutenant Breton, who slept at the farmhouse last night, gives a bad account of our hussars, who, not content with living at free quarters, completely sacked it this morning before they marched—one of their officers taking away a beautiful pony in spite of the old farmer's entreaties, who begged with tears in his eyes that it might be spared, since it was a pet of the whole family. The pony, however, marched.

After marching some distance on this plateau by very good gravelly cross-roads, we rejoined the chaussée from Pont St Maxence to Senlis, and soon after began descending towards the latter place, which is separated from the former by this ridge of hills, covered in most parts by the forest of Balatte. Though not to be compared to Pont St Maxence in point of situation, yet Senlis stands in a pretty country, well wooded, surrounded by fine meadows, watered by the little crystal Nonette. Just beyond the town, on the Paris side, commences the forest of Pontarme, a continuation of that of Chantilly.

Senlis being the first place of any importance through which we have passed, was of course approached with much interest, and this was heightened by its picturesque appearance: antique walls, pierced by an arched gateway, the summit decayed and irregular, fringed with verdure. Spires, and lofty houses showing themselves above it, appeared to advantage through the foliage of the trees, which ran scattering and in clumps up to the very gate, through which crowds of peasantry, with little carts and asses laden with the produce of their farms, were passing to the market. When we passed in our turn, we found the street so thronged that it was with difficulty we could get along, for the market was held in it. The passage of our column, threading its way through the crowd of stalls and baskets of poultry, vegetables, &c., did not seem to excite any very lively emotion, or to interrupt the business of the day. Some of the more idle, or more curious, left their stalls to get a nearer look at *les Anglais*. Nothing like apprehension was visible even among the women, and the boys were as bold and familiar as usual. Here and there I heard a shout of "Vive le Roi!" once or twice it looked in earnest. To try the sincerity of this versatile people, I stooped in passing near some of the most vociferous, and in a subdued tone treated them to " Vive l'Empereur!" The result was always the same—staring first at me, then at each other, with a sly expression of countenance, some one of them, slapping me on the thigh, would reply in the same tone, " Mais oui, monsieur, vive l'Empereur — vive Napoleon! C'est bon, monsieur, c'est bon—vive l'Empereur!" seemingly delighted at being able to express their true sentiments. This might have been mere fun, certainly, but I thought them in earnest. I found this the case everywhere. To us they were never backward in avowing their attachment to Buonaparte or their hatred of the Bourbons, of *Louis le Cochon*. The animated scene in the streets prevented me paying much attention to the town. The impression I retain of it is, that it is gloomy and the streets narrow; but that there are many most respectable-looking houses, some of them very prettily situated amongst shrubbery, and particularly one just as we left the town and crossed the Nonette—the long open windows of which enabled us to peep into spacious and handsomely-furnished apartments, looking most deliciously cool. Just beyond the town we overtook the rear of the Prussian baggage, escorted by a corps of lancers, whose simple and serviceable costume pleased me much : plain blue frocks, buttoned close up to the throat,* and drab trousers or overalls ; not a particle of ornament, nor a superfluous article about their appointments. I think they are the most soldier-like looking fellows I have ever seen. This is our first meeting with any of their army since the 18th. Continuing our route through the forest of Pontarme, we soon came out on a more open but still well-wooded country—the chaussée constantly bordered and overshadowed by lofty elms, the cross-roads by apple, pear, and cherry trees, all now loaded with fruit. Here a sudden and disagreeable change took place in the aspect of the towns and villages. We had got on the route of the Prussian army, which was everywhere marked by havoc and desolation. What a contrast! In Senlis, a few miles back, all was peace, plenty, and confidence,—here traces of war in its most horrid form, desolation and desertion. The inhabitants had everywhere fled, and we found naught but empty houses. Troops and their usual followers were the

---

* The close Prussian collar, now so well known to the British army, was a novelty to us then : our collars were low, and cut down in front. The cavalry and horse-artillery particularly affected very narrow sloping collars.

only human beings we saw now. The village of Loures,* where we arrived about noon, presented a horrid picture of devastation. A corps of Prussians halted there last night, and, excepting the walls of the houses, have utterly destroyed it. The doors and windows torn out and consumed at the bivouac-fire—a similar fate seems to have befallen furniture of every kind, except a few chairs, and even sofas, which the soldiers had reserved for their own use, and left standing about in the gardens and orchards, or, in some places, had given a parting kick to, for many had fallen forward on the embers of the bivouac-fires, and lay partially consumed. Clothes and household linen, beds, curtains, and carpets, torn to rags, or half-burned, lay scattered about in all directions. The very road was covered with rags, feathers, fragments of broken furniture, earthenware, glass, &c. Large chests of drawers, *armoires*, stood about broken or burned. The very floors had been pulled up and the walls dis-

* This must have been a mistake, for the Duke dates his despatches from Loures on the 30th June, and the headquarters would hardly have been established in a place so utterly destroyed as is here described. Perhaps the place was La Chapelle, which I find in the map. My recollection of the scene here portrayed is quite perfect even now, although not of the name.

figured in every possible way. It were needless to add that no human being was to be seen amidst this desolation. It was with no small pleasure I found we were not to halt amid this disgusting scene, as I expected, but to move on somewhat farther; and with still greater pleasure I received the order to quit the chaussée for the village of Chenevière,* about a mile to the left. This removing us out of the Prussian line of march, we hoped to find things somewhat better. The village, like most others we have seen, consisted of a number of farmhouses with their barns and outbuildings, &c., all standing amidst orchards and gardens — the whole surrounded by corn, corn, corn! The place, I should think, has not been visited by the Prussians, for no pillage or destruction is to be seen; but it is deserted—not a soul except our soldiers to be seen. Besides our brigade of cavalry, two or three other troops of horse-artillery are here, so that the place is pretty full; and as we are among the latest arrivals, we have not got under cover, but are bivouacking in a very nice orchard, separated from the village street by some large open sheds; but as the weather is fine, and probably from

* This makes it appear that my notes are right, answering with the map as they do.

OUR NIGHT-QUARTERS.

habit, my people have *littered themselves down* as usual under their guns instead of profiting by these—this they are enabled to do very comfortably here, for there is no want of straw. The people, in their retreat, seem to have taken little with them, except their animals, so that we have all kinds of pots and pans, jugs, basins, &c., *ad libitum*. In short, we should be pretty comfortable but for one want, and that a most important one. The weather is dreadfully hot, and we have scarcely any water; there is but one good well in the place, and that has been surrounded by a crowd ever since we arrived. It is impossible to imagine what a gloom this throws over everything: were it not for the abundance of ripe cherries growing along the roadsides (not of the best flavour, but juicy), we must have suffered to-day terribly from thirst in this burnt-up plain. The corn (standing) is almost bleached—it should have been cut long ago.

CHAPTER XVII.

July 1*st*.—Tiresome work this—very! Here we are in Chenevière with little to do but smoke and sleep, or saunter about the hundred yards of street, which is all the place can boast of; and that can hardly be called a street, being formed of stone enclosures or the backs of barns, &c., the dwellings being in the yards. A rivulet once enlivened one end of this street, but now, alas! when most needed, it is not there—the dry bed with a slimy pool or two, still unevaporated, are all that remain to tell the tale of its quondam existence. How melancholy! I scribble *pour passer le temps*. Some good, however, results from this tiresome halt. Marching at or before daybreak, and not halting until dusk, our shoeing was in a bad state, which Farrier Price and his myrmidons are now busy remedying. The forge is established on the bank of the *ci-devant* rivulet in the rear of our orchard, and under two or three spreading elms. As it is on the edge also of the corn, we have been on the eve of consummating the ruin of the poor fugitive *habitans*, for it has been once or twice on fire. Another piece of service the halt has rendered, is the allowing Hincks with the guns and carriages left at Waterloo to overtake us. He brings also a remount of tolerably good horses, though rather fatigued, since he has made tremendous marches to overtake us. These arrive most opportunely; for with all care we have a number of galled backs and shoulders, though in this respect we are not half so bad as the cavalry, amongst whole squadrons of whom there is scarcely a sound horse.

Another reinforcement has just joined us. That beautiful but unfortunate regiment the Cumberland Hussars has been broken up for its retrograde movement on the 18th ultimo, and distributed amongst the different corps, to be employed as forage escorts, &c., for the commissaries. Being all gentlemen in Hanover, it is easy to imagine they are rather irate at this degradation. A corporal and four privates have joined us. They are all amazingly sulky and snappish with every one, forgetting that neither I nor Mr Coates, nor any of our people, have anything to do with their disgrace. They come, however, very opportunely, since for the last day or two Mr Coates has been resisted by the peasantry, and only this morning several shots were fired at him and his convoy of forage from a wood near which he was obliged to pass. In general, during the above period, he has been obliged to help himself from the barns and granaries, having found every place deserted.

Lord Edward ordered a sale to-day of the effects of the slain. This occasioned a little stir in the village, and passed away an hour or two. I have purchased a good large cloak, erst the poperty of poor Colonel Fuller of the 1st Dragoon Guards. Things sold well in general.

From the front we heard (I don't know how) that the French army are in position at Montmartre, where they intend to fight us again. If they are beaten—of which we entertain no doubt —the fate of Paris is certain; every one fully expects it will be plundered and burned, and thus my prediction verified, the campaign ending with a *grand embrassement*, as I have already written down! There is some firing just begun in front. The Prussians commencing, no doubt!

July 2*d.*—Having no candles last night, could not write up as usual, but was forced to sit in the dark smoking our cigars and listening to the incessant firing in front. This morning is beautiful again, but terribly hot. The latter part of yesterday evening we passed on the tiptoe of expectation, for the firing became constantly heavier and more distinct; that a battle was fighting could not be mistaken. Lieutenant Bell, our adjutant, came to tell me my troop was for the reserve. He also told us that many messages had passed between the Duke and the French authorities. Anxiously we gazed across the top of the waving corn, hoping every moment to see the messenger bringing orders for our advance. Twilight began to shorten our ken, and still the cannonade continued without intermission. At last an orderly dragoon did come, but he brought an order for the rocket-troop only to advance, whilst we were to be saddled and ready to move at a moment's notice. The rockets soon moved, and our bivouac became more gloomy than ever. Fatigued more from excitement than anything else, I lay down at a late hour to sleep; but though I slept I did not rest—feverish dreams of Paris in flames; of plundering, mutinous soldiers, and all sorts of horrors; so that I could hardly believe my eyes and ears when I awoke this morning at three o'clock and looked round me. The orchard presented a scene of the most perfect tranquillity; the firing had ceased; my people, ensconced in the straw, their blankets drawn over them, lay quietly sleeping under their guns; no sound broke the silence of this most delicious summer morning save the jingling of our horses' collar-chains, and the sweet songs of birds, with which the trees were filled. I could scarcely credit the agitation of yesterday evening—it all seemed part of my dream. By degrees our village was all alive; and as the morning advanced, so has our excitement, for the cannonade in front has recommenced. Evening approaches again; the firing has lasted all day without intermission; and yet here we are, doing nothing, or worse, for both our horses and ourselves are drying up with thirst. We cannot stay here much longer, for our only well is almost exhausted.

July 3*d*.—Fine and hot morning. Yesterday morning I awoke and found myself under the trees of a thick orchard; this morning I am lying amongst artichokes, and the Lord knows what, upon a soil somewhat like that one sees about Hammersmith, and, instead of the warbling of birds, the air is filled with the hum of a multitude and the monotonous beating of a watermill close at hand, which has never ceased its "thump, thump, thump, thump" all the livelong night, the quartermaster of some regiment having been placed in it with a detachment to grind corn for us all. Yesterday evening, near sunset, an order arrived for all the artillery at Chenevière to move to the front, but that the cavalry should remain, which puzzled us a little. Accordingly we marched forthwith in company with Major Bull's troop; but I saw nothing of the others, for we were all left to march independently. The order was scrawled out on a scrap of dirty paper and hardly legible, so that neither Bull nor I could make it out perfectly, and were consequently in some doubt as to the exact point to march upon, although in none about going forward in the direction of the cannonade. Instead of returning to the chaussée by the way we came,* as I believe the other troops did (they were not so quickly ready as we were), Bull and I took a road which appeared to lead straight to the front. The country we marched through, though perfectly flat, was still interesting:—one vast expanse of golden wheat, divided as it were into beautiful fields by the crossing of numerous roads, all bordered by two, or even four rows of most magnificent elms. A few vineyards, with here

* We did this to be enabled to march more expeditiously and freely, observing this road to be quite clear of troops.

and there a village, diversified very agreeably this scenery. For a time we seemed to approach the field of battle—the firing became more distinct; and at times we saw, or thought we saw, the slate-coloured smoke rising over the tufted tops of the elms. By-and-by it drew off more to the right, and insensibly became less intense, though still kept up with great vigour. Notwithstanding some little anxiety as to the correctness of our route, and an impatience to arrive on the field of action, still I could not be insensible to the beauty of the noble avenues, umbrageous and cool, along which we marched. They are at all times superb, but become exquisite when seen as we saw them, illumined by the blaze of a cloudless sunset. At a place called Vauderlan we rejoined the chaussée, and had marched little beyond when I observed Bull's troop, which was ahead, suddenly come to a halt at a point where another chaussée came in from the left. What was my surprise, on riding forward, when Bull told me we had run in upon the French outposts: and sure enough, not far in front of us, a long line of vedettes extended across the fields to a village—Blanc Menil, with its white houses and white garden-walls—about a mile on our left; and to our right were lost behind the little woods with which that part of the country was covered. In rear of the vedettes, on the chaussée, was an intrenchment, with an abatis in front of it; beyond was another village;* and to the right the lofty spires of St Denis, towering above the woods, showed us that we were nearer that place than we had expected.

What was to be done in this dilemma? Two troops of horse-artillery, totally unsupported, within musket-shot of the enemy's lines! During our march we had not fallen in with a single corps, and every house was deserted, so that we had no opportunity of gaining information. I had relied on Bull's experience, which, however, in this instance, was at fault. We both agreed as to the necessity of a retreat; as also that we ought to betray no hurry and confusion in so doing. The French pickets and those within the intrenchment were evidently watching us very attentively, but made no move, nor did we for a short time. Whilst thus hesitating, a few of the staff corps made their appearance in the fields on our right, and from them we were rejoiced to learn our neighbourhood to the main body, which occupied all the country in that direction; the staff corps being on the extreme left in the village

* Bourget.

of Dugny, which, though close at hand, was hid from us among the trees. This accounted at once for the inactivity of the enemy; so, reversing, we followed a miserable cross-road through some low swampy ground to Dugny, where the officers of the staff corps succeeded in deciphering our ticket, and gave us directions for finding Garges, the place mentioned. The infantry must have advanced whilst we halted at Chenevière, for these people appeared settled in their quarters. The route pointed out led us for about half a mile between meadows surrounded with high trees and intermingled with little thickets; then, after crossing a small muddy rivulet, we debouched upon more open ground, and a most interesting scene burst upon us. On our left, and very near, the Abbey of St Denis with its elegant spires reared its venerable form above the intervening thick masses of foliage, formed by the converging of several chaussées with their noble bordering of elms, to a point near the town. Beyond, in the distance, appeared the heights of Montmartre, with its telegraph and numerous windmills and chalky cliffs; a narrow gap, through which was seen the dome of St Genevieve, separated them from the heights of Belleville, where a succession of

FIRST GLIMPSE OF PARIS.

the same sort of white cliffs encouraged the idea of a gap having here been broken through the range of heights, leaving Montmartre an isolated mass. Through this gap we obtained the first view of Paris, and the heights were everywhere gay with white buildings, gardens, shrubberies, &c.

To our right the ground ascended by a gentle slope to the village of Garges, whose numerous villas and summer-houses (*kiosks*), intermingled with shrubberies, yet illuminated by the warm mellow light of the western sky, crowned the summit; whilst the intervening space presented one vast bivouac alive with men and animals, and all busy with preparations for passing the night. This ground a day or two ago was covered with the most luxuriant crops of flowers, fruits, vegetables, and some corn—now all trampled under foot; in like manner the chaussée descending from the village had been bordered with fine trees — now lying prostrate in the form of an abatis a little to our left. In our front the dense foliage and rounded summits of the trees in the Park of Stains cut strongly against the yellow sky of the west. It was certainly an animating, interesting scene. Here at length was assembled the advanced-guard of our victorious army, in full view of the devoted, fickle, guilty city—of that city which, in the days of her prosperity, arrogated to herself the empire of the world; that city which for years—nay, for our whole life—had been the great centre of our most intense interest; that city which both historical and romantic reading had rendered perfectly classical, and over which the long exclusion of Englishmen from the Continent had drawn a veil of mystery, rendering her doubly interesting. There she lay, as it were, prostrate at our feet, awaiting in breathless anxiety the fiat of her conqueror.

The firing had now become very indistinct, and ceased to occupy our attention, for here we found the troops quietly establishing themselves, and no appearance whatever of any fighting. There, to be sure, was the intrenchment and abatis similar to that we had seen near Bourget; and there were the French vedettes extending across the plain and those of our Rifles opposite them; but all remained peaceable and quiet. The troops in bivouac presented in the twilight many a picturesque group as we marched along, none more so than a corps of Brunswick lancers, with their sombre uniforms and drooping black plumes—the horses, all saddled, picketed in a line, and in rear of them the lances stuck upright in the ground. The dark mustachioed visages of these men completed the colouring of the picture. Amongst these I met some old acquaintances, who were lounging at the roadside to see us pass. They were all elated and eager for the morrow, which they confidently expected would see Paris delivered up to the punishment she deserved. Leaving them, we turned to the right up the treeless chaussée and soon reached Garges, which we found principally occupied by our artillery; but here the scene we passed through greatly cooled the excitement caused by our march through the bivouacs. The village, or town I should call it, is composed of one long and broad street of good houses—generally, I fancy, the country residences of the Parisian cockneys. These have all been gutted and disfigured in the same manner as at Loures: torn carpets and paper-hangings, broken furniture and glass, and even pianofortes, encumbered the streets in all directions. Inhabitants there were none—not a cat remained in the place; and our soldiers and their horses were the only living animals to be seen. The sight of this devastation cast an inexpressible gloom over me; and I shall never forget the sickening sensation I experienced whilst traversing the street of

Garges in search of some unoccupied garden in which we might establish ourselves for the night. All the best houses and gardens were already occupied; so, after marching through the whole place, on arriving at the end of it we were obliged to content ourselves with a great unsheltered market-garden, close to a muddy sluggish rivulet; and here we are, Hitchins and I, sitting amongst potatoes and artichokes. This fine rich soil does not make the most agreeable parlour-floor. In short, contrasting our position with that of our other troops, we think we have a right to grumble. Every one that I looked in upon in my search had a house and offices more or less convenient (shells, to be sure), and the troop-horses and men who could not be accommodated under cover found themselves almost equally well off amongst the *allées, berceaux*, and shrubberies of the gardens. On the contrary, we have a damp location; no shelter of any kind higher than an artichoke, or, much the same thing, a vine. There is a well on the premises, certainly, but the water is so brackish that it is not drinkable; and that of the neighbouring rivulet, naturally foul, is now so impregnated with soap-suds, from the multitudes of washermen and washerwomen at work in it, that we are at a loss how to water our horses, for they won't touch it. Bell (our adjutant) has just found us out, and communicated an order to remain harnessed and ready for an alert, as it is expected the enemy will attempt something during the night. The firing which we have heard these two days has proceeded from the Prussians having attempted to force the French lines; but they met with a more determined opposition than they expected, and kept fighting their way round to the right to a place called Argenteuil,* where, throwing a bridge over the Seine, they have crossed that river, and Bell says are at this moment in possession of St Cloud. So that Paris is, in a manner, invested.

July 4th.—Last night passed very tranquilly; and, *malgré* our position, I never enjoyed a sounder sleep or woke more refreshed. If the French intended an attack, they thought better of it, and let us sleep quietly. We have had some visitors already this morning from some of the neighbouring bivouacs. They tell us the Prussians are reported to have lost 15,000 men in the last three or four days' fighting, and, what is more

* Mistake. They passed at St Germain on the 30th June, and were in position between Plessis Picquet and St Cloud, with reserve at Versailles, on 2d July.—See Duke's despatch.

interesting, that the Duke, *en grande tenue*, and followed by a numerous retinue, also in their smartest uniforms, has just galloped down toward St Denis—that a rumour of negotiations is afloat, and not a word about advancing. Pretty mess, then, we are in. If this be true, we may stay in this mud-hole for a week yet. Fortunately for us, Dynely, who occupies a very fine house and garden a little way up the street, has a most abundant well of excellent water, to which he has given my people free access, although he guards it most jealously from everybody else. My poor horses suffered last night in getting no drink after their hot march.

7 P.M.—I have already got some little confusion in my notes from not writing them at once, therefore must jot down to-day whilst daylight enough yet remains to do so. *Imprimis*, then : This has been a completely idle day ; very fine, very hot, and very dusty. Having nothing else to do, I have amused myself with rambling about the place, smoking a cigar here and a cigar there, &c. &c. Bull was more fortunate than we were last night —he stumbled upon a most excellent bivouac, which I paid my first visit to this morning, as it is not far up the street. The place is said to belong to the Prince of Eckmuhl (Davoust), and

must have been a delightful residence; it is now *tout à fait abimé*. The pleasure-grounds and gardens, laid out in the English style, are quite delicious, not only from the lovely shady walks and prettily-disposed shrubberies, but also from the splendid terraces, and the views they command of Paris and the neighbourhood. Bull's guns, &c., are packed amongst parterres of the choicest and rarest flowers: the *berceaux* and shady walks form excellent stables, and there his horses are picketed. The officers occupy a charming *kiosk*, partly embosomed in wood, but open to the extensive view over the country toward Paris. Here I found some of them sleeping on the floor, whilst the vacant blankets of others marked the spot they had chosen as their own.

The house itself, large and magnificent, had already been completely pillaged. The doors and windows, where not torn from their frames, were all flying open; furniture of every kind, broken to pieces, and partly thrown out into the garden or courts, and partly littering the rooms; pier-glasses of immense size shivered to atoms; the very walls defaced and smeared with every species of filth. A few of the rooms had escaped this species of pollution, and, except the destruction of their furniture, remained in pretty good order. One of these (which I wondered at) was very handsome, of fine proportions, well lighted, and the walls exquisitely painted (*not stamped*), to represent an Oriental landscape through the open sides of the room, the roof being supported on pillars, which stood so strongly forward that, at the first *coup d'œil*, the illusion was complete. Unless this were saved by the interposition of some officer—a man of taste—I much marvel at the barbarians leaving it untouched; perhaps whilst I write the destruction is accomplished, for I left numbers of Dutch, Nassau, and Belgian gentry wandering about on the hunt for plunder.* A large room adjoining was hung round with very fine prints from Vernet's paintings of the French ports, all in rich frames. These, by some miracle, had all escaped destruction, though not one article of furniture was left. My friend Hitchins, an amateur, thought it a pity they should be left for destruction, and appropriated the whole of them, and not only them, but some fine paintings which he found elsewhere, and cut out of their frames

* Several regiments from America marched through Garges this evening, and took up their station in front—fine corps of veterans, all having served in the Peninsula, and subsequently in America. Many a cheer from old comrades greeted their arrival. It was a soul-stirring sight, the proud march of these well-tried troops into our camp.

with his penknife. This certainly is not justifiable, but his argument is a specious one—better save them at any rate than leave them to be destroyed by the Belgians. At the back of the house, on the same floor, had been a handsome library, but here as elsewhere the genius of destruction had been busy. The furniture was broken to pieces, the books pulled from their shelves, scattered over the floor, many of them torn to pieces, and many, thrown out of the windows, lying in heaps on the pavement of the court below. The foreigners were not the only busy people in Garges—our own troops were not idle. Leathes' servant in this very house has found a magnificent work in three folio volumes, splendidly bound—a series of views of the principal buildings and scenery in France, in the best style of line-engraving. This appears to have been considered the greatest treasure in the library, being the only work attempted to be hidden. He found it under a cask in the wine-cellar, where he had no business. In the gardens and shrubberies the foreign troops were searching for plunder very systematically. Armed with watering-pots, they proceeded regularly over the ground, watering as they went, and whenever the moisture was quickly absorbed, dug. In this manner I understand they have already found many valuable things—certes, whilst I was at this chateau they found a batch of very fine wine buried under a flower-bed. Our men are not so indefatigable; they certainly take what they want when it presents itself, but do not give themselves much trouble in hunting things up. A party of Dutch (Protestants) broke into the church this morning, and after amusing themselves for a time with dressing themselves in the priests' garments, &c., and turning into ridicule the Roman Catholic ceremonies, finished by breaking to pieces the altar and destroying everything they found in the church or vestry. Our allies are by no means an amiable set, nor very cordial with us. If an English corps (as Bull's troop) occupy a chateau and its grounds, still they leave free ingress and egress to any others so long as they do not interfere with them. On the contrary, a single Dutch, Nassau, or Belge, will sometimes (if a commanding officer) occupy a whole place himself: sentinels are placed at every gate, and the place strictly *tabooed*. They are a brutal set. The Dutch appear the best. They are all uncommonly insolent to us.

July 5th.—Our conjectures as to the business which took the Duke to St Denis yesterday prove to be correct. It is rumoured this morning that the preliminaries of peace are signed, and that the *war is at an end!* So terminates, then, our campaign—short, but active, brilliant, and honourable to all concerned. Another fine but hot day.

This morning rode to Gonesse, the headquarters, through a country no doubt pretty enough before our arrival, but in which armed men now occupy the place of vines and fig-trees, &c.—in short, one continued bivouac. Arnouvilles, through which I passed, is a pretty village, and, although the houses were filled with soldiers, did not seem to have suffered like many other places, especially that unfortunate Garges. Four short but well-built and clean streets branch off from a pretty circus, the area of which is a nice smooth turf planted round with young elms. The shrubberies and pleasure-grounds of the Archbishop of ——— (I forget who), all untouched and in good order, added to the pleasing appearance of the place, forming, as it did, such a contrast with the desolate state of the surrounding country. Louis XVIII. occupies the palace, and his Suisses, gardes du corps, &c., the village. Gonesse is a nasty, dirty, gloomy place, and I made little stay there after getting my English letters. My garden begins already to be *home*, spite of its *désagrémens*.

July 6th.—All quiet; not a word about moving. Hitchins and I were both very ill last night after drinking some coffee. This we had brought with us, and therefore it was good: the horrible water here must have caused our illness. Passed the whole morning in idling about the street. There is a very pretty house with (apparently) delicious gardens at the upper end of the town; but some Dutch colonel has got possession, and his sentry turned me from the gate rather rudely. This evening the Doctor and I rode down to St Denis to see the lions. The French outposts had been withdrawn and their barricade removed, so that nothing impeded our progress until we arrived at the entrance of the town, and had a glimpse of the long dusky perspective of its principal street; but here we found an English guard, whose orders were to permit no one (officer or soldier) to enter the place. This was somewhat of a disappointment, but we must see it soon. Just at the entrance to the town is a very fine barrack of grey stone, with a spacious parade, separated from the road by a handsome *grille* or iron railing. The little muddy rivulet which runs through Garges and Dugny crosses the road, just by the entrance, into St Denis, and then falls into the Seine. This feature had been taken advantage of in the intended military defence: the bridge removed and a battery constructed with earth and casks quite across the road. The approach to St Denis on this side is very fine; for at a short distance from this battery three chaussées converge to a point, and a more magnificent *coup d'œil* cannot be conceived than that which presents itself to a person placing himself at the point of union, which at once commands three splendid avenues of the finest elms joining overhead and forming so many lofty arches. From Garges to this point our bivouacs extend; and the rich harvest of wheat which had covered the adjacent fields is completely trodden down. Just by the *etoile* formed by the meeting of the roads, we found Dick Jones encamped with his corps (about 500) of Flemish waggoners with their horses and waggons — a motley and not unpicturesque crew, with their blue smock-frocks and *bonnets de nuit*, wooden shoes, &c., as they sat in groups cooking, or smoking their short pipes. As it was yet early, we did not relish returning immediately to Garges and therefore made a detour to the left through the vineyards, plantations of artichokes, rose-bushes, &c. It was quite refreshing to find this part of the country untouched, everything uninjured and thriving. But there were no vine-dressers, no inhabitants of any kind—not a soul; field and houses all alike deserted. Philosophising as we went on the horrors of war and the beauty of the scenery we were passing through, which contrasted so strongly with that about Garges and every other place where the army halted, we rather unexpectedly entered a pretty village—that is, it had been once so; now devastation had visited it, and the forlorn deserted street was everywhere encumbered as usual with broken glass and fragments of furniture, &c.; every window in the place was destroyed. In front of the church was a small open space, whence a handsome lodge and *grille* gave a view of a long avenue terminated by a chateau. In this place about twenty or thirty hussar horses were standing linked together under charge of one hussar. I believe these people were Prussians, but I can't say. From this man we learned that his comrades were at the chateau, and thither we went, curious to ascertain what they did there. We were certainly not quite so much shocked at the scene of ruin and havoc which presented itself as we went down the avenue as we should have been a week ago; they are becoming familiar now. The fragments of sofas, chairs, tables, &c., lying about the grass, bespoke a richly-furnished house, and the nearer we drew to the house the thicker became these signs of vengeance. Large pieces of painted paper torn from the walls, remnants of superb silk window-curtains, with their deep rich fringe, hung amongst the bushes; broken mirrors and costly lustres covered the ground in such a manner as to render it difficult to avoid hurting our horses' feet—the brilliant drops of these last, scattered amongst the grass, might, with a little stretch of imagination, have induced us to believe ourselves traversing Sinbad's valley of diamonds; slabs of the rarest marble, torn from the chimney-pieces, lay shattered to atoms; even the beds had been ripped open, and the contents given to the winds, and conveyed by them to all parts of the park, covering in some places the ground like newly-fallen snow. The trees of the avenue were cut and hacked, and large patches of bark torn off—many were blackened and scorched by fires made at the foot of them, with the mahogany furniture for fuel; the shrubs cut down or torn up by the roots; the very turf itself turned up or trampled into mud by the feet of men and horses. Hitchins and I dismounted at the grand entrance into the house; and, by way of securing our horses, shut them up in a little room to which a door was still left, and proceeded to inspect the interior of this once splendid mansion. Shouts and laughter resounded through the building. The hussars were busy completing the work of destruction; and as we passed the magnificent stairs leading up from the hall, we narrowly escaped being crushed under a large mirror which these gentlemen at that very moment launched over the banisters above with loud cheers. The ground-floor on the side fronting the park consisted of a suite of magnificent rooms, lofty, finely proportioned, and lighted by a profusion (as we should deem it) of windows down to the floor. These had been most luxuriously and richly furnished; now they were empty, the papering hanging in rags from the walls, and even the cornices destroyed more or less. Every kind of abuse of France and the French was written on the walls. In one room was the remnant of a grand piano. The sad reflections awakened by this sight may be more easily conceived than described, and I turned from it with a sickening and overwhelming sensation of disgust, in which I am sure Hitchins fully participated. The next room seemed to have been chosen as the place of execution of all the porcelain in the house, which had there been collected for a grand smash. The handsomest Sèvre and Dresden vases, tea and dinner services, formed heaps of fragments all over the floor, and a large porcelain stove had shared the same fate. Another room had been lined with mirrors from the ceiling to the floor; it appeared these had been made targets of, for many were the marks of pistol-balls on the walls they had covered; little remained of these except some parts of their rich gilt frames. The last room of the suite had the end farthest from the windows semicircular, and this end had been fitted up with benches, *en amphithéatre*. The whole of this room was painted to represent the interior of a forest, and on one side was a pool of water, in which several naked nymphs were amusing themselves. The plaster was torn down in large patches, and the nymphs stabbed all over with bayonets. The upper floor consisted of bed-rooms, dressing-rooms, and baths, and exhibited the same melancholy destruction as those below; even the leaden lining of the baths, the leaden water-pipes, &c., were cut to pieces. On inquiring of one hussar why they so particularly wreaked their vengeance on this house, he said because it belonged to Jerome Buonaparte, whom every

German detested. Having seen enough here, we looked into another chateau somewhat smaller, but which had also been something very fine; it was precisely in the same state. A very fine library had been here, but the books had been thrown out of window; a small pond below had received multitudes of them, and the rest were scattered all over the park. In the pond I saw several beautiful Oriental MSS., and I fished out a pretty little edition of 'Seneca,' which I pocketed. Disgusted, we returned to our garden, which, by the by, begins to look rather the worse for wear, and I hope if we stay any longer we may be able to get into some house.

July 7th.—Fine hot day. Since early morning the road from Paris has been crowded with people of all ages, sexes, and conditions flocking to Arnouvilles to greet their *beloved monarch.* The whole population seems to have turned out, so continuous is the stream. Berlines, caleches, equestrians, and pedestrians, flow along without cessation or diminution of numbers. All are in their *habits de Dimanche,* and all gay and merry. It is a perfect holiday, which all seem to enjoy without alloy. I could scarcely persuade myself that the gay throng passing before me was the same that, after being accustomed for a quarter of a century to look upon themselves as invincible, then twice within a twelvemonth saw themselves humbled to the dust, and those whom they had so long been accustomed to trample on in military possession of their capital, who now were hastening to do homage to the family twice driven from their throne—and who, in traversing the bivouac of their conquerors, saw on all sides the wreck and ruin of their own houses, fields, and gardens; —yet, nothing daunted, on they went, laughing, chatting, and even singing, in the gayest of all possible moods. For them it was a *jour de fête*, which they seemed determined to enjoy, no matter what its origin. The smart dresses and lively colour contrasted strongly with the dingy clothing, hardy embrowned visages, and apathetic demeanour of our soldiery, who lounged at the roadside, amused by the passing crowd. There were the members of the Legislative Assembly in their embroidered uniforms, some in carriages, some on horseback, others walking and looking dignified; near them, perhaps, a group of pretty brunettes, with brilliant black eyes and coquettishly arranged *cornetts*. Then comes a National Guardsman with his blue and red uniform, with white breeches and *brown-topped boots*, strutting along most consequentially, a handkerchief in hand, which ever and anon he applies to wipe away the dust from his fair face. High and low, rich and poor, jostle along together; and not the least remarkable amongst them is the *limonadier*, in his light cotton jacket and cocked hat. On his back is suspended a tall machine of lustrous tin or some such metal, picked out with brass. Its shape is that of a Chinese pagoda, and from the lower part of it two long slender leaden pipes, terminating in brass cocks, lead round under his right arm. *Chemin faisant*, the tumblers which he carries in his left hand are filled from one or other cock as may be called for, and handed to his fellow-travellers. One cock furnishes lemonade, but of the produce of the other I am ignorant— perhaps a light beer, for the French seem fond of such thin drinks, although the constant repetition of the words "*Eau de vie*" (sometimes "*Au de vis*") indicates that they are not altogether averse to something more stimulating. In the afternoon I mounted Cossack and joined the throng. There was no choice but to go at their pace, so completely filled was the road. The easy, natural, good-humoured manner in which my companions, right and left, chatted and laughed with me, left no room to feel one's self a foreigner, much less an enemy. We were all "*hail fellow well met.*"

Occasional openings allowed me from time to time to push on, and thus change my company. There was, however, no difference between them in one respect—I always found my new friends just as chatty and good-humoured as those left behind.

At Arnouvilles, still following the stream, I was swept into the palace gardens, and found myself in the midst of a most gay *fête-champêtre*. All had come provided with a little basket, or something of the sort, and now, seated round a clean white cloth spread on the grass, numerous parties were enjoying at once the coolness and fragrance under the shade of fine trees or thickets of acacias, laburnums, syringas, &c. &c. Merry laughter, and an occasional " Vive le Roi ! " resounded on all sides, and was from time to time responded to more loudly by the crowd assembled without, all anxious to get a sight of their *new old* King. I longed to try the same experiment as at Senlis, but did not dare.* Handsome young men of the Garde-de-Corps, in their classical helmets and brilliant uniforms, were strolling along the gravel walk, their countenances radiant with joy. I

* Amongst these parties some were of the *haut-ton*, and I saw many very elegant women. Indeed, amongst the bourgeoise there was no lack of beauty, and in manner much to admire, since they infinitely surpass our countrywomen of the same class in gracefulness of carriage and gentility of address.

could not but sympathise with them in thus returning into the bosom of their country, and again meeting with those dearest to them after an absence which, though short, had at its commencement promised a most hopeless duration. Indeed, I did witness more than one tender recognition and affectionate embrace. In the palace his majesty was holding a levee, which, judging from the numbers crowding in, must have been very fatiguing work. Whilst strolling about amidst this scene of festivity, the sharp notes of a trumpet recalled me to the palace, where I found all bustle. It was the *bout-selle* that had sounded, and the Garde-de-Corps was already formed on parade to accompany the advance of the royal cortège. As I wished to see this, and had as yet not dined, I returned forthwith to Garges, which a diminution of the throng fortunately allowed me to do speedily, and having got my dinner, regained the highroad (which crosses at the higher end of our village) just as the cortège and crowd came up. First marched the Garde-de-Corps, resplendent with steel and silver; then came the Garde Suisse, about two hundred as handsome young men as can well be imagined, and such as I never before saw in one body— tall, straight, even genteel figures. They owed nothing to their dress, which was shabby in the extreme—old threadbare frock-coats, once blue, now of any colour, and sufficiently ragged; trousers to match, and mean misshapen forage-caps; arms and accoutrements all wanting—to be sure, some of them carried sticks; knapsacks of long-haired goatskins, once white, but now of a reddish-yellow hue. To these succeeded five or six 4-pounders, in style and equipment a fitting match for such soldiers, who, I should have added, marched along very dejectedly, as if ashamed of their mean appearance. The guns were drawn by little ragged farmers' horses, with their own common harness, driven by the *cultivateur* himself in his smock-frock, night-cap, and *sabots*; carriages, deplorably in want of paint, and further disguised by Belgic mud still adhering to them, were loaded (limbers, trails, and all) with women, children, and bundles; a few old cannoneers, quite in keeping with all the rest, walked beside the wheels; —the whole corps more fit to march through Coventry than to accompany the triumphal entry of a monarch into his capital, and that eminently military. The royal carriages, drawn by post-horses, came next, and in outward appearance were little better than those of his majesty's guns. Louis was in the last carriage, and a dense cloud of pedestrians, with a plentiful admixture of British officers on horseback, closed the procession. I accompanied the throng as far as St Denis, which took up a considerable time, since its movements were necessarily slow. No complimentary movement was made by our troops, although his majesty passed through the midst of us. The more curious crowded to the roadside, which was lined by them, but all in their fatigue-jackets, or even without any—but numbers remained at their occupations, or sitting smoking at a distance. The brigade of Highlanders alone cheered as the King passed through their bivouac. Why was this? Is there any connection between this and the protection afforded the Stuarts by the Bourbon family? Certain it is that the Highlanders alone cheered! The entrance to St Denis was almost impossible, such was the multitude choking up the street, peasantry as well as citizens; and, as the royal carriages approached, they made the air ring with their shouts of "Vive le Roi!" "Vivent les Bourbons!" Only a short month ago, perhaps, these same people, and on this very spot, had shouted as lustily, "Vive l'Empereur!" "Vive Napoleon!" "A bas les Bourbons!" &c. &c. I never felt prouder of being an Englishman! From Garges to St Denis I kept close to the royal carriage, watching the countenance of his majesty in order to detect any emotion. He betrayed none. It was calm, serious, and unvarying in general, occasionally illumined by a faint smile as he returned salutations, but the smile was evanescent—very—and the features immediately resumed their calmness. Our troops seemed to attract considerable interest, particularly the Highlanders; and to every English officer he paid most marked attention, returning their salutes with eagerness and punctilio.

CHAPTER XVIII.

July 8*th*.—Here I am in heaven, as it were—in *Colombes!*—in a *perfect paradise!* More of that hereafter. I am sitting scribbling at last in a handsome room, all to myself! But to begin at the beginning. This morning was (as usual of late) very fine and very hot. At an early hour we received orders to hold ourselves in readiness to march, and understood that we were about to move on the Loire, where the French army had mustered in force and refused to acknowledge the capitulation. Hitchins and I had just found a very pretty little house vacant near our bivouac, and little damaged. Into this we proposed getting to-day, and were rather disappointed when the order for moving came. It was no small comfort, however, to escape from Garges and all its horrors of plundered houses and bad water. The filth of the bivouac, from such long occupation, was becoming intolerable, and the water, bad as it was, was failing fast.

Being sufficiently occupied, I did not notice at what hour we marched, but it must not have been late; for, notwithstanding delays, we arrived here early in the afternoon—the distance probably six or seven English miles. A column of cavalry, composed of our brigade and some other regiments of heavy dragoons, preceded us, and all together took the road to St Denis. Arrived at the point of junction of the three chaussées, instead of marching through the town we struck off to the right. This was not the road to the Loire, and we were puzzled. Wherever we were going the road was beautiful, and the cool shade of the green vault under which we marched peculiarly agreeable in so hot a day. All the country right and left was like a garden; laid out in little square plots of vegetables or roses, an astonishing quantity of which flower is grown in this neighbourhood. Passing through the pretty village of Epinay on the banks of the Seine, we soon after came to a singular ridge of chalky hills separating the road on which we marched from the river. Here then we quitted the chaussée for a cross-road skirting those hills on the side next the river, which we now understood was to be crossed by a pontoon bridge thrown across a little lower down.

Quitting the delicious shade of the elms for the open fields, and these lying on a southern slope, the heat was intense, and when, getting between vines and fig-trees (of which we found whole fields here), the little air there was became shut out from us, it was quite suffocating. The ripe, cool, juicy figs with which the trees were loaded, relieved us, however; the poor fellows placed to watch these looked on rather piteously, but we committed no waste nor destruction beyond eating a few as we went along. These were the first peasantry we had found in the fields since passing Senlis. All along our route dead horses in abundance poisoned the air, and marked the line of operations of Blucher's army. The bridge was at Argenteuil, another pretty village; but on arriving there we found so many corps to pass before us, that, having got into a shady spot, we dismounted and disposed ourselves to rest. The Seine here appeared to me such another river as the Thames at Vauxhall Bridge. The ground on our side sloped rapidly down to it; on the other the banks were low and rushy, an extent of flat meadow-land lay beyond, and thence arose gently swelling hills, covered with shrubberies, villages, villas, &c. The scenery was animated by the masses of our troops and the novelty of the pontoon bridge, together with the interest excited by a number of women and pretty girls who brought us in abundance (for sale) flowers and very fine cherries.

What a change from the sickening, desolated, deserted country we have left, where everything breathed war! Suddenly we enter a land of peace, plenty, and happiness, fields covered with luxuriant crops of various kinds of vegetables, amongst which the large, dark-tinted leaves of the artichoke predominate; vines, figs, and myriads of roses are extended over the face of the hills; whilst the meadows beyond the river exhibit a vast tract of the richest pasture. Innumerable villages, all full of people; their dwellings comfortable and in good order. No desertion here; no sign of military exaction or plundering; no apprehension betrayed at our approach. We are received as countrymen might be. The people are confiding and happy; nor would one imagine that the blast of war had passed so near and left them scathless.

At length our turn to pass arrived, and we crossed the Seine. It seems there were not pontoons enough by half for this bridge, consequently what they had were placed at double distance; the bridge was therefore so weak that the utmost precaution was necessary in passing it, and our guns and detachments (the latter dismounted and leading their horses in file) were obliged to go over separately; but it was also necessary to take the three pair of leaders (eight horses to a gun) off, and let the wheel horses alone take over the guns. Even then, each pontoon sank until its gunwale was within two or three inches of the water as the gun passed over it.

My tutelary genius, Major M'Donald, met me in the meadows, and, as we rode along together, pointed out a village on a rising ground peeping through the trees as my destination—the village of Colombes. "Are we to halt there to-night?" I asked. "Yes, a good many nights;" and then, for the first time, I learned that our army was going into cantonments. On entering the village I found we were not to have it all to ourselves. Bull's and M'Donald's troops were here before me; but as it is very large, and there are plenty of good houses, we have all got abundance of rooms and capital quarters. The place consists principally of two long streets, with a good many detached country-houses of citizens; and as the houses of these streets are generally two or three storeys, it holds us well. We have divided the village into three districts: Bull has all the upper end towards Courbevoie; M'Donald has a fine chateau and park at the bottom of the hill, in the meadows, with the adjacent parts; I have the end where the two streets join on the road to Nanterre—by far the pleasantest.

The peasantry all remain here quietly; but whether fled in alarm, or that it is not the fashion to be seen in the country at this season, I know not; but, certes, all the villas and better description of houses are either entirely empty or only a few servants left in them. Such is the case with this house I now write in. My men and horses are all well put up with the cultivateurs, and the officers are superbly lodged in the different *quintas*. My own is charming; and no one can imagine the delight of such a residence, nor the pleasure I enjoy at again having a place to myself, and that, too, such a paradise. One drawback there is; I have been obliged to park my guns in my own pleasure-grounds—a sad invasion of my privacy this; but I have made it as little annoyance as possible by forming the park close to the further gate, with orders to the sentry to allow no one to pass beyond; and as there is a thick shrubbery between that part of the grounds and the house, it is completely excluded. Another very sad one was the loss of my poor old dog Bal, who had been my companion day and night about eleven years, always sleeping under my bed or by my side. In 1807 he accompanied us to South America. On arriving at Colombes he was first missed. I sent Milward back to Garges, but never heard more of him. *My establishment* appears to be small; I have only seen one old man-servant as yet, though I know there are more. He is extremely obsequious and attentive to my wants, apparently somewhat alarmed, and not quite certain whether I mean to eat him up alive or not. He gave me an excellent dinner to-day and delicious wine—so that he hopes his fate is deferred. A most luxurious-looking bed tempts me, and as I am somewhat tired, and more lazy just now, I shall consign myself to it without delay, and describe my house, &c., to-morrow, when I shall have had time to examine it more leisurely.

July 9*th*.—Hot, beautiful day. A haziness in the atmosphere—the effect of this great heat—makes the distance quite *dreamy*. After so many bivouacs and cottage-beds, the delicious sensation with which I took possession of my voluptuous couch last night is not to be set forth in words, any more than the puzzled astonishment with which I gazed around on awaking this morning. It was some time ere I could clearly recollect where I was — surrounded by everything rich, beautiful, and luxurious. From my bed, too, I could see the meadows below, the silver current of the Seine, and the vine-clad hills beyond. It was impossible to jump up in my usual abrupt manner immediately on waking. I was loath to bring so much pleasure to a conclusion, convinced as I was that it must be less keen to-morrow; so I lay on until hunger reminded me that there were other duties to attend to—other pleasures to be enjoyed.

I have now completed the inspection of my domain, and a right lovely one it is. Let me try and preserve a *souvenir* of it. Architectural pretension the house has none—its charm consisting in the elegant and luxurious fitting-up of its interior, together with the exterior accessories by which it is surrounded. A neat (not small) house of two storeys, with dormitories under the usual very high roof characterising most French houses, seated on the very brink of the rather steep *coteau*, and thus overlooking the meadows, the Seine, the country beyond; and having in the foreground, and immediately below it, the fine massed foliage of the noble trees in the park occupied by Major M'Donald's troop. From the village you enter by a *grande porte cochère* into a neat gravelled courtyard—having the house in front, offices on the left, and a range of excellent light airy stables, and one or two coach-houses on the right. The lower floor of the *corps de logis* consists of a suite of handsomely-furnished saloons, in one of which is a billiard-table—a most delightful solace in such a situation. The end room, having a large window opening to the floor upon a flight of steps leading down to a pretty terrace, is ornamented with some good statues. The corresponding rooms up-stairs are all fitted up as bedrooms. The opposite side of the house from the court looks upon a charming garden presenting every variety of parterre and shrubbery, among which wind cool and shady walks; whilst the innumerable flowers of the parterres fill the air with their perfume; and the sparkling waters of a fountain continually playing under the windows impart a refreshing coolness and throw an air of romance over the whole. A broad terrace, over-shadowed by linden-trees and acacias, runs along the edge of the *coteau* from the end of the house, as above mentioned, to the extremity of the grounds, commanding a charming prospect through its whole length, but particularly from its termination, where, from a picturesque little *kiosk* seated on an artificial tumulus-shaped mound, the eye wanders down the sweet scenery of the valley until in the extreme distance it rests on the palace and park of St Germain-en-Laye. Masses of roses, carnations, lavender, geraniums, and a multitude of other flowers, planted in beds along the upper side of the terrace, contribute their fragrance to enhance the delight of this lovely walk. Immediately beneath the terrace, enclosed by a wall covered with vines, and roofed or coved with large picturesque tiles, is a spacious kitchen and fruit garden, covered just now by its luxuriant crop of all kinds. The more distant part of the grounds is laid out in lawns of smooth turf, interspersed with a variety of shrubs and forest-trees, scattered about singly, in clumps, or sometimes in close thickets or open groves. A lofty stone wall encloses three sides of this domain, the terrace forming a fourth, and a gateway in the further part permits access to my park without trespassing on my *homestead*. The house is elegantly furnished with articles of the most costly and luxurious description, and exquisite statues of white marble decorate the corridors, staircases, and the large saloon before mentioned. The apartment I have chosen for myself is immediately over and corresponding to this, and is a perfect *bijou;* it is fitted up with a taste and splendour that bespeak the inhabitant at once voluptuous and refined. Separated from the other apartments by a small antechamber, it occupies the whole extremity of the house, overlooking the Seine, &c. In this end, like the saloon below, one large window opening to the floor, but into an iron balcony, commands a most delicious view. Immediately below is my well-stocked rich-looking garden; beyond that, yet still, as it were, under me, the finely-rounded luxuriant masses of foliage of the stately elms in the park; then stretch out, like a verdant carpet, the spacious meadows, the sameness of their level expanse diversified and rendered interesting by thickets of underwood, bushes, and occasional clumps of trees. These are bounded by the silvery waters of the Seine, above which rises rather abruptly a curious chain of hills, round-topped, and broken in places by gypsum cliffs, their slopes clothed with vineyards, and separated from a similar isolated hill,* evidently a continuation, by a sin-

---

* Three windmills and an obelisk stand upon the summit next the gap, and a single mill on the isolated hill beyond it. The

gular gap, through which is seen a rich country extending far back, and in the extreme distance the chateau and park of the Montmorenci. The contrast between the purply haze enveloping this country, and the more vivid colouring of the nearer landscape, gives it a dreamy and indescribably mysterious appearance. At the foot of the hills on the river-bank, and immediately opposite my window, the white buildings of Argenteuil, mingled with foliage, form a pleasing object, its church tower decorated by the sacred *pavillon blanc*, which waves continually from its upper window. To the left the picturesque little village of Bezons and its ruined bridge, and beyond a wide extent of open, not picturesque, though rich country, covered with wheat, vines, and fig-trees, extends to St Germain — the sombre trees of whose park terminates the view in that direction. The other windows look over the garden, and the bubbling, sparkling fountain throws its glittering drops quite up to them, if not actually cooling the air, at least refreshing to the imagination. Here the view is bounded by the thick foliage of the shrubbery ; but the contrast between this and

neighbourhood of Paris may be said to be characterised by the windmills which occupy every height, and thus testify to the sluggish nature of the streams watering the plains by the want of water-power.

the extended view from the balcony only serves to enhance the one and the other. The balmy fragrance arising from the parterres, the splashing of the water, and the cheerful songs of innumerable birds, with which the trees are filled, make this a most luscious apartment. But for the interior!—the walls are nearly covered with large mirrors, reaching from the floor to the ceiling, encased in frames richly carved and gilt. The compartments between these are filled up with fine engravings or drawings. In a recess (as the French fashion is) stands a spacious and sumptuous bed, which may be concealed at pleasure by curtains of green silk with deep rich yellow fringe. The bedstead is of mahogany, highly varnished, sculptured, and enriched with gilt ornaments, but looks unfinished to an English eye not yet accustomed to the absence of posts and curtains. The bed itself the most luxurious and fastidious must be content with; the silk counterpane matches the curtains of the recess; the enormous pillows, encased in the finest and most delicately white linen, are edged with rich lace; the sheets are as the pillow-cases, and in texture rival cambric. An elegant little table, standing between the two side windows, serves as a stand for beautiful vases of Sevres porcelain, holding large bouquets of the choicest productions of the garden; a large round table of mahogany, covered with oil-cloth and edged with gilt bronze, occupies the middle of the floor;—the rest of the furniture, in short, is of a piece, and the accessories of a bedroom are of porcelain or fine crystal. A little door beside the recess opens into a narrow passage leading round to the rear of the house, where a small cabinet, lined with mahogany and lighted by an *œil de bœuf*, leaves no want on the score of conveniences unsupplied. At the other end of the room a small closet, fitted as a library, contains a collection of the most splendid editions of the best French authors. Here, however, the voluptuary was conspicuous; the licentiousness of Voltaire, Louvet, and others, is innocence itself compared to many works in this collection. My establishment consists of the old butler (Monsieur Ferdinand), the gardener, the cook, and, I believe, a girl as a scrub. These, with the addition of William and my two grooms, make up a snug little family. M. Ferdinand is attentive, and seems solicitous to please. Cook sent me up yesterday a remarkably nice dinner; and the gardener brought a fine fresh bouquet this morning for my vases, which he promises to do daily, also fruit for my dessert. My larder seems well stocked, and so does my cellar, for I had a bottle of excellent wine yesterday; therefore I have every reason to be satisfied with my good fortune.

The houses in which my officers lodge are all either entirely or nearly deserted; so that, having the only convenience for the purpose, I have acceded to their request, and allowed our mess to be established here, though it is hardly fair upon the proprietor, on whose resources we shall draw largely; however, I have given orders for the dinner to be prepared to-day, and M. Ferdinand has made no scruples.

July 10*th.*—Splendid morning, but heat excessive. Sorry to say that at the parade this morning I found we had no less than thirty horses with sore backs. This is terrible! but I know others are worse. Yesterday we dined together, and a capital dinner and excellent wine we had. After dinner, the evening being so fine, Hitchins, Breton, and I, mounted our horses for an exploration. We first crossed the meadows to the river, and rode a little way along the banks; at the ferry we found the ferryman asleep in his boat, and I could not prevent Breton from launching him into the stream—how far he went down we have not yet heard. This was childish, certainly. Quitting the river-bank we made for a high hill, whence we expected a view of Paris. *Chemin faisant*, we stumbled on some singular quarries, immense caverns cut in the soft calcareous stone, and going farther in than we thought it prudent to follow. These were in the middle of the fields, in the low ground between Colombes and Nanterre. As we enjoy the privilege of travelling over fields, &c., and are therefore quite independent of roads, we made straight for the hill, and gained its summit just as the sun was setting in all the glory of a fine summer's evening. We had judged rightly, for Mont Valerien (so it is called in my map) commands a most lovely view. Before us all Paris lay extended as in a plan; we could see every part of it, and even the far-away country beyond. Here was no dingy, orange-coloured smoke, like that which obscures the London atmosphere, and blackens the country for miles round. *Au contraire*, the clearness of the Parisian atmosphere was scarcely deteriorated by the very light transparent vapour floating over the city, which rather increased the interest and beauty of the scene by the softened outlines, and by the rich purply tint communicated to all parts of the landscape seen through it. The country immediately around, and the slopes of the hill itself on which we stood, had the appearance of one vast and productive garden, being divided into rectangular patches planted with rose-bushes, cherry-trees, vines, fig-trees, artichokes and several other sorts of culinary vegetables, all growing in the greatest luxuriance, and presenting a most extraordinary mass of verdure. Amongst all this, the white walls and red-tiled roofs of several neat villages and picturesque villas harmonised charmingly. The foot of the hill towards Paris was washed by the gently-flowing waters of the Seine, on whose placid bosom a few boats occasionally appeared.

The lively verdure of a long narrow strip of meadowland lying on the opposite bank of the river, and the white walls of several large-windowed Italian-like houses bordering on them, contrasted strongly with the sombre tones of the Bois de Boulogne behind them, amongst whose thickets several columns of blue smoke, and a line of white tents seen here and there on the lawns, attested the presence of some part of our army. Along the line of the river were the villages of St Cloud, with its bridge; Suresnes, Puteaux, and Neuilly, from the end of whose bridge a most superb avenue of elms stretched away toward the city. Beyond could clearly be discerned the column of Austerlitz, the dome of the Pantheon, Nôtre Dame, with its high-pointed façade, circular window, and two flanking Gothic towers. A little to our right the elegant dome of the Invalides, its gilded decorations glittering in the last rays of the setting sun; the cream-coloured portico of the Hotel de Bourbon; and the more deep-toned architecture of the Hotel des Monnaies and its dome. Still further to the right the scene was closed by the wooded heights of Bellevue, which appeared continuous with the Park of St Cloud. These, wrapped in deep shadow, formed a mass of sombre verdure, balancing well the other parts of this brilliant picture. In the distance beyond the city were the smiling heights of Belleville, covered with villages and country-houses, gradually descending into the vale of the Seine, of whose waters an occasional glimpse might be caught winding their tortuous way like silver threads through the rich plain. To the left the buildings of the city spread up the steep slopes of Montmartre, the summit of which presented a formidable appearance with its lines of fortifications. Windmills and a telegraph occupied the higher end of its ridge, whilst that next us terminated in a perpendicular precipice, the white face of which overhung the tufted groves of Monceaux and Clichy. Still further to the left extended the plains of St Denis, yellow with the golden harvest, beyond which arose the town and abbey. The horizon on this side was bounded by a low range of blue hills, of pleasing though not very varied outline. The balmy softness of the evening air—the varied noises, softened by distance, arising from the village below—the sounds of music, mirth, and revelry coming up more distinctly,—all contributed to heighten the interest of this charming panorama. Long did we linger on Mont Valerien, until the coming shades of night reminded us that we were strangers to the intricate maze of vineyards, &c., which we must traverse to regain Colombes, and we turned our backs on the lovely scene.

July 13*th*.—This is our first wet day. Hitchins and I went to Paris this morning; but the rain set in so much in earnest that we returned forthwith, and I have devoted the remainder of the day to bringing up my leeway; for, between much occupation and much idleness, I have let my journal drop astern, and now I hardly know how to begin what I have to record, which, though trifling for others, is to me worth its

MY LANDLORD. 113

weight in gold — at least will be so years hence.

Imprimis, then, I have discovered my landlord to be a M. L'Eguillon, who is an old bachelor (seventy-four years of age), and resides in a handsome town-house, Rue des Enfans Rouges. He is said to be very rich, but I cannot find out whether he has or had any employment under Government. I find that I can in some measure repay him for my good living here by sending his hay, oats, or anything else he may want, under an escort, as otherwise it would not be allowed to pass the *barrière*.* I suppose Ferdinand has reported us as good people, for I have received a most polite and obliging note asking this favour, and at the same time assuring me that Ferdinand has orders to pay us every attention. I sent Bombardier Ross up the other day, as he speaks French, with a load of hay, and he reported that nothing could exceed the kindness with which he was treated, and that the old gentleman's town residence is a magnificent one. A very pretty girl of sixteen (Mademoiselle Ernestine), whom the servants call his niece, lives with him. There

* The Prussians seize all forage not under escort and for our own use. Had they known this last was not the case, our non-commissioned officer would have availed little.

VOL. II. H

seems a mystery, however, in the matter, for the gossips of the village declare she is not his niece. It is Mademoiselle Ernestine's apartment which I have taken possession of, it seems.

Up to the present moment nothing could have been more delightful than my residence here—so much so, that it was some time before I could tear myself away from it to go to Paris, though only about six English miles distant, and then with reluctance. To me the country at all times has so many charms, and the city so few, that it is never without regret that I exchange the one for the other. Situated as I am here, during this fine season, and surrounded by luxuries, it is a hard task to think of sacrificing even a single day to the close, disagreeable streets of a large town. Rinaldo in the gardens of Armida was not more completely enthralled than I am in this little paradise. On first awaking in the morning, my delighted ear is saluted by the melodious warble of innumerable pretty songsters in the shrubbery, which comes accompanied by the soft murmurs and splash of the fountain. My toilette occupies a much longer time here than it ever did anywhere else, so great is the luxury of wandering about in a dressing-gown: finished, however, it must be, and then I descend to my stable, talk nonsense to my horses, examine poor Cossac's wounds, which were not improved by our lengthened march, and then stroll into my garden, cool my palate with some of the delicious fruit, take a turn or two on the terrace under the linden-trees, look at St Germain, think of the unfortunate James who died there in exile, then at Argenteuil, where Heloise pined for her mutilated lover, return to my penetralia and find that William has arranged a delicious little breakfast. A parade of the troop in the village street follows; a visit to the quarters, stables, &c.; an inspection of carriages; concluding with a little peroration with Farrier Price and Wheeler Rockliff. All this occupies the first part of the morning; the remainder is passed in lounging about the village, visiting the other troops, or wandering about my own delightful grounds; sometimes a game at billiards, sometimes a little scribbling. So pass my mornings. Five o'clock usually finds us all assembled in the *salle de compagnie* awaiting M. Ferdinand's annunciation, " On vient de servir, M. le Commandant," throwing open the *battants* with a bow and an air worthy a groom of the chambers. Dinner consists of a *potage* and several other dishes, always excellent; it is followed by a dessert of fine fruit from my *own* garden. Our wines, too, are not only of the best quality, but we have an astonishing variety—in short, we live like fighting-cocks. After passing a reasonable time at table, and drinking a reasonable allowance of M. Eguillon's wine, we break up for the evening. Some resort to the billiard-room, some to the neighbouring troops, and I either take a ride or saunter about my terrace as I did in the avenue at Strytem, smoking some of the few remaining excellent cigars I have brought all the way from Brussels—doubly precious now, since I find there are none such to be got in Paris. Cigars are, I think, a government monopoly here as in Spain—at least there is some mystery which I don't understand further than that the French Government has been concerned in forcing the lieges to smoke bad cigars or none at all. Only two kinds are procurable here : the one, a little black thing made of the commonest tobacco, they call Dutch, *des cigars Hollandais;* the other, a large cigar of very common bad tobacco also, has a wheaten straw stuck into it to suck the smoke through ; and this, besides the villanous taste of the tobacco, burns your palate horribly.

The other evening I had retired after dinner to the terrace to enjoy, as usual, the charms of a fine sky and fine landscape. Twilight crept gradually over the valley, and, by obscuring the distant parts, allowed play to imagination, and gave additional interest to the scenery. Light airs from time to time sighed amongst the overhanging foliage; the joyous laugh of the villagers comes softened on the breeze, united with the monotonous splash of the fountain. I had seated myself in the little *kiosk* at the end of the terrace; the smoke of my cigar arose lazily in the air; my eyes were fixed on the silver Seine, and my mind travelling over again the events of the last three or four weeks, drawing comparisons between the feverish excitement prevailing through the former but greater part of that time, and the delicious tranquillity of the present, when suddenly the grating sound of angry voices wounded my ear and dissipated my reverie. I listened; the speakers appeared to be at our park, or near it. There were English voices and foreign of some sort. A quarrel between my men and the natives, no doubt. But how came the latter in the grounds? The voices became louder and fiercer; there was a rattling of sabres, too. Good heavens! are the French renewing the Sicilian Vespers? Whilst asking myself this question, I was already hurrying along the tortuous path leading to that part of the grounds, and soon came upon the scene of action. Here I found Quartermaster Hall and several gunners struggling with our hussars of Brunswick, whose horses, bridled and saddled, seemed the objects of contention from the way in which they were alternately seized by one or the other and most unceremoniously dragged about by both.

High words and threatening gestures, pulling and scuffling, seemed the order of the day, but no blows were interchanged. Both parties seemed equally enraged, but neither understood the other, —for one swore in German, the other in English; the gestures, however, spoke a sort of universal language which all parties comprehended perfectly. At the moment of my arrival one of the hussars, having rescued his horse from the grip of his opponent, had raised his foot to the stirrup, and was in the act of mounting, when an athletic gunner, seizing him by the waist, swung him to some distance, rolling on the turf. The fellow, springing up again, had half drawn his sabre as I emerged from the shrubbery with an authoritative "*Halt da!*" which was instantly obeyed by all; whilst old Hall, the moment he saw me, cried, "They are off, sir—they are going off." The hint was sufficient. I despatched a gunner with orders to the guard to shut the iron gates and allow none to pass, then proceeded to investigate the origin of this quarrel. I had placed these people in the grounds from the first, that they might be more under surveillance. They have a tent for themselves, and their horses are picketed near our guns. This I have found necessary, from the sulky mutinous spirit they have always evinced since the first day of joining us. They have always been a source of considerable worry to me, and have been getting worse lately. According to their own account, they are all *volunteers* and *gentlemen*; therefore they feel very severely the degradation of their present position, particularly being put under a vile commissary, whom they affect to treat with the utmost contempt. Their present complaint was about their bread, which they said " was not even fit for *common soldiers*; " and they accused Mr Coates of having purposely given them this bread as an insult. In their rage they had saddled their horses with the intention of returning home, or the Lord knows where, when Hall interfered, and the scuffle took place. The corporal (a fine young man) was particularly indignant, and held forth most vehemently on what was due to a gentleman, partly in German, partly in French. Hall's insolence he spoke of with great bitterness, giving me to understand that he expected my men should pay him somewhat of the same deference as to their own officers. My answer to all this was short : " The bread is of the same quality as that served out to our own men ; therefore, if the *gentlemen* disliked it, they might leave it. As to their rank in civil society, I know nothing about it ; they were put under my orders as any other soldiers, and as such should do their duty." Two or three of the most refractory I made prisoners of, and if they still remained discontented, they at least remained quiet. This disturbance, however, spoilt my evening; so, having consumed my cigar whilst lecturing the gentlemen, I retired to my room and spent an hour or two over Voltaire's 'Philosophical Dictionary.'

Notwithstanding the raptures in which our people spoke of Paris, which some of them visited the very first evening of our coming here, yet it was only a day or two ago that I could tear myself from the country and go thither. The village and *les villageois* had not yet lost the freshness of novelty. Strolling about the street gossiping with the people has been a source of infinite amusement to me, and I have been much interested in observing their peculiar manners and habits. The harvest, which has just commenced, causes considerable stir in the village, as all the produce of the fields is brought to be stored in their granaries here. The villages round Paris have anything but a rural aspect : houses of stone, roofed either with tiles or slates, from two to three and even four storeys high ; large windows, like those of town houses; the attics are their granaries, hay-lofts, &c., and a window or door, furnished with a crane and tackle similar to those of our merchants' stores, furnishes the means of hoisting in the sheaves, bundles of hay, &c. The consequence of this is, that our streets are all in a bustle—loaded carts continually arriving from the fields, and drawing up under the entrance-window of their respective houses. Bundles and sheaves are mounting into the air, and various gossiping groups are formed below. The peasantry in this neighbourhood are almost all of them proprietors of the lands they cultivate. As with us, the law obliges every man to put his name, &c., on his cart ; so we see continually "Jacques Bonnemain, cultivateur," "Jean le Mery, proprietaire," &c. The figures composing these street-groups are sturdy well-made men ; much more active and springy than our clowns, although sufficiently rustic. Their costume, too, widely differs from everything we are accustomed to associate with rusticity. The bronzed visage, surrounded by its setting of black locks, surmounted by the *bonnet de nuit*, usually white, or having once been so, round jackets of blue-striped cotton stuff, and trousers of the same—bare feet, thrust into a pair of clumsy *sabots*, complete the costume. Amongst the young men and boys I have remarked a much greater proportion of handsome intelligent faces than one usually sees in any English village; our rustics are generally coarse-featured, and have a most unintellectual expression of face. The French peasant not only has the advantage in point of person and carriage, but infinitely so in his address. The women partake of the labours of the field, and enter largely into the composition of our village groups. Their general costume is not unpicturesque. They are always without gowns, the exposed stays (not always very clean) sometimes laced up, sometimes quite loose and open; blue and white, or pink-striped petticoats; neck partially covered by a coloured handkerchief (*fichu**); the head by another, gracefully turned round it, something in the shape of a turban;† large gold or silver hoops in the ears, and a small cross of the same

---

* In English we have no word which will translate.
† The *cornette*.

THE WOMEN.

suspended by a black ribbon from the neck; stockings of grey or blue thread, or bare legs; large *sabots*, the insteps frequently garnished with a strip of rabbit-skin. Such are our village belles. At a superficial glance one does not see amongst them such gradations from youth to age as among our own women. All are either old or young, hideously ugly, or pretty, or very pretty. About the age of puberty (which seems to be earlier than with us), they become masculine and coarse, though still handsome. But about thirty (or earlier, if they have children) they lose all pretensions to good looks, and immediately assume the appearance of old age—wrinkled, skinny, with sunken cheeks, hollow eyes—and such necks! Like the men, these women are vastly superior to our female peasantry in carriage of person and in manners. The former is invariably erect and commanding, giving to the ugliest old woman an air of dignity never or very rarely to be met with among our working classes, and not always amongst our ladies. Some of the young ones, well made and tall, with their firm determined step, are really majestic creatures.

The ordinary diet of these people seems little calculated to enable them to go through the portion of hard labour that falls to their lot. Bread, black, coarse, dry, and diabolically sour, a bit of hard tasteless cheese, compose the usual breakfast and dinner, with the occasional addition of haricots, or some other vegetables; for supper, broth (*potage aux herbes*), in which a bit of lard or some kind of grease is melted to give it richness and perhaps flavour. Their beverage is a poor sort of *vin du pays*, very sour, and very inferior to the sound rough cider used in our apple-counties, Hereford and Devon. In the *cabarets* beer is to be had of a pleasant quality, although not strong. The *bonne double bierre de Mars* is of a superior caste, and, when bottled (as it is sold), a refreshing, agreeable drink in hot weather.

March is to their brewers what October is to ours. This *bierre de Mars* (from the month, I presume) one would suppose exclusively military, from the numerous coloured prints stuck on the window-shutters of most *cabarets*, representing officers and soldiers in the acts of drawing, pouring out, or drinking this favourite tipple. The most common of these represents two officers in *grande tenue*, plumed hats, swords by their sides, spurs on the heel, &c., seated at a small round table. Each holds in the right hand an uncorked bottle, in the left a tumbler, the *bierre* rising in a jet from the bottles, forming two intersecting arches, terminating precisely in the opposite and apposite tumblers. The shutters frequently bear both pictorial and scriptorial annunciations not a little amusing. I have seen numbers on our march, but thought no more of them; and it was only the other day, at Courbevoie, that "*audevie à vandre*" upon a shutter gave rise to the idea of making a collection of them. The universal "*Ici on loge à pied et à cheval*" is parallel to our entertainment for man and horse.

I have before noticed that on arriving here we found all the gentry fled. That was not quite the truth. A few days since I discovered that a certain handsome house, in Bull's quarter of the village, is still inhabited by the proprietor, an old lady of seventy (la Marquise de * * *), very partial to, because somehow connected with, the English, and therefore remaining at home in full confidence of good treatment. She has judged rightly; not a soul has trespassed upon her except as visitors, of which she is very proud, and holds a sort of daily levee, which we sometimes find a convenient lounge. Brought up in the Court of Louis XVI., Madame la Marquise is a strict observer of all the etiquette of the old *régime*. A light active figure, and a natural (or perhaps assumed) sprightliness of manner, added to a very juvenile costume, give her at a little distance quite the appearance of a girl. A nearer approach, however, spite of rouge, &c., most liberally applied, betrays the *septuagénaire*. At my first visit I found this extraordinary old woman alone, dressed, and evidently expecting visitors. I introduced myself, and was received with almost affectionate kindness. Our *tête-à-tête* was a long one, for she would make me listen to the whole of her family history, and how one of her ancestors, having married some English lady of rank, she considers herself *à moitié Anglaise*. She was not content with telling me her history, but showed me her whole house and gardens (both very handsome and in excellent order), even her own boudoir, *chambre à coucher*, &c. On taking leave she exacted a promise of being a good neighbour, which I have endeavoured to perform by devoting to her a small portion of my leisure time. It is to her that I am obliged for breaking the spell that bound me to the village, and at last *visiting Paris*. The other morning she expressed such unfeigned astonishment at my want of curiosity that I resolved to see the place forthwith, if only for a few minutes. Accordingly, after dinner I mounted Nelly, and set off by what I guessed must be the road thither. The day had been exceedingly hot, the roads were very dusty, and, half irresolute, I rode slowly over the uninteresting parched-up plain between Colombes and Courbevoie, made disgusting, moreover, by the trodden-down corn and carcasses of horses, &c., which marked the old bivouacs. The handsome cavalry barracks for the Imperial Guard at the entrance of Courbevoie detained me a moment, and then I descended the winding shabby street, and came suddenly on the beautiful Pont de Neuilly. The lovely scenery here, above and below the bridge, and the magnificent avenue beyond it, put an end to my Paris trip. For the life of me I could not resolve to exchange such scenery, and pass such an evening in the streets of a city, however fine they might be. This bridge, and the one at St Maxence, are elegant things, certainly; but the straight line, which is one of their great beauties, must not be claimed by the architects as an original idea. The Roman bridges at Alcantra and elsewhere no doubt have been their prototypes. I found here defences similar to those at St Denis —the road to the bridge broken up and obstructed by carts, and a sort of abatis; this was commanded by a 2-gun battery, built across the road on the Paris side, secured at each flank by a stockade. These mementos of war were unpleasing objects certainly, yet they could not divert the mind from the sweet scenery on every side. The Seine came gliding tranquilly along through green meadows, fringed with willows, bordered on each side by villages and villas; several verdant islands, also, decorated with large umbrageous willows, divided its stream into different channels, on which floated boats of various descriptions—some plain and of coarse construction, laden with goods; others of a more elegant construction, gaily painted, and filled with joyous light-hearted people, already forgetful of the downfall of their idolised Emperor—of their national glory tarnished—even that, in these their moments of mirth and recreation, they were in the presence of their conquerors—of their ancient enemy. British soldiers stood on the river-bank as they passed along—British soldiers occupied the barracks of the late Imperial Guard, under which lay their course, and yet the laugh was as joyous, the countenances as bright, as they could have been after the bulletins of Austerlitz or Jena. Not so, I ween, on the slimy Thames had England fallen as low, were London the cantonment of French legions.

A most superb avenue is the road which gradually ascends from the Pont de Neuilly to the

Barrière de l'Etoile, the unfinished works of which terminate this unrivalled perspective. I forget whether there are two or four rows of elms on either side—and such trees! This splendid road was alive with carriages, equestrians, and pedestrians, as I rode up it to the *barrière;* and here another magnificent scene burst upon me. Hence the road descended gradually towards the city, handsome houses, and even rows of houses, intermingling with the masses of foliage on either side ; and far away, in hazy, dreamy distance, this avenue was terminated by the heavy but imposing mass of the Tuileries, with the spotless banner of ancient France waving gracefully in the evening breeze from the elevated central mass. I returned from this interesting excursion just as the fading tints of the western sky began to sober down into the greys of twilight. My curiosity was excited by this peep of Paris, and the next morning actually found me riding slowly down from the Barrière de l'Etoile towards the Place Louis Quinze, delighted with the novelty of the scene by which I was surrounded. On either side of the road, among the noble trees, were handsome houses, the large open windows and balconies of which were filled with green shrubs and brilliant flowers. Beyond these I came to a wide open space everywhere covered with trees, but poor ones compared to the giants forming the avenue. Under these a regiment of English hussars, and a band of Cossacks, were in bivouac together — a novel and amusing scene. The soldiers and their horses were objects of curiosity (English as well as Cossacks) to a crowd of idle Parisians who stood by, not in silent contemplation of the *strange animals*, but chattering like a pack of monkeys, and explaining what they saw to those of their neighbours less gifted with the powers of conception. Carriages, too, as they passed, and groups of young men on horseback (looking half-military, half-bourgeois, from their mustachioed upper lips, erect carriage, holstered saddles, and cavalry bridles), paused to contemplate the foreign bivouac. If these last were amused with my countrymen and their friends, I was no less so with them. There was something irresistibly comic in their self-satisfied air as they paraded their managed cats of steeds before the fair ones in the carriages, and the affected, contemptuous looks they cast on the hardy fellows who had so recently chased their own braves (perhaps some of themselves) from Brussels to Paris. The equipages, too, were worthy of notice : they reminded me of Ireland

—"*Nothing of a piece.*" Handsome carriage, well-dressed servants, dog-horses and shabby harness; or shabby servant and beautiful horse, new harness, and an old jarvey of a carriage—the fair dames within invariably smart. No comparison can be instituted between French and English equipages. The neatness and perfect completeness, beauty, finish, lightness, and goodness—all are on the side of the latter. Their cabriolet, however, is something *sui generis*, and worthy of admiration. They are generally drawn by one horse, sometimes a postilion on a second horse attached as an outrigger. It was one of these that captivated my fancy near the *barrière*. Such a turn-out! The carriage was just like other cabriolets, only a very smart one; and here I must acknowledge an exception to what I have just written—the whole *was* of a piece—good, smart, and respectable; but, *mon Dieu!* what a spectacle! The heavy harness under which the horses were almost buried was covered with plated buckles, bosses, &c. On the outrigger sat a fine, well-made fellow, six feet if an inch, erect as a grenadier. On his head an enormous cocked-hat, bound with broad silver lace and loop, stuck square on; a blue coat, collar, skirts, and sleeves, all covered with silver lace; the clothing of his nether limbs hid in a tremendous pair of boots, sticking six inches above his slightly-bent knee, and armed with a most formidable pair of spurs; like all the rest of them, riding exceedingly long, consequently bumping along at a moderate trot with most imperturbable gravity. How I should have liked to see this equipage trotting down St James's Street! A passer-by, of whom I asked the question, informed me that this was Les Champs Elysées. I could hardly credit him. What! the far-famed, much-vaunted, much-bescribbled Champs Elysées! Impossible!—or, if true, what a disappointment! I hardly know what sort of an idea I had formed of the Champs Elysées—certainly nothing like the reality. No turf, no verdure, in short, no fields, but a gravelly dusty space, surrounded nearly by buildings, and barely shaded from the scorching sun by a parcel of miserable-looking half-grown trees, sufficiently powdered to conceal whatever verdure they might have. If ever the grass had grown here, every trace was now obliterated. Bivouacs are sadly destructive of nature's beauties. "Thus, then," said I, "here is one illusion dissipated. Let us see farther, perhaps all will equally vanish in smoke and dust." A certain feeling of exultation, a tumultuous rising of spirits came over me as I rode into the Place Louis Quinze, and pulling up, regardless of the moving throng of people, contemplated at my leisure the scene around me. I have now got a map and a 'Guide de Paris,' both of which I have since had opportunities of elucidating or confirming by inquiry and *vivâ voce* evidence. Then, I knew not that I stood precisely on the same spot where the martyrdom of Louis Seize and the fair Marie Antoinette had been consummated. I knew that the walls in front of me as I entered the Place from the Champs Elysées were the ramparts of the Tuileries; that the bowery trees which overtopped them were in the gardens; and that the immense pile seen again over these was the chateau itself: but I did not know that the magnificent ranges of buildings, with their rich sculptures and Corinthian colonnades on my left, were those of the Garde Meuble; nor that the fine but short perspective by which they were separated was the Rue de la Concorde; nor that the handsome bridge on my right was the Pont de la Concorde, and the imposing portico which reared its lofty Corinthian columns beyond was the entrance to the Salle des Representatifs. Although ignorant of the names and destinations of the noble objects, I could not but be sensible of their effect individually and as an *ensemble;* and I did acknowledge that nothing could be more imposing, more strikingly magnificent, than this entrance to the city of Paris.

Every faculty absorbed in the contemplation of the various and varied novelties around me, I progressed mechanically, and without knowing or seeking to know where I was going, found my way down the Rue de Rivoli, and so into the Place Vendome, where the column of Austerlitz, by its beautiful workmanship, and the historical recollections associated with it, arrested my course for some time. Strange, however, that a nation like France should borrow from Rome—that she could not produce an original idea to commemorate a great national triumph. It is nevertheless a superb monument; and at least the idea of using the guns taken in the battle to decorate the city —was not *that* an original idea? The Place itself I do not like. Its houses are certainly fine, and uniformly built, but the style is heavy, the material dismal, and the want of *trottoirs* gives the whole the air of a "mews." In approaching the Place Vendome by the Rue Castiglione, I crossed the Rue St Honoré, the busy stream flowing along which would have induced me to follow it, but the column in front drew me forward like a magnet. The streets of Paris are infinitely more amusing than those of London, inasmuch as they everywhere teem with animation, from the pavements to the roofs. Nowhere do we meet such long, tiresome, dull avenues of brick and mortar as Baker Street, Gore Street, Gloucester Place, &c. In London, " home's home," &c.—and when people are at home, they like quietude and retirement. In Paris *au contraire*, people cannot exist in quietude, and solitude is abominated. To see and be seen seems the universal maxim. The varied forms of the houses, too, and the still more varied styles of ornament, render the streets much more picturesque and interesting in Paris than in London. There is something very picturesque and interesting, I think, in the immense long perspectives between the tall houses of such streets as the Rue de Richelieu, into which I was led by the Rue Neuve des Petits Champs. This is the Bond Street of Paris, and is a most amusing one. Here every thing savoured of the fashionable world. Shops of a more respectable description richly decorated; goods of the most costly kind arranged for display with a very superior degree of taste and even elegance. Numerous equipages with liveried attendants driving about or waiting at the doors. Numberless loungers sauntering up and down, or philandering in the shops, a striking feature among these the foreign officers, particularly English, all indicating the Rue de Richelieu as the focus of fashionable resort. After all, however, there is something about this as well as all the other streets of Paris, with a few exceptions—such as the Rue de Rivoli, de la Concorde, de la Paix, and some part of the Boulevard—that displeases an Englishman's eye and nose. The buildings in general have a worn and shabby appearance; their great height, and the narrowness of the thoroughfare, throws a degree of darkness and gloom over everything; but, above all, the olfactory nerves are continually offended by a certain pervading odour, difficult to be accounted for, since it is everywhere the same—not arising from any visible cause, but omnipresent and unvarying. In the Rue de Richelieu not all the fragrant odours issuing from that *magazin* of odours, the Cloche d'Or, and fifty others, were sufficient to overpower this most unsavoury of smells. It may be said to characterise Paris—to stamp it as the sulphureous city. My attention was attracted by a broad avenue crossing one end of it, and along which flowed a dense and continuous stream of passengers and carriages. I directed my horse's head thither, and in a few minutes found myself in the Boulevard des Italiens. The excitement and interest of that moment will not soon be forgotten. The breadth of the street, the mixture of trees and houses, the number and variety of the immense multitude moving on, all contributed for a moment to electrify me, and I should have forgotten Colombes and the lateness of the hour had not Hitchins at that moment rode up and asked me if I was not going home to dinner. Colombes and M. Ferdinando's good cheer regained their sway, and we trotted off together, vowing an early return to explore the wonders of this mine of novelty and excitement.

CHAPTER XIX.

July 17*th.*—Alas! how transient is all earthly happiness! To-morrow I quit Colombes and my delightful residence for ever; except, indeed, I pay it a casual visit, and that I shall hardly have heart to do. A few short days passed in this elysium have endeared it to me beyond expression, and, spite of certain little differences, M. Ferdinand and I have become quite friends. The old man's manner is always so kind that I really believe he likes me; but then these French are consummate *blagueurs*. Our principal quarrel has been invariably about wine. At first he always produced such as would have done honour to any table, but by degrees he began from time to time to introduce a bottle of inferior quality. It was, however, too late; our palates were formed, and could bear nothing but the best, which we insisted on having, spite of his equivocations and harangues to prove to us that we were no judges of wine. Some droll scenes have arisen out of this; for we discovered that M. Ferdinand has the greatest horror of our invading his territory, and availed ourselves of the discovery whenever he tried to play us a trick. Nothing could be more comical than the expression which his countenance assumed on these occasions. "Ferdinand!" "Monsieur!" "Ce vin ci n'est pas bon!" "Ce vin n'est pas bon, monsieur?" arching his grey eyebrows. "Non, il est exécrable, vilain." "Mais, monsieur," with emphasis, "c'est du meilleur vin de la cave, je vous assure;" and then, with an "Excusez, monsieur!" he takes the bottle, pours a little wine into the palm of his hand, tastes it, makes a grimace indicative of pleasure, rubs down his stomach with feigned ecstasy, and exclaims, "Dieu merci, comme il est excellent!" "Eh bien, M. Ferdinand, vous ne savez plus plaire à notre gout; allez vous en, cherchez une chandelle et la clef de la cave, j'y descendrai choisir moi-même," &c. &c. This always produced the desired effect—the comic expression of his countenance would give place to one of extreme anxiety. "Tenez, monsieur! —tenez! cela ne sera pas bon; la cave est si obscure, si humide. Ah, je ne le permettrai jamais.

Si monsieur le trouve bon, je descendrai chercher d'autre vin, et peut-être je serais plus heureux." Without waiting for a reply, he would brush off with the activity of a man twenty years younger. In due time, allowing for the supposed search, re-enter M. Ferdinand with a joyous countenance and bottle in hand, from which, the long cork duly extracted, he would deliberately fill a *large* glass, look exultingly around, and, making a most profound bow (without, however, spilling one drop), drink " au bonheur de Monsieur le Commandant et des braves Anglais," then triumphantly plant the bottle on the table with renewed assurances of the excellence of its contents, which we invariably found to be perfectly true. On the whole, however, as I before said, we were excellent friends, and Monsieur le Commandant a special favourite with honest Ferdinand, whose attentions were unremitting. It grieves me, certainly, leaving Colombes—but go I must.

Yesterday Sir George Wood received despatches from Lord Mulgrave appointing Sir John May and Major William Lloyd to the two troops vacant by the deaths of Ramsay and Bean. This is a disappointment, for I had fully expected one of them; however, it is somewhat softened by the handsome manner in which his lordship directs that I be retained as a supernumerary captain of horse-artillery until a vacancy may occur, which it is known must be soon, for poor Lloyd is too severely wounded to survive. But the worst part of the story is, that my old troop, in which I have now been nine years, is to be taken from me and given to Major Wilmot, who has just arrived from England, and I am to go to D Troop, late Bean's, now Lloyd's, and no doubt soon to be mine. This morning Sir Augustus Frazer inspected G Troop, previously to my giving it up to Wilmot, in the field by the side of the road from Neuilly Bridge to L'Etoile. I took the opportunity of complaining that certain malicious reports had been circulated by persons unknown, to the injury of my character. These set forth that the great loss sustained by G Troop on the 18th arose from my culpable stupidity in having unnecessarily exposed my detachment, gun-horses, &c. Sir Augustus acknowledged having heard such a report, which he had taken every pains to contradict, and added, "I have told everybody that the imputation is false; and, moreover, that if blame attach to any one, it must be to myself and Major M'Donald, for I placed you in your position, and both of us visited you repeatedly during the action, and ought to have corrected anything that was wrong." This has been some ill-natured, jealous person, who envies us the little credit we got on that occasion.

After our inspection I sent Newland home with the troop, and accompanied Sir Augustus to La Chapelle under Montmartre, on the road to St Denis, where he inspected the D Troop, now commanded by Major D., previously to his giving it up to me to-morrow. It is a wretched troop, and very badly officered; the state of discipline such as I never thought could have existed in such a perfect service as the horse-artillery. Frazer flattered me by saying, in answer to my complaint, "Never mind; I am sure you will soon have it in a very different state." I hope so. To-morrow, then, I depart hence—give up my elysium, and exchange one of the very finest troops in the service for the *very worst*. But I must try and bring down my journal, if possible, to the present day, so as to begin a new score at my new station, wherever that may be. The 13th was the wet day on which I last wrote, and then did not finish up to the date, I think the 12th. Hitchins and I breakfasted at seven, and set off together immediately after for Paris. The road thither, with the exception of the naked plain between this and Courbevoie, is most interesting. At the Place Louis Quinze we dismounted, and Milward brought the horses back, whilst we continued on towards the Louvre by the Rue de Rivoli, &c. The Louvre is now in all its glory—nothing has been touched, although restoration is talked of. The Place du Carrousel we found occupied by Prussian infantry in bivouac. Not far off, near the Boulevard de la Madelaine, are several large timber-yards. Blucher, less scrupulous than Wellington, has emptied the contents of one of these on the Place du Carrousel, where his people have constructed a little town of sheds or shanties with the planks. A singular spectacle is this bivouac. The sheds form regular streets parallel to the Grille; along the centre of these are lines of fires, with camp-kettles suspended over them, and soldiers in most slovenly (even beggarly) *deshabille* sitting round, peeling potatoes, turnips, onions, &c., or cutting up very carrion-like meat for their messes. A chain of sentries kept back the crowd, which was immense—all eager to see the warriors so often beaten by their own troops, now in their turn conquerors, and enjoying the fruits of their victory on the very ground where the mighty

Emperor of the West had passed in review those *soi-disant* invincible legions, and whence they had successively departed for Madrid, Vienna, Jena, and Moscow.

Except a scowling ex-*militaire* here and there, nothing could exceed the *bonhommie* apparent in every countenance. Curiosity—pure curiosity—had drawn them thither, and their staring physiognomies did not betray an idea beyond the gratification of it. What a holiday for the Parisians this is, after all! The city seems in a continued state of festivity, and at the same time of fever. Amidst such a crowd and such excitement it was not possible to indulge reflections; yet, spite of these, a confused jumble of very curious ones flashed across my mind as, *en passant*, I contemplated this host of foreigners, domesticated, as it were, on the *sacred territory;* beyond them, and overtopping their temporary dwellings, the celebrated triumphal arch, surmounted by the four Venetian horses; and beyond these again, the immense façade (dark and gloomy) of the Tuileries, scene of such strange and startling events. Struggling through the crowd, our approach to the Gallery of the Louvre was announced by a host of boys and women, "A bill of the play, sir?" "Please to buy a bill of the play?" which was soon exchanged for "Catalogue du musée, monsieur? un franc, monsieur." "Voulez-vous un catalogue du musée, monsieur?" &c. &c. These people are more persevering than our vendors of these articles; however, the purchase of one was a mouth-stopper, and we were then suffered to proceed unmolested to the great doors, where two servants, most respectably dressed in blue and silver, with white waistcoat and breeches, received us, and pointed out the way to the first *salon*. A perfect stream, almost all foreigners, was setting in, and the *salons* were already pretty full, although so early in the day. I cannot set up for a connoisseur either in painting or sculpture, therefore have little to record of this celebrated collection beyond my unfeigned admiration of what I there saw. My emotions in each individual *rencontre* with the different *chefs-d'œuvre* here assembled might be a source of amusement to myself at some future period had I faithfully noted them down at the moment, but that was impossible in such a crowd; moreover, I had a companion, the most complete hindrance imaginable in my estimation to the enjoyment of anything admirable either in art or nature. Now they are nearly obliterated, and I can only say that I was delighted, though in some cases disappointed. This was particularly the case with the Venus de Medici. I scarcely know what I expected to see; but when a statue, patched and cracked, the marble discoloured and disfigured with greenish stains, such as one sees in our garden Neptunes, Tritons, &c., was pointed out by the number in our catalogue as the Venus, I could scarcely believe but that it must be a mistake. Such was the effect of the first *coup d'œil*. Upon a more attentive examination, however, I could not but admit the thing to be a most beautiful piece of workmanship as such; and the lady represented a very pretty woman, but I felt no raptures. The colossal group of the Laocoon, occupying, like an altar-piece, the whole extremity of the same apartment, hence called the Salle de Laocoon, had no charms for me. In the first place, I dislike colossal statues as much as I dislike allegorical paintings; both are a departure from nature, which I am not poetical enough to appreciate. Secondly, I hate such subjects—I hate a gratuitous contemplation of horrors and suffering—and to me there is something exquisitely disgusting in this subject. Thirdly, I dislike all attempts at representing violent action either in painting or sculpture, except for a momentary glance; they cannot deceive the senses

—there is no illusion. Specimens of either should be subjects to dwell upon, to contemplate, to study. But who can dwell upon action that *stands still?* What can be more tiresome than the continually-uplifted arm of the Laocoon, or the immovable struggles of the two little (by comparison) men (for they are not boys), with formal curly wigs, on each side of him. In short, I hate this so far-famed group. Occupying the extremity of the next *salle,* is the Apollo. Here I was not disappointed. The action has just ceased—the figure is in a sufficient state of repose to keep up the illusion and bear continued looking at. And who could ever tire of this? Such grace and ease, such lightness and activity—activity written in broad characters upon a figure not in movement—such an elegant and perfect form, and such a divine head! How often I have returned to gaze upon this most perfect conception of the human mind—this most perfect execution of the human hand! How often have I turned into the *musée,* and, heedless of the Venus, the Laocoon, and all the other celebrated statues in my way, have passed along, seeing nothing and heeding nothing, until I stood once more before this most exquisite piece of statuary! In collections of this kind too many choice *morceaux* in juxtaposition, or in immediate neighbourhood, injure each other—they distract the attention; and it is only after repeated visits that we become cool enough to attach ourselves to particular pieces. It was thus with me at my first visit both to these and the *galerie;* and I have felt the same effect in passing through a wild and picturesque country exhibiting beautiful features and pictures at every turn. I have been cloyed, even fatigued; and looked with pleasure on, and found relief in, a landscape of a tamer description.

From the *salons* we ascended to the Galerie du Louvre by a most superb staircase. English riflemen were posted, not only on the landing-place, but also distributed at intervals through the whole length of the gallery—whether to preserve order or the pictures, I know not; but I do know that the appearance of their green uniforms, as they stood leaning on their rifles all along this magnificent perspective, was another of those sights calculated to excite in our minds such strange tumultuous feelings. What must have been those of the Parisians, of whom a part of the immense crowd that thronged the *galerie* and anteroom was composed? They apprehend that the spoliation will commence directly, and are therefore assiduous in their worship of those treasures about to quit them for ever, and with them, they think, their national glory. The only record I make of the *galerie* is, that Poussin's "Deluge" fascinated me. Never did I see a picture inspiring so much awe. Paul Potter's "Bull" pleased me as an inimitable copy from nature, but as a picture it struck me as wanting in poetry. Some beggar-boy, by Murillo, perfectly ravished me, *malgré* the disgusting subject: here was nature and the most delicious colouring imaginable.

As both Hitchins and I proposed paying many more visits to the *musée*, we did little more than walk to the end of the *galerie* and back, and then departed, crossed the Prussian bivouac, and wandered into the palace of the Tuileries. We went as we listed, no one offering us the slightest obstruction; and the sentinels (I think they were of the National Guard), although they did not salute us, yet drew up respectfully at their posts as we passed them. Ascending a magnificent staircase, we found our way into a large handsome saloon, over the fireplace in which was a very fine painting of a battle. I think this was the Salle des Maréchaux. There was not a living soul to answer our questions; but I have since learned that what I took for a painting was a piece of Gobelins tapestry. Unheeded, we rambled on from one large room to another; indeed we met but few anywhere, until at last we walked most unceremoniously into one where a number of servants in the royal livery were laying a dinner-table, which, to our astonishment, we found was for his Majesty. They hardly noticed us, and answered all our questions in a most good-natured but most respectful manner. There was a beautiful service of Worcester ware, and, for a private gentleman, a decent display of plate, but nothing more—so far all was respectable; but what a table-cloth! I doubt whether most of our gentry of even the second table wouldn't turn up their insolent noses at such a one. Sure I am that no gentleman in England ever sits down to so coarse a thing. As dinner was just coming up, the butler (I suppose) very civilly begged us to retire, as his Majesty would be in immediately. We descended to the gardens. I had heard and read so much of the gardens of the Tuileries, that here I experienced a disappointment similar to that inflicted by the Champs Elysées. Nevertheless they certainly form a very agreeable promenade. That part immediately under the windows of the palace is laid out in parterres of flower-beds of different geometrical figure. I should say that the garden is a dead level.* Between the parterres are broad walks, well rolled and well swept. The further part is a grove, forming a cool and pleasant promenade or lounge, much taken advantage of by the Parisians, who may be seen lounging in one or two chairs, as may be, in all directions. These chairs are the property of individuals who bring them there, and make a livelihood by letting them out at two or three sous the chair. Similar accommodation, it appears, is to be found in every public place, even in the Boulevards. The ramparts (rather grandiloquent, when speaking of a mere terrace), which surround the garden on three sides, are planted also, and afford a most interesting promenade from the views they command; yet, strange to say, people appear to prefer the more confined one below. Although I do not like the formal laying out of these gardens, yet can I not but confess there is something very lordly (or kingly) in them. The broad, well-kept gravel-walks, the play of the fountains, the numerous orange-trees in boxes, which fill the air with their delicious but rather overpowering perfume, the multitude of statues, the view down the centre *allée*, which is pro-

* Le Nôtre had five feet (French) difference of level between one side and the other to remove. There is no accounting for taste.

longed into an immense perspective by being on the same line with that of the Champs Elysées, and on the other hand the ancient and venerable pile, with its numerous windows, long covered verandas, &c., overlooking the whole. The gaily-dressed crowd, too, by which the garden is almost always filled, gives it a holiday air very pleasing. Passing once more through the palace and traversing the Place du Carrousel, we soon reached the southern entrance of the Palais Royal. It was "change time," and the place in front of the gate was filled with business-like people, exactly as in our Royal Exchange. What a strange propensity the French have for misnomers! On entering the so-called "*garden*"* of the Palais Royal, I was for the third time disappointed. Instead of a garden I found myself in an immense arid esplanade, surrounded (at least on three sides) by lofty uniform buildings, the façade of which was decorated by Corinthian pilasters, and surmounted by vases, &c. An arcade ran all round the base. The side by which we entered was disfigured by a shabby wooden erection, under which were numerous stalls of petty dealers in every sort of articles, but apparently all of inferior quality. Under the arcades were shops of

* It once was a garden, but was destroyed by the great fire.

a better description, intermingled with cafés, restaurants, &c., and here was certainly a splendid display of goods of the richest kind. Watchmakers exhibited the most elegant little toys, enriched with pearls and chased-work; jewellers the most splendid articles in precious stone, gold, silver, &c.; shops of *gourmandise* (if I may be allowed the term)—everything that could stimulate or pamper the appetite. Many were entirely filled with knick-knackery, or articles of *vertu*; others with steel or cutlery; in others, again, were tastefully displayed the finest cashmere or merino shawls and *fichûs* of the most brilliant colours. In short, I cannot remember the tenth part of the rich display under these arcades.

In the esplanade were a few shabby trees, some benches, and piles of chairs. The crowd of loungers, &c. (for I presume most there were so), under the arcades, was very great, principally, I think, military. Prussian and Russian officers in blue or green uniforms, waists drawn in like a wasp's, breasts sticking out like a pigeon's; long sashes, with huge tassels of gold or silver, hanging half-way down their legs—pretty red and white boyish faces, with an enormous bush of hair over each ear; lancers in square-topped caps and waving plumes; hussars in various rich uniforms, one more remarkable, sky-blue, curiously laced with a sort of chain-lace, very ugly to my taste; Austrian officers in plain white uniforms, turned up with red—very neat, very soldier-like, very becoming, and the men who wore them more gentlemanly in their appearance than any of the others; English officers in all sorts of dresses, fancy, half-military, and quite so. To say that women abounded amongst these would be almost superfluous — some very handsome, some quite the contrary—all wearing looks of the boldest and most meretricious character. Boys, too, abounded, as in the Pays Bas, following and pestering you with their odious propositions. The cafés and restaurants were principally filled with officers smoking, drinking, playing chess, &c. &c. A few turns in the promenade, and then it was so late that we returned to the Place Louis Quinze, whence a cabriolet in due time brought us to our quiet peaceable village.

The next day (13th), although it looked black and threatening, we went to Paris; but the rain set in so heavily that we returned forthwith, most completely drenched, to Colombes, having seen nothing.

The 14th was fine again, and I resolved on an expedition to Malmaison and Versailles if possible.

The road lay through Nanterre, on the *coteau*, but a little elevated above the meadows through which the Seine holds its course. The scenery, without being very striking, was very pleasing and pretty. On my right at some little distance ran the river, beyond which rose a ridge of vine-clad hills, a continuation of those behind Argenteuil; on the left, the vineyard, corn-fields, and rose-gardens terminated in a range of high ground, wooded, continuing from Mont Valerien towards Marly, where the water-works, projecting from the there steep acclivity, formed rather a picturesque object—following the windings of the Seine through a less interesting country (because all corn). In the distance one sees the chateau of St Germain, with its long white terrace, backed by the dark foliage of the park; beneath, the waters of the river glitter like silver in the bright light. Malmaison is on the higher ground; and on ascending to the park-gates, I was pleased to find two neat little lodges, and an entrance perfectly English, which was the style all around. The house had nothing extraordinary in its appearance, but the little lawn in front was redolent of the perfume of the orange-flower, numerous trees being ranged around all in full blossom. I found but few servants in the house; on asking to see which, a lady-like person was called, who acted as cicerone with the easy and graceful manner so characteristic of French women. Had it not been for the interest one attaches to whatever is connected with great or extraordinary people, the houses at Malmaison perhaps were not so much worth seeing as many houses even of our commoners. There was only one room remarkable for its fitting up, and it was in other respects the most interesting. It was Josephine's bedroom. A little scene took place here. My companion idolised her former mistress; the recollections of past times and of her beloved Empress, renewed by my questions, overpowered her. I believe she was sincere. The furniture of this room (which was, I think, an octagon) was certainly splendid. Scarlet cloth (very fine) with trimmings of broad gold-lace, and deep gold fringe of bullions. The bed-curtains and coverlet were of the same, and the walls were covered with it instead of paper, the gold-lace serving as a border to the panels, &c. I did not admire the taste of Josephine in this. Here it was she expired. Running at right angles to the front of the house is the *galerie* —a beautiful *salon*, full of exquisite morsels of sculpture, all modern, but in my estimation many of them rivalling the antique. Taking leave of my amiable conductress, I set off to pick my way without a guide through a woody, intricate, wild country, where the openings were of no extent, so that no view could be obtained. After riding up one avenue and down another for some time, I began to fancy I was lost, when suddenly riding out upon an open I saw several peasants, male and female, at work near a *bergerie*,* which occupied the centre of the place. I rode forward to inquire my way, when lo! down went hoes, and away went men, women, and dogs as fast as their legs could carry them into the neighbouring woods, leaving me as much at a loss to account for their fright, as to which of the many roads *(forest)* diverging hence I should take to extricate myself from my dilemma. As the English nowhere inspire terror, these people must have taken me for a Prussian hussar, from my pelisse and enormous mustache. As no information was to be procured, I had nothing left but to push

---

* These *bergeries* are very numerous in the neighbourhood of Paris, where it seems the fashion among the great proprietors to keep flocks of merinos. Almost every chateau has its *bergerie* and *vacherie*. We have one here in Stain belonging to M. le Marquis de Livry, as I know to my cost. The *bergerie* consists of low sheds, forming a square. Within, they are fitted up with low racks for hay. The sheep are kept in these all the winter, and at night during the summer.

on and take my chance. I had not ridden far when the ground began to descend (I had been travelling on an elevated plateau), the thickets and wood became thinner and more scattered, and below me I saw several farmhouses. From subsequent inspection of the map, this must have been La Selle de St Cloud. I rode up to the first substantial-looking house, tied my horse up in a shed, and without ceremony marched into the kitchen, where the mistress and her maids were busily employed in their household concerns. My entrance did not in the least disconcert them, or even occasion them any apparent surprise: they entered gaily into conversation without for a minute interrupting their work. No running away here. I was very hungry, but, *malgré* the opulent appearance of the house, the good lady could give me nothing but bread (sour, as usual), some very fine cherries, and delicious milk. For this she would accept no remuneration, but her maids thankfully accepted the trifle I offered them for their trouble. I found that my deviation from the direct road to Versailles had not been great; and having received instructions for my future progress, and taken leave of my kind hostess, I once more plunged into a forest, from which, however, I soon emerged upon a cultivated country sprinkled with farms and villages, and very agreeably diversified with hill, dale, and woodland. At last the palace of Versailles, overtopping the trees and buildings in its neighbourhood, burst upon me with imposing grandeur, and I soon after entered the town.

In front of the palace is a large, almost triangular, esplanade, narrowing from the palace until it terminates in the road to Paris. A clumsy thing enough, for when building the palace they might as well have laid out a handsome square in front of it. The place looked dull and lifeless, few people, except some Prussian soldiers, being visible. The number of hotels, taverns, &c. &c., announced it as the resort of strangers and idlers. The palace itself, from all its window-shutters being closed, looked as dismal as the rest. Having secured my horse, I sounded the bell at the palace-gate, which brought out the *Suisse*, who sounded another bell, which brought a most gentlemanly, but very melancholy-looking, young man in the royal livery, who, upon being informed of my wish to see the palace, made a very polite bow, and requested me to follow him. It were needless repeating the history he gave of each splendid apartment, and they appeared innumerable. Solitary and silent, an overpowering sensation of melancholy came over me in comparing their present deserted state with that which had for ever passed, and I no longer wondered at the pensive manner of my interesting young companion, though he was too young to have known Versailles in the days of its splendour. I believe, with the exception of ourselves and the *Suisse*, whom we had left at the gate, this immense fabric did not contain another living soul. So long did we continue wandering from room to room, that at last, on returning to the vestibule — no time was left to visit the *Trianon* as I had intended, or even the gardens—all that I saw of them was from a terrace upon which we were admitted from one of the central *salons*—unless I remained all night. It became necessary to depart forthwith, or find my way in the dark back to Colombes.

The great road to Paris is a superb avenue, but it was disfigured by dust, which, spite of yesterday's rain, I found a real nuisance.

Numerous were the villas along the road, but, like those in the neighbourhood of London, the shrubberies in which they were embowered, and everything about them, was grey and dingy with the dust with which they were powdered. A great part of this line seemed inhabited only by washerwomen. The foul linen of all Paris seemed assembled here. The abundance of fine water, perhaps, is the cause of this. Pity that some portion of it were not employed in making this otherwise beautiful ride somewhat more enjoyable. It was growing so late as I passed Sêvres, that I merely can say I saw the exterior of the celebrated manufactory of porcelain. A thick dark avenue of trees, turning to the left, here seemed to promise a short cut to St Cloud; so up it I turned, but had not proceeded far ere I stumbled on a guard of Prussian jägers in an old summer-house. The sentry stopped and ordered me back. The corporal coming out, and finding that I was an English officer, very civilly informed me that, as Prince Blucher had his headquarters in the palace of St Cloud, no one was allowed to cross the park. Back, then, I went, and descending to the Seine found a good road, by which, passing through St Cloud, Suresnes, &c., I returned hither just as it got so dark that I was obliged to my horse for bringing me safe home. The latter part of my ride along the charming banks of the river, and in the cool of a fine evening, was truly delightful.

15*th*.—I went to Paris again, wandered about the streets without any fixed plan, and quite by accident stumbled upon the Hôtel Dieu. I like this random mode of proceeding much better than following any fixed plan of sight-seeing : it is more independent. I walked into the hospital and through its wards. Nothing could be cleaner or better arranged; but the whole place, especially about the main entrance, had such an overpowering smell, that I was glad to make my escape and find my way to the Cathedral of Nôtre Dame. There is something exceedingly impressive in the interior of a Gothic cathedral at any time. Mass was performing as I entered the church, the solemnity of which, from the little light and rather heavy style of the architecture, was increased by the fine bass voices of the canons who assisted in the service, every one in his stall. From Nôtre Dame, after taking an omelet in a neighbouring restaurant, I had a long stroll by the quays to the Invalides. The old soldiers lounging or walking about the approaches to this fine establishment, although perfectly respectful, I thought looked displeased at seeing me. There were even some who did not attempt to conceal looks and gestures of hatred and contempt. They are to be pitied more than blamed for this feeling, since these were the men who fought and *always* conquered in Italy and

Germany. Notwithstanding their scowling looks, I could not help regarding these fine veterans with the most profound veneration. I found no difficulty, however, in procuring a cicerone to show the lions, and under his guidance walked through the halls, where the tables were already laid for dinner; through the dormitories, where the beds were all clean and neatly made up, and looking comfortable, &c. &c. In the officers' dining-rooms the tables were also laid—round ones for four or six persons each—not as with us, all at one long table. A bottle of wine was here placed by the side of each man's plate. Nothing could be more comfortable or more respectable. We then visited the church under the dome where are the tombs of Turenne and Vauban.* All this was not very amusing, but my guide, leading the way up several staircases, at last ushered me into a large but low room, immediately under the roof, filled with beautifully-finished models of almost all the frontier fortresses in France. Here I passed the remainder of the day most delightfully. The most interesting of these models were Chateau Trompette; Brest, with its harbours and

* I cannot FEEL in public, especially when a *showman* is telling me in a garbled manner that which would spontaneously flash across the memory if left to one's self. When we do not *feel*, we *can't write*.

the adjacent country for three or four miles round; Strasbourg and neighbourhood; but one of the most amusing was an exquisitely-finished model of the battle of Lodi, under a glass bell. A fine boy of about fifteen or sixteen, to whom my quondam guide had delivered me over on entering the model-room, excited my surprise, not only by the clearness with which he explained everything to me, but also by the shrewdness of his remarks, and the great knowledge he evinced of military affairs in general; quite an incipient Buonaparte, I should say—only Buonaparte was never half so handsome. I could have lingered for a week over these interesting models, but the diminution of light obliged me at last reluctantly to leave them. Whilst we were wandering from loft to loft, for there were several, we came accidentally into one where two or three Prussian officers were superintending the dismemberment and packing up of all such as had any relation to the possessions of their monarch; and my young companion told me he suspected they meant to take away Strasbourg, and that they had already packed up several which could not come under that denomination. The poor boy spoke very feelingly on the subject, and seemed heart-broken at losing his favourite models. I shall frequently visit the Invalides, unless the Prussians quite strip it of the models. It will be a delightful lounge, those lofts.

Yesterday, being Sunday, our three troops assembled, under Major M'Donald, in the park, where Captain M'Donald's troop is quartered, and had divine service. Passed the afternoon in riding about the neighbourhood, and the evening in the enjoyment of my beautiful terrace, &c. &c.

To-morrow I go in search of my new troop, somewhere about St Denis.

CHAPTER XX.

Sunday, July 22*d.*—This is the first time I have been sufficiently settled and quiet to sit down to write since the evening of the 17th, my last at Colombes — dear Colombes! The intervening space has not been passed in idleness. On the morning of the 18th I was fully occupied in giving over my troop and stores to Major Wilmot, who takes possession also of my charming apartment, and Mademoiselle Ernestine gets a new neighbour. After an earlier dinner than usual, Hitchins accompanied me to St Denis; my servants and horses started in the morning. At St Denis I could gain no immediate and distinct information. Some of Ross's non-commissioned officers whom I met with said they thought the troop must have halted in Stain. I shuddered at the very name of the place; it was the worst I had anticipated. As Hitchins knew the desolation of Stain, and the utter impossibility of my giving him a bed, even if I could get one myself, he took his leave, and I proceeded thitherward alone. It was with a heavy heart that I traversed the once rich crops of grain, now trodden into mud by having been the bivouac of our troops, and still heavier that I rode through the dismal street of the ruined village. I soon met some of the gunners, who confirmed my worst fears—viz., that the troop actually was stationed here. The officers were living and messing in a house close to the church, and opposite the *grille* of the great chateau; and thither I repaired, and found them accordingly sitting at their wine. My servants had been here some time, and had taken possession of the Petit chateau, already mentioned. The house I found my officers in belongs to the Sœurs de la Charité. I was sensibly struck on entering it at the contrast with my villa at Colombes; mean, gloomy, dirty, and scarce an article of furniture in it, and what there was, of the poorest description. To counterbalance all this, it is the only house in the place (at least so they thought then) that has any glass in the windows, and how it escaped is extraordinary. They were seated in a dismal room, very low, and having a very disagreeable odour, overpowering even that of the dinner, in which the flavour of onions predominated. After introducing myself, and drinking a glass or two of wine, as the daylight began to fail I set off to inspect my new quarters. The appearance of this in its best days would not have been pleasing after Colombes; but now, forlorn, deserted, plundered! The handsome furniture which had once adorned it, mutilated and torn to pieces, was yet fresh when last I saw it; the fragments retained their paint or gilding, the mahogany its varnish; the tatters of silk fringe and curtains, scattered over the lawns and walks, or hanging from the branches in the shrubberies, yet retained their colour in all its freshness: now, after having been drenched by rain, and bleached in the sun and wind, all remains of former beauty were gone —all associations with splendour and magnificence vanished; they conveyed to the mind no feeling but that of squalidness and wretchedness. Amidst all this I entered the house. There things looked even worse. The winds of heaven had freely coursed through the paneless windows, the rain had inundated the floors, decay had already commenced, and the place looked as if it had been years deserted. Chilly, comfortless, and wretched, the floors still covered with fragments of glass, which, crunching under one's feet, added not a little to the misery of the scene, still further enhanced by a most gloomy evening, and the dismal sound of the wind through the branches foretelling a stormy night. At length, after wandering from room to room, always finding one worse than the last, the approaching darkness obliged me to decide quickly, so I pitched upon a large one, with a recess for a bed, where I could at least be at some distance from the windows. My men had already made themselves tolerably comfortable in the stable, and I now summoned all hands to make me so too. Brooms were speedily made by stripping the branches from some acacias or laburnums in the courtyard, and all the rubbish and broken glass swept out of the window; candles were procured from the mess, my bed made in the recess upon a bedstead, nearly sound—the place began to look a little better, and I a little more cheerful. Though not so luxuriously, yet I slept as soundly as ever at Colombes, *malgré* the forlorn feeling that crept over me as I fell into unconsciousness at the idea of being the only person in the great rambling mansion, with doors and windows all open, and admittance free to whomsoever might come.

My gloominess had construed the sighing of the wind among the foliage into a presage of rain and storm. Neither came; and the next morning I was awakened by the sun streaming full in my face, the carol of birds innumerable, and the soft, balmy, yet fresh air of a most lovely morning. As our mess-breakfast was not very early, I jumped up determined on a thorough examination of the whole village, in hopes of finding something better than the Petit chateau. After looking into several, all equally miserable, I found the one where I ought to have begun, the only one habitable. It was only across the road, shut in by high walls, overtopped by acacias. This house had escaped the observation of others as it had mine; and, strange to say, had scarcely been visited by the spoiler. All the windows were perfect, and the only injury visible on the premises was the breaking to pieces of a number of paltry plaster Cupidons and their pedestals, that had erst disfigured the garden. I took possession immediately, and here I sit in my cabinet about to give a description of it. The house is tall and narrow—four storeys counting the ground-floor to the front, and three towards the garden, which is higher than the court. The ground-floor consists of stables, wood-houses, &c., opening on this court, which is planted with acacias and shut in from the village by a high wall with great close

MY NEW RESIDENCE. 171

gates. On the next (or garden ground-floor), is the only decent-sized room in the whole house: all the rest are divided into those useless little cabinets of which the French seem so fond, many of them with glass doors. All the rooms have the abominable brick or tile floors so common here: however, all the windows are sound, which is the grand object. I have chosen the floor above the garden—that is, third from the court—where I have a narrow slip, with glass door at one end and window at the other, the view from which certainly does not rival that at Colombes, for it is bounded by the four high walls of my garden; another piece, with a recess in it, serves me for a bedroom, and into these two I have collected all the furniture remaining in the house, which is but little, and that of the meanest description—a few clumsy, old-fashioned chairs, and a table or two. One of the former is a curious article: the seat lifts up, and behold a *bidet;* the top of the thick back has two or three little boxes in it for holding soap or what not. My three domestics occupy the floor below me, and are next the animals. The garden, which rises in a gentle slope from the house, is a long narrow strip, neatly laid out and abundantly stocked with flowers, vegetables, and fine fruit

—particularly grapes, plums, and peaches, &c. The whole is the property of two old maids, Les Demoiselles Delcambre, Marchandes des Modes, who, on the approach of the Allies, removed all the furniture worth removal, and left the place in charge of an old Flemish servant—a virgin, like themselves. Mademoiselle Rose, as she is called in the village (and I should have mentioned that most, if not all, the peasantry have returned, and that only the chateaux and country seats of the citizens remain unoccupied)—Mademoiselle Rose is a character. Strong in the confidence of her want of charms, she is said to have remained faithful to her charge,* even when the Prussians entered and plundered the village, and thereby, the villagers assure me, saved her mistress's property when all else was destroyed. A short, squat figure, clad in coarse black frieze, a face of the ugliest, set off by a pair of black mustaches fit for a hussar, which gives her a fierce and masculine aspect, like the dragon of the Hesperides, for she performs the part of watching the fruit most unremittingly. The moment I enter the garden she skulks after me; and on looking about I am

* Angélique told me since that Mademoiselle Rose fled to the woods with the rest of the villagers, and only returned when they did.

sure to detect her ugly phiz watching my movements from behind some bush, not presuming, however, to interfere. More than once I have noticed the sudden disappearance of fruit from some particular tree; and William tells me that Mademoiselle Rose strips the trees at night and sends the fruit to Paris. I should suspect my own people, only that they would not take it in such quantities. This, however, is not of any great consequence, since we have several other well-stocked gardens in the village from whence to help one's self without trespassing on those attached to the officers' houses, which are, of course, considered as private property. There are, *par exemple*, the chateau belonging to Jerome Buonaparte; the Petit chateau to M. Domer, who, I believe, is something in the Admiralty; another large handsome chateau, with very extensive, well-kept gardens, to Admiral le Comte Rosilly; a very pretty villa, garden, &c., the property of some rich shopkeeper; and several little boxes of minor importance. The village itself may be said to consist of two streets, short, and neither of them continuous. It is situated on a dead flat, consequently has no other beauty to boast of than what it derives from the foliage of the trees in the grounds of the chateaux, &c. The fields about it are corn and vines—principally the latter, I think.

It was at first certainly rather a nuisance changing from Colombes, though I have already got pretty well accustomed to the new situation. The difference was not only in the style of my lodging, beauty of the surrounding country, &c. &c., but also most particularly in our living. Instead of the comfortable, well-served table, and excellent wine of M. Ferdinand, and the new milk, nice fresh butter, and new-laid eggs—produce of my dairy and poultry-yard — here we daily sit down to miserably-cooked soup and *bouilli*, made of ration-beef, and a bad steak of the same, served in ill-cleaned tin (canteen) dishes. Vegetables, to be sure, we have in abundance. Then for wine, we have some very poor stuff, which Ambrose (my surgeon) bought somewhere in Paris, and, from not understanding French, got cheated. At home here I have managed to get up a breakfast, though a poor one; the bread is so abominably sour, and the butter so cheesy. Nor have I been able to dispose of my time in the same agreeable manner as at Colombes; for between the constant attention my wretched troop requires, and the plague of the villagers, I have but little left for amusement. The former of these, the troop, I have quieted a little, by giving one of them a severe flogging ; but its disorganised state may be guessed at, when it is known that the payment (contrary to our regulations) is in the hands of the sergeant-major, and that my predecessor, poor Bean, died in debt to this man at least £300. Of course everything was winked at.

The villagers (unlike those of Colombes, who have never been disturbed), after being scared from their dwellings by our advance, have returned to them, only to find everything ruined and destroyed. Of course they are not in charity with us, and full of complaining. This is all brought to me by the Maire, who pays me a regular visit every morning, and frequently in the evening also, waylaying me, besides, whenever I go from home. The Duke's system of discipline is well known, and these people seem disposed to take every advantage of it, fair and unfair. One complains of our occupying his house and stables, another of his field being mowed, another of something else, and so on. It is inconceivable that a conquered people, and a people whose armies have shown no forbearance in foreign countries, should thus dare lift up their voice and complain that the conqueror disturbs them, and puts them to some inconvenience. So it is ! If I attended to one-half the complaints brought before me, we should soon be turned out of the place altogether. The very morning after my arrival, M. Bonnemain (Maire, &c.) called, and was introduced—a dry, thin, old man, rather above the middle height, in a suit of rusty-brown clothes, snuff-box in one hand eternally, and the other gesticulating in aid of his drawling voice and interminable oratory. After the introductory bow, he commenced by welcoming me to Stain, eulogised the village and villagers, expressed his satisfaction at my appointment, having already heard of my high character as an officer; under the command *d'un tel* Monsieur, everything must go on in the happiest manner possible. Then followed butter, thickly laid on, after which he cautiously and dexterously introduced his business, no doubt guessing that, having placed me on so elevated a pinnacle, I should be more cautious of a fall. "Mais, Monsieur le Commandant," he continued, "nous sommes des pauvres malheureux, pour nous tout est perdu —tout abimé, &c.;" and so he went on expressing his confidence in the justice of M. le Commandant, and that he would not oppress the poor. Then followed a long—very long—story about a worthy industrious man, with a large family, whose house was occupied by our men, and stables by our horses, and a request that I might have the goodness to relieve this unfortunate family from so oppressive a burden. He had not reckoned without his host: Monsieur le Commandant swallowed some, at least, of the dose; was softened; the quartermaster is called, and orders given that the detachment should be removed from the farm in question. Monsieur le Maire is still more profuse in bows and compliments, amidst which he retired, to my great satisfaction, for I was tired of him. The next day Monsieur le Maire again appeared, and in similar manner pleaded the cause of another excellent *malheureux*, whose crop of oats our people were cutting. Again he was successful; but as Monsieur le Commissary-General had begged us to supply ourselves in this manner from the fields, I requested Monsieur le Maire to point out how we might do so with the least possible injury to the inhabitants. He did so, and I gave the necessary orders for confining our foraging parties to the fields indicated, and to avoid unnecessary waste. Again Monsieur Bonnemain is announced; but this time he came accompanied by a genteel but rather important-looking personage, just arrived in a handsome cabriolet, whom Monsieur le Maire introduces as the postmaster of St Denis. They are somebody these postmasters. An exordium of a most complimentary character ushered in, as usual, a complaint, or rather a protest, against our cutting this gentleman's oats. Monsieur le Maître des Postes condescended (and he made the condescension evident) to inform me that he farmed the land in question at an exorbitant rent; that the produce was absolutely requisite to enable him to fulfil his contract with Government; that he should suffer much inconvenience from our depredations; and that, the public business of the Government being thus obstructed (with a most ominous shrug and extension of both hands), it was impossible to answer for the consequences. Hereupon the great man, with an air of perfect indifference, turned his back on me, and began asking trifling questions of some villagers who had flocked in to witness the negotiation. My answer was very brief: "Monsieur le Maire had himself designated the fields we were to cut." (Here a most portentous glance was shot by Monsieur le Maître at Monsieur le Maire.) "That if the public suffered in the business of posting, it was of infinitely less consequence than that any part of the British army should become inefficient for want of forage. As, in the present case, somebody must suffer, it were

better that the burden should fall on those best
able to afford it." Monsieur le Maître then
shifted his ground somewhat, complaining of the
waste committed by our foragers, who, he said,
trampled down more than they cut. I promised
this, if found to be the case, should be remedied,
for our own sakes; and, at his request, that one
particular non-commissioned officer should superintend the foraging. Monsieur, finding he could
get no more, bade me adieu with more politeness
than he had condescended to use on our first meeting, mounted his cabriolet amidst bows of the
assembled peasantry, and drove off. This fellow's
opposition has not been without consequences.
My villagers have become more bold, and even
begin to draw up petitions to the Duke. Some
of these have already been sent to me, with an
intimation that I must not oppress the inhabitants unless it be unavoidable. This happens to
be the case—therefore I have taken no notice of
them.

July 25th.—Yesterday our army (British only)
was reviewed by their Imperial and Royal Majesties. I marched early, as the line was to be
formed by 9 o'clock. After passing through St
Denis, we took the great road to the right by St
Ouen, and came on the Neuilly road just above

the village, where we formed, being on the left of the whole, except the 18 - pounder brigades. Ross and Bull's troops were on my right. We had a long and tedious wait; and as the day was very hot, it was no small treat to discover that an apothecary hard by had some excellent raspberry vinegar, which, I think, we exhausted. At length the approach of the sovereigns was announced, and they came preceded and followed by a most numerous and brilliant *cortège*, in which figured, perhaps, some of almost every arm of every army in Europe. It was a splendid and most interesting sight. First came the Emperor Alexander and the King of Prussia, in their respective green and blue uniforms, riding together— the former, as usual, all smiles; the latter taciturn and melancholy. A little in their rear followed the Austrian Emperor, in a white uniform, turned up with red, but quite plain—a thin, dried-up, thread-paper of a man, not of the most distinguished bearing; his lean brown visage, however, bore an expression of kindness and *bonhommie*, which folk say his true character in no way belies. They passed along, scanning our people with evident interest and curiosity; and in passing me (as they did to every commanding officer), pulled off their hats, and saluted me with most gracious smiles. I wonder if they do the same to their own. Until yesterday I had not seen any British infantry under arms since the evening the troops from America arrived at Garges, and, in the mean time, have constantly seen corps of foreign infantry. These are all uncommonly well dressed in new clothes, smartly made, setting the men off to the greatest advantage—add to which their *coiffure* of high broad-topped shakos, or enormous caps of bear-skin. Our infantry—indeed, our whole army—appeared at the review in the same clothes in which they had marched, slept, and fought for months. The colour had faded to a dusky brick-dust hue; their coats, originally not very smartly made, had acquired by constant wearing that loose easy set so characteristic of old clothes, comfortable to the wearer, but not calculated to add grace to his appearance. *Pour surcroit de laideur*, their cap is perhaps the meanest, ugliest thing ever invented. From all these causes it arose that our infantry appeared to the utmost disadvantage—dirty, shabby, mean, and very small. Some such impression was, I fear, made on the sovereigns, for a report has reached us this morning, that they remarked to the Duke what very small men the English were. "Ay," replied our noble chief, "they are small; but your Majesties will find none who fight so well." I wonder if this is true. However small our men and mean their appearance, yet it was evident that they were objects of intense interest, from the immense time and close scrutiny of the inspection. At length they finished, and, taking their stand in the Place Louis Quinze, we marched past in column of division. The crowd assembled to witness this exceeded anything I had ever before seen. Not only were the people packed as thick as they could stand in the area itself, but the buildings of the Garde Meuble, the ramparts of the Tuileries, even the roof of the Hotel Bourbon over the river, were all crowded— windows, roofs, and every cornice that could hold human beings. After passing, we took our route along the Rue Royale, Boulevard and Rue Poissonnière, starting off at a good trot, and got home about 6 o'clock. In St Denis I met Captain Gaffon and the little doctor of the Brunswick Hussars, neither of whom I had seen since we were in barracks together at Woodbridge. The meeting really seemed to please them, as they had heard I was killed at Waterloo. It seems somebody is determined I did or ought to have died. One of our people told me the other day, that the day after the battle a staff-officer had shown him my name in a list as dangerously wounded.

And during the retreat of the 17th, whilst I was with the cavalry at Jemappes, one of the Blues who overtook my troop on the road told them that I was killed, for he had himself seen me cut down by a French dragoon—*Cependant me voici!*

July 30*th*.—More trouble, more complaints Another memorial to the Duke from my subjects, complaining of cutting their oats. This I have very easily disposed of; but lo! here is a more formidable adversary to deal with—no less than M. le Marquis de Livry, *rentier* or *propriétaire* of the gambling *salons* in the Palais Royal, and, as such, a man of immense influence. He has property in this commune, and a *bergerie* in the village, where he keeps a flock of merinos. The sheep being absent when the troop arrived, the *bergerie* was converted into a stable; but having lately returned, under their shepherd, part of the building has been appropriated to their use. The shepherd, a perfect Sancho Panza in person, not content with this, has ever since been intriguing to obtain entire possession. I have been fairly pestered to death about this *bergerie*. Almost daily M. le Maire and M. le Berger de M. le Marquis de Livry make their appearance at my quarters, or intercept me in the street to tell me the same story over again, and to get the same answer. Finding his perseverance useless, M. le Berger (no doubt assisted by M. le Maire) draws up a very moving petition to the Duke, which M. de Livry takes care shall be presented under proper auspices, and behold the consequence: A positive order from his Grace to evacuate forthwith the premises of the Marquis de Livry, and *to put up our horses elsewhere in the best manner we can; that is, respect the rich man's property and oppress doubly the poor*—for we must divide the forty horses hitherto stabled in the *bergerie* among the poor villagers, who already have more than is good for them. The Duke of Wellington's ideas of discipline, &c., are rigid—his mode of administering it summary; but he is frequently led into acts of the grossest injustice. A notorious instance of this I am now suffering under, and one that makes the *bergerie* business a mere flea-bite. Only a few days ago, whilst sitting after dinner at our little mess, an officer of the mounted staff-corps (*gendarmerie Anglaise*) was announced. He regretted being the bearer of disagreeable orders, &c. &c., but Colonel Scovell, commandant of the mounted staff-corps, had directed him to show me the paper, which he produced, and to inform me that his Grace had ordered it should be immediately complied with. Further, that the Duke was excessively angry, and had expressed himself very harshly on the subject; therefore Colonel Scovell recommended me to make no remonstrance, as he could not foresee what might be the consequence. The paper was a petition from a certain M. Fauigny (an Italian), setting forth, I think, that he is proprietor of the Grand chateau which has been miserably plundered; but more particularly that the English troops now quartered in the village have stripped the lead off the roofs, from the baths, water-pipes, &c. &c., and sold it. This is, as nearly as I remember, the petition. A note written with a pencil by the Duke himself on the margin was too brief and pithy not to be remembered, and here it is, *verbatim:* "Colonel Scovell will find out whose troop this is, and they shall pay.—W." I was thunderstruck at the complaint and the decision—the one so unfounded, the other so cruelly unjust. I signed an acknowledgment of having seen the order; and the officer took his leave, recommending me to try and compromise with M. Fauigny, who stated the damage at about 7000 or 8000 francs. Upon inquiry of M. Bonnemain, he asserts that this M. Fauigny is the agent of Jerome Buonaparte, to whom the chateau actually belongs, as we were told by the Prussians who plundered it.

The next morning I had just ordered my horse, and was about to set off for Paris, when William announced a gentleman who wished to see me; and a rather genteel-looking man sailed into my little parlour with an air of *nonchalance* and easy familiarity quite amusing. My friend seated himself with the utmost coolness, and drawing out his snuffy pocket-handkerchief, displaying it— whilst he spat all about the floor, to my utter disgust, for I had been in the act of finishing my breakfast—informed me with a slight inclination that he was M. Fauigny, and had called to know when it would be convenient to settle this *leaden accompt*. Finding him already acquainted with the Duke's order, I was obliged to make the best of it and put him off with excuses, which he did not seem to relish, having evidently counted on touching the cash forthwith. However, the man behaved like a gentleman, kept his disappointment to himself, and turning the conversation on general subjects, proved himself a man of very general information and a most agreeable companion. Although he would not partake of my breakfast, he paid a very long visit; and the moment he was gone, I set off also for Paris, and went straight to Sir George Wood's quarters in the Rue de Richelieu. From Sir George I learned that the affair was much more serious than I had imagined. The Duke is furious about it, and Sir George says my only chance is by evading payment as long as I can, in hopes some favourable opportunity may offer of inducing the Duke to think more leniently on the subject; in the mean time, to make every inquiry into the truth of the statement. Accordingly, we have been at work, and the result is a discovery that M. Fauigny is a villain—has made a false statement to the Duke in hopes of gaining payment from us for what has been actually done by others, but from whom he knew nothing could be recovered. The villagers themselves have informed me how the thing happened, and have denounced one of their own body as the robber, for the lead has in reality been stolen, as set forth in the petition, only not by us.* M. Plé is *couvreur* by trade, and did precisely the same thing last year when the village was occupied by a Russian

* I suspect a fact I have since remembered must have suggested the idea of charging us with the lead. Finding the horses very ragged when I first joined the troop, I ordered all their manes to be plaited and loaded with lead, of which a sufficiency could have been picked up about the chateau or lawn, or off the ends or remnants of the *already* cut pipes.

corps, against which a charge similar to the one against us was brought, but not with the same success. Their General did not condemn his people unheard like the Duke of Wellington. However, having gained this piece of intelligence, I set off to St Denis, and stated the whole affair to the chief of the police, who smiled, and anticipated me by himself mentioning M. Plé as a culprit and an old acquaintance, adding that he would lose no time in sifting the business thoroughly. A *procès verbal* was drawn up, and I took my departure, well pleased with the politeness and urbanity of the French civil authorities.

Two *gens-d'armes* were despatched to arrest M. Plé and search his premises. A day or two afterwards, I received a note requesting my attendance at the police the next morning at eleven o'clock. Thither I went, and was met at the door by M. le Chef, who addressed me with a smile and an assurance that the lead was secured. Accordingly in the office stood M. Plé between two sentinels, and on the floor lay several enormous rolls of lead. This was only a part of the plunder, the rest having already been sold. In short, with admirable dexterity and perseverance, they followed up the business, and finally ascertained beyond a doubt that M. Plé was the thief, both now and last year; but although there is some suspicion of collusion between him and M. Fauigny, nothing has been brought out that throws any light on it. I don't think he seems known to our villagers, as one would suppose the agent ought to be. M. Plé is lodged in some prison in Paris, but I have no idea what eventually will become of him. The exposure of the affair has not in the least altered my position with the Duke of Wellington, for none dare tell him the story; and even Sir Edward Barnes, who kindly undertook it, met with a most ungracious rebuff, as he himself told Sir G. Wood. Meanwhile M. Fauigny continues to pay me an occasional visit. Sometimes I see the scoundrel *par nécessité*, but always keep out of his way if I can. Knowing, as he does, the Duke's humour, he continues dunning me with most unblushing effrontery for payment.

Were it not for these complaints, and most particularly this horrible affair of the lead, I could be happy enough here. I am getting quite reconciled to my house and to the village, and getting acquainted with the people, who have pretty well put things to rights again. Old Bonnemain I find quite manageable and very useful. Another ally has turned up in the person of the *garde champêtre*, who has at last ventured back and resumed the insignia of office. A very different character this from Petit Jean of Strytem; fat, pursy, stupid, dressed in shabby plain clothes, with a broad embroidered belt over his shoulder, altogether looking like a rat-catcher, for which I at first mistook him.

Moreover, to be completely on a peace-establishment, our village church has been reopened, and mass is now regularly celebrated there. The curé fled with the rest at our approach; but, unlike them, has never returned to his lair, and for some time the church remained closed. The other morning, shaving with the windows open towards the garden, I was astonished at hearing a most stentorian voice chanting in the church, which is not far from my garden-wall; and as nothing does or ought to take place without my knowledge, William was forthwith despatched to ascertain what was going on. In a few minutes he returned accompanied by M. Bonnemain, who, with his usual profusion of bows, commenced a most humble apology for the step he had taken without first obtaining my permission, which, however, he trusted would not on that account be withheld. He had sent to Pierrefitte (a neighbouring village) and engaged M. le Curé, a most worthy and exemplary man, to come over and "faire la messe;" and further, provided it met the approbation of M. le Commandant, and was no disturbance to him, he had engaged M. le Curé to come over every morning. So we have had mass ever since, and my morning shave is regularly accompanied by the bass, nasal chant of M. le Curé performing *l'office* to about a dozen old women; for, sometimes when I have been earlier and gone in, I have never found any other congregation. Yesterday (Sunday) it was more numerous, for then the girls go; but I am uncharitable enough to believe only to exhibit their finery. Even on that day very few men attended; indeed, throughout, since we entered France, we have found religion at a very low ebb: the churches always thinly attended, and principally by women; the Sabbath observed, if at all, only as a holiday, apparently totally unconnected with any religious idea; shops everywhere open; and agricultural labours, as well as every other kind, going on as usual, unless people choose to rest and make a holiday of it.

In looking back at this journal (if so we may term what is written by fits and starts, as an otherwise idle day occurs), I find omitted altogether the review of the Prussian army, which took place some days ago in the Place Louis Quinze as usual, only in this case the line was formed along the Boulevard, and the column entered the place by the Rue Royale. I have neglected this so long, that I remember few particulars of the review. The troops looked well, their equipment appeared good, the men young, active, and well drilled, countenances full of animation, and apparently proud of being soldiers; cavalry well mounted, and the cuirassiers wore black cuirasses, instead of polished ones like the French. The crowd was as great as when we were reviewed, and the ground was kept by a parcel of wild-looking Cossacks in blue frocks and very shabby-looking horses and appointments—*voila tout!* But there was one occurrence at that review that I shall never forget. The Cossacks were under an old chieftain, evidently of high rank, whom I understood to be no less a person than their Hettman Platov, besides whom several Russian general officers rode about giving directions to the Cossacks.

It was with some difficulty that I made my way through the crowd and gained a front place, not far from the *debouchement* of the Rue Royale. The only military man near me was a proud-looking Russian officer, who, from his large epaulettes and numerous decorations, I took to be a man of some consequence, and, from the sidelong glances at my plain and rather shabby pelisse, somewhat annoyed at my near neighbourhood. We were, however, knee to knee, and, *bongré malgré*, destined to keep company, for the throng was too dense to admit of changing place; and so, as it fluctuated backward and forward, we were forced to advance or retire like files of the same squadron. The Cossacks were very actively employed with their long lances keeping us all back, but still the crowd continually pushed us forward until we were sometimes almost in the ranks of the advancing column. At length, tired of his ineffectual attempts at restraining us within bounds, the Cossack who was our immediate sentry made an angry complaint to one of the general officers, and, from pointing our way, evidently particularised me and my neighbour. The general, flying into a passion, first looked thunder and lightning at us, and then, cane in air, rushed to the charge. It will readily be imagined that the ferocious gestures meant to drive us from the field only roused my John Bullism, and caused me to assume an air of defiance. Not so my superb neighbour; on him it had full effect. He looked intimidated, reined back his horse, and, turning, endeavoured to push through the crowd and make his escape, leaving me to bear the brunt of the attack. The general, however, knew his game; so, passing me with a scowl which I smiled at, and a grumble which I did not understand, he pursued my friend with uplifted cane, which every moment I expected to see descend on his back. The scene was the most degrading I had ever witnessed—an officer in full uniform, his breast covered with decorations, actually bending low on his horse's neck and making a back to receive a caning, whilst with upturned face his looks seemed abjectly craving mercy. I wonder what the French thought of it. I blushed for the cloth, and most sincerely congratulated myself on being an Englishman. The chase continued until the discomfited hero was fairly driven from the field, when his bully returned fuming and chafing and looking very fierce, and apparently very much vexed at the insolent indifference with which I purposely surveyed him.

Being on the subject of reviews, I may as well note here one that took place yesterday, which I have just heard of, but did not see. It seems that we have been the *raræ aves* of the day ever since our review. The rapidity of our movements, close-wheeling, perfection of our equipment, &c. &c., excited universal astonishment and admiration. The consequence of this was an application to the Duke for a closer inspection, which he most magnanimously granted, and ordered Ross's troop out for that purpose. They paraded in the fields near Clichy. The reviewers, I understand, were *maréchaux de France*; but there was also a great concourse of officers of all nations. After the manœuvres the troop was dismounted, and a most deliberate inspection of ammunition, and even of the men's kits, appointments, shoeing, construction of carriages, &c. &c., took place. I believe they were equally astonished and pleased with what they saw, and, as there were several among them taking notes, have no doubt that we shall soon see improvements introduced into the Continental artillery.

Paris, and the country for leagues round, form one immense garrison. The Prussians have their headquarters at St Cloud, where Prince Blucher occupies the palace. Their army occupies all the country west of Paris—Versailles, Sêvres, Bellevue, &c., and round to the southward as far as Charenton. In Paris they occupy the arsenal, and at first had a bivouac of infantry in the Place du Carrousel, and of light cavalry in the Champs Elysées, both of which have since been withdrawn and sent somewhere into quarters. They also had infantry in bivouac in the Jardin du Luxembourg, Place Royale. I do not know whether they are withdrawn yet or not. Our headquarters are at the Elysée Bourbon; and our cantonments, commencing at Suresnes, extend along both banks of the Seine to Argenteuil and St Germain en Laye, all round the north side of Paris to the heights of Belleville. The greater part of our cavalry is, I believe, on the left bank of the Seine. The Life Guards, Blues, &c., are at Nanterre, Rueil, &c.; hussars at Suresnes, Puteaux, &c., and Gardiner's (Sir Robert) troop of horse-artillery. This last is, I think, quartered on the Duc de Feltre (Clerk). The 12th, and another light dragoon regiment, at Courbevoie, in the fine barracks. Infantry at Anières, Villeneuve, and Genevilliers. Colombes—my old troop, Bull's, and M'Donald's. Bezons — the rocket-troop. Neuilly—two troops of Hanoverian horse-artillery. St Ouen—Brunswick cavalry and infantry; some in the village, some in bivouac. Epinay—pontoon-train. Pierrefitte—waggon-train. St Denis — commissariat magazines, &c., two regiments of English infantry (64th one of them), a brigade of 18-pounders, and Sir H. Ross's troop* of horse-artillery. Malmaison—cavalry headquarters. I think there are cavalry at Marly, St Germain en Laye, &c. &c. Stain—my troop;* communication kept open by the bridge of Neuilly, and pontoon-bridges at Argenteuil and Anières. Clichy, Courcelles, and Villiers—the fifth division, partly in camp, partly in quarters. Bois de Boulogne—infantry, encamped. Passy— English artillery. Rue Poissonnière—a regiment of English infantry in the barrack. La Chapelle — Hanoverian dragoons and a brigade of 18-pounders. Montmartre—English infantry. Clignancour — 21st Regiment of do. Faubourg de Montmartre — English infantry. Faubourg de Clichy—Rifles. Chaussée d'Antin—Foot Guards. Vertus, or Aubervilliers—English infantry and Major Morrison's 9-pounder brigade. Gonesse— English infantry and artillery. Chenevrière— do. do. do. Luzarches, and along the line of road to Chantilly—Belgic contingent. Dugny—Staff-corps. Garges, Arnonville, &c.—Nassau troops. Headquarters of our artillery, Rue de Richelieu. Belleville and the neighbourhood is occupied by Russian infantry. Abattoirs de Montmartre (the

* The two reserve troops.

barrack at)—a regiment of cuirassiers, in white, with black cuirasses; I think they are Russian—not sure. Faubourg St Denis—Austrian or Hungarian infantry. The Emperor of Austria lives on the Boulevard (I think des Italiens). The Emperor of Russia and King of Prussia I know not where; but the Hetman Platoff (as well as our Colonel Sir A. Fraser) lives at the Hotel du Nord, Rue de Richelieu, where his guard of wild-looking Cossacks, with their little shabby horses picketed in the court, furnish gape-seed for the *badauds*, a crowd of whom are continually at the gate. It is a singular spectacle to see the public places in town all doubly guarded—a French and an English or Prussian sentry. When I ride into Paris by the Barrière de Clichy, as I generally do (that way being so much pleasanter than passing through La Chapelle and Faubourg St Denis), I am at once amused and interested at seeing the two sentries soberly pacing backward and forward, opposite each other, one on each side of the street. As I draw near they simultaneously front and pay the usual compliment (there is something piquant in receiving a salute from a French soldier), each after his own fashion. There they stand; on the one side a tall handsome fellow, with a fair face and prim shopkeeper-like air, with his high fur cap and trim uniform, almost speck and span new; the other, a shorter but more sturdy figure, bronzed visage, and jacket of brick-dust red, marked in various places with bivouac stains, and faded from exposure to sun and rain, but with arms and accoutrements in far better order than those of his smart neighbour. On first taking possession of Paris, the Prussians posted one or two field-pieces at each of the bridges, with a guard of infantry. These guns were kept constantly loaded, and slow-match lighted. Latterly they have been withdrawn; but we still have guards at every public building —such as the Louvre, Palais Royal, &c. These are generally English.

Yesterday I made a most interesting excursion over all the scene of last year's battles,—the plain of St Denis, Vertus, the heights of Belleville, Montmartre, &c. Independent of historical associations, these heights are extremely interesting, from the fine commanding views they afford; but particularly in a geological point of view. Rising abruptly to the height of some hundred feet from the (almost level) Plain de St Denis, their appearance is very remarkable as we approach by the great northern road to La Chapelle, almost everywhere terminating in lofty white precipices of gypsum (or sulphate of lime)—hence called plaster of Paris. Montmartre appears once to have been a continuation of the heights of Belleville, from the similarity of the gypsum cliffs opposite to each other. It is now isolated, and, with its precipitous terminations and crest covered with windmills, forms a very remarkable object from the plain below. These windmills are principally on the end over Clichy; towards the other is the celebrated telegraph—known by fame to all Europe—whence were transmitted at various periods orders for the invasion of Italy, Austria, Russia, Prussia, and Belgium, and by which Paris was so often roused to the boiling-point of vanity when it brought intelligence of Jena, Wagram, &c. But *revenons à nos moutons*. The heights are separated by a narrow gorge, in which, under the cliffs of Montmartre, is a small hillock* (Mamelon), crowned by three windmills, which appears to have been formed by detritus from above. The dome of St Genevieve seen through this gorge gave us the first notice of the French capital the evening we arrived at Garges.

* Under the cliffs at the other extremity, near the Barrière de Clichy, is a similar mound, originating, no doubt, in the same way. It is now covered with fine trees, and forms an agreeable object as one approaches the Barrière. Its name (*Monceau*) perhaps points to its origin.

The intermediate part of Montmartre, though not precipitous, descends by a very rapid slope towards the plain. About midway of the descent is the pretty village of Clignancour, the houses of which, having their first floor on a level with the ground behind, command from their windows and balconies a most extensive and pleasing view over the country below, and are delightfully intermingled with shrubberies and gardens. The descent towards Paris is less steep, and is covered all the way with the suburb of Montmartre. The whole summit is enclosed by Buonaparte's celebrated, but, as it has turned out, useless lines, erected last year for the defence of the metropolis. Of these I need say little, as I know they are surveying by our engineers, who will no doubt give us a detailed account of them—a piece of slavery which I am not at all disposed to engage in. All I can say of them is that, considering the hurried manner in which the work has been done, they are very creditable—that they cover all the ground in front with their fire—and that a tremendous concentration of fire, direct and flanking, commands every important point. They are continued partially across the gorge, the bank of the Canal de l'Ourcq, and fully up the opposite heights of Belleville. They may, however, be easily turned on either flank. The gorge is occupied by the humble and uninteresting suburb of La Chapelle. The heights of Belleville are extremely pretty, being almost covered with a succession of cheerful and sometimes elegant villas, gardens, shrubberies, vineyards, and the village. I envied the Russians such pretty quarters; yet they would be just as well pleased here as there, perhaps. From these heights I got a peep at Vincennes, with its park, chateau, and tower, on which the Lilies of France have at last replaced the Tricolor. The governor (*un vieux moustache*, with one leg) refused for a long time to surrender; and the sovereigns, out of respect for the old man, did not insist; but after a time he grew insolent, and I understand either did or threatened to fire at some officers who went too near his stronghold. This was too much, and preparations were making to reduce him when he was fortunately persuaded to surrender. Having rambled about until I had seen all worth seeing, and got an omelet in one of the *ginguettes*, or whatever they call them, I descended from the heights ot Belleville, and crossing the fields (all without hedges here), and the great road to Soissons, made straight for Vertus. As far as the road to Soissons, the number of gardens, with summer-houses perched on one angle of the enclosing wall, thick shrubberies, and the fine umbrageous avenue which the road itself with its quadruple rows of elms presents, made the country interesting in spite of its flatness; but beyond, when one comes on what may more strictly be termed the plain of St Denis, there is no redeeming point—it is a vast extent of monotonous corn-field, unrelieved by tree or shrub, and only broken by the buildings of the village of Vertus and the elevated bank of the Canal de l'Ourcq. The great road to Compiègne, which crosses this plain from La Chapelle to St Denis, once had its trees also; but they were cut down, I think, last year; and the only objects one now sees along this dreary line are a mile (or a league) stone on the left going to town, and a cross or Bon Dieu on the right. Young trees have been planted along part of the line, but at present they are mere sticks. Met Major Morrison in Vertus; his 9-pounder brigade is stationed there, together with a regiment of infantry. By the way, the name of that place is Aubervilliers, or Notre Dame des Vertus, but one never hears any more of its name than the last word—so that it is Vertus *par excellence*, and all the rest is superfluity.

I have had a long scribble this morning; so

now, having jotted down nearly everything to the present date, I have a right to go and idle a bit with the girls. This is a lounge of which I have as yet said nothing, because I thought it commonplace; hereafter, however, it will be interesting to look back and see as in a picture all that is now transacting—*allons donc!* Through the middle of our village runs a little sluggish rivulet, very like that at Garges. On the banks of this, every fine day, may be seen assembled the scraggy-necked dames and black-eyed nymphs of the village, all pretty much alike in costume— that is, arms bare, stays loosely laced, and petticoat of *siamoise*, with the eternal blue stockings and wooden shoes; each has her bundle of linen, her heavy bat, and generally a bit of board to kneel on. Here, then, kneeling in a line along the banks of soapy waters, they laugh, chatter, and sing; whilst the bat incessantly goes slap, slap, slap. Just where the street leading to St Denis joins ours, in the centre of the village, a bridge of very humble dimensions spans the stream, on the parapet of which I have established my divan; and thither I repair to smoke my weed and enjoy a little badinage with the fair daughters of Stain—to gain a little information from their wrinkled mothers. Amongst our village maidens there are several exceedingly pretty—some one or two would be beautiful, were not their feminine *delicacy* (perhaps the word may be used morally as well as physically) much injured by their being constantly employed in the fields, which cannot but make their persons coarse. There is one exception to this, however, in Josephine Chamont, who is really a beautifully-delicate, lady-like girl; but then she does not go to the fields. Angelique, on the contrary, is as fine a woman as ever I saw; she is about twenty—a perfect Juno—tall, erect, with a beautiful countenance and splendid black eyes; she walks like a queen. When our invasion was expected, the women of the commune formed themselves into an amazonian regiment, and Angelique was their sergeant-major.— But I must to the bridge.

M. Fauigny paid me a visit this morning: I did not see him.

CHAPTER XXI.

August 1*st*.—Our fine weather still continues—
with the exception of one or two days, we have
scarcely had any rain since we arrived here. Our
army is breaking up from hence and going into
Normandy. Some of our troops of horse-artillery
marched the day before yesterday, and yesterday
some regiments of cavalry. The infantry are also
preparing for their departure. Ross's troop and
mine, belonging to the reserve, are to remain in the
neighbourhood of Paris. This appearance of peace
has, I suppose, induced the Beguines, or Sœurs
de la Charité, to return to the village, much to
our annoyance; for their house is the one in which
we mess, and where Ambrose and Maunsell live.
Five of the sisterhood called on me this morning
for the purpose of obtaining the restoration of
their house, and permission to return and inhabit
it. I was at breakfast, but these good dames

would take no refusal, and William was obliged to show them up. My little room was crammed.

I have always up to this date associated most inseparably in my mind youth and beauty with the term nun. It was, therefore, not without some trifling emotion that I awaited the five nuns whom William had announced, and heard them bustling along the narrow bricked passage leading from the head of the stairs to my room. Such being the case, it may easily be imagined that it was not without disappointment I saw entering, one after another, four ugly old women, in shabby black dresses, and at the same time became sensible of a very unpleasant odour accompanying the ladies. All this was enough; and, in the politest manner possible, I hastened to meet their wishes as soon as known, in order to get rid of them. Here I reckoned without my host. The good dames found my politeness so winning, that they were in no hurry to move, nor did they until they had inflicted on me the whole history of their adventures and sufferings from the first invasion by the Allies last year down to last night. When, at length, they did depart, I thought I could never sufficiently inhale the fresh air of heaven.

Having got rid of the ladies, after visiting the parade (which we hold in the park of the great chateau), I rode to St Ouen and Clichy. In the last and neighbourhood our fifth division is quartered, and I was astonished to see the Prussian-like manner in which the place is occupied. One very handsome villa I visited had its pretty pleasure-ground trampled and spoiled as much as the chateau at Stain; and, to my surprise, in the house I found two formerly splendid *salons* converted into stables, and actually occupied by officers' horses. I don't know what the Duke will say when he comes to know this. The neighbourhood of Clichy is pretty—all villas and gardens, &c.

August 2d.—Another beautiful day. More regiments marching towards Normandy. In consequence of the return of our nuns, we moved our mess establishment to-day into the Petit chateau, having prepared and made as comfortable as circumstances would admit the grand *salon* in the centre of the front. This is a very fine room with a boarded floor in little squares (*parquet*), which looks very well, but is very creaky, as all these floors are. We collected what chairs were still serviceable as seats, and as they were few, the wheeler patched up others; a table was a more difficult article to procure; the floor served as a sideboard. There being no glass in the window, we are obliged to make the venetians (which fortunately are unbroken) answer, lowering those to windward when the air is too much. We are raised about six feet above the lawn, and two winding flights of steps afford the means of descending from the windows of the bowed front to the turf below. Fatigue-parties have been employed all yesterday and this morning clearing the lawn of the fragments of furniture, rags of curtains, torn books, and broken glass, that encumbered and disfigured it—so that now our domain looks decent, and we have actually wondered we could stay so long in the gloomy old house we have left. By way of a house-warming I gave my champagne on promotion, and we have had a merry evening, without excess, or I should not be able to write this.

3*d*.—No headache this morning; our champagne was excellent and very cheap. In England we should pay from 10s. to 15s. per bottle. This cost me precisely 5 francs, or 4s. 2d., a bottle —some little difference. But to my journal. Rode to Paris, and as usual put up Cossack at a stable I have discovered in Rue de Malle, just by the Place du Carrousel, consequently very convenient. When I arrived, there were several people in the stable, who gathered round me and Cossack, asking with apparent curiosity if he was in the battle of Mont St Jean. I told them Yes, and all about his eight wounds—the scars of which were visible enough. This seemed to excite great interest; and I walked off, leaving them assembled round the fellow's stall, having first, however, warned them of his heels. The Palais Royal, Rue Vivienne, and Boulevard were the scenes of my promenade. The first I have spoken of before, and hope to do so again; the second is a kind of Bond Street, leading straight away from the northern entrance of the Palais Royal. Like Bond Street, it is narrow—so narrow, indeed, that the London street becomes broad by comparison, and is infinitely its superior in the convenient *trottoir* which the Rue Vivienne totally wants. In short, in London this narrow, badly-paved avenue, with its gutter down the centre, would only rank as a lane. Here is to be seen all the beauty and fashion of Paris; for here, as in Bond Street, are all the fashionable shops. If some of those under the arcades of the Palais Royal are more splendid, the articles in these are more substantially rich and good. But the Boulevard is the great point of attraction for me, and there I passed this morning, until it was time to return here before dark, lounging from the Rue Royale to the Boulevard du Temple and back again, with an occasional turn down the Rue de Richelieu, or the Passage des Panorama and Feydeau, into the Rue Vivienne and Palais Royal. The Boulevards (for there are many, every few hundred yards having a different designation) form a sort of circular road round what once was Paris, separating it from the Faubourgs, now forming part of the great whole; and these Boulevards form a street about as broad as Oxford Street, perhaps broader. This, without excepting the Palais Royal, is the most amusing part of Paris. The houses along this immense avenue are neither regular nor uniformly handsome, but high and low, rich and poor, wood and stone—from the cottage to the palace. A broad footway (not a paved *trottoir*) next the houses is in many parts shaded by rows of lime-trees, and separated from the road by a shabby wooden railing. The road is incessantly thronged with carts, fiacres, cabriolets, private equipages, and horsemen; every now and then a detachment of *gens-d'armes* is seen urging their way soberly through the crowd. This forms a lively and amusing scene enough, particularly just now, from the contrast between numerous well-appointed English equipages and the clumsy vehicles and tinsel finery of the native. But it is in the footway one finds the greatest source of amusement, and most food for philosophical contemplation. Here one meets promenaders or passengers in every variety of European, and even some Asiatic, costumes. Some, you may know by their lounging gait, are employed only in killing time and dispelling *ennui*; others, bustling from shop to shop and from table to table, are people whose money burns in their pockets, and their amusement consists in getting rid of it as quickly as possible for articles utterly useless to them, and which, laid aside to-morrow, will quickly be forgotten. Again, a third, and by far the most numerous class one sees here, have a directly contrary employment to the last—they are people whose pockets burn to have money in them; and accordingly here, in this great thoroughfare, we find them resorting to all sorts, even the most ludicrous, the vilest, and the most degrading means of obtaining their end. Here tables innumerable are set out under the trees covered with all sorts of cheap articles—toys, perfumery, cutlery, combs, and articles in horn, bone, wood, metal, glass—every thing and every article upon each table of the same price. In passing along, one is deafened by the incessant and rapid vociferations of these dealers enumerating the various articles upon their tables, eulogising them in the most ridiculous terms, and announcing their price: "Dix sols pour chacun!—dix sols, dix sols—dix sols seulement, messieurs!" Then there are jugglers, mountebanks, and importunate beggars. My great torment in the Boulevard is a little wretch of a girl, about ten or twelve years old, whose ostensible business is the sale of toothpicks, but in reality is begging. This little animal fixes herself on one with the tenacity of a leech—running by one's side, occasionally holding up the articles of her pretended trade, and unceasingly plying her song: " Ah, monsieur! cure-dents, monsieur? En voulez - vous, monsieur? deux sols, monsieur! Ah, monsieur! le pauvre père, monsieur; il est malade, monsieur!" and then, when she becomes convinced of the inutility of perseverance, suddenly stopping and entering into an indifferent, perhaps merry, confab with some chum, and again starting after some other likely-looking customer. She frequently follows me from her stand, which is at the end of the Rue de Richelieu, to the Rue de la Paix. Other characters there are of different descriptions, and many of them forming a feature in this motley and daily crowd. Amongst these I have particularly noticed an old man, with long grey locks flowing in a most picturesque style over his back and shoulders, strumming a cracked guitar; and a female, somewhat advanced in years, dressed in shabby old finery, her faded charms partially concealed under a rusty-black veil, who attempts to excite interest in and extract metal from the passengers by warbling a pathetic love-song in a most ominously husky voice. A little farther, a proud and stately Mohammedan, in full Turkish costume, offers for sale I know not what, and evinces much indignation at the itinerant sausage-vendor, who pushes steadily through the crowd, the fiery brasier suspended before him by a strap passing round his neck, everywhere opening for him a free passage. Over the brasier a square pan contains the savoury-smelling, hissing sausages, which as they fry he is able, from having his hands at liberty, to keep turning, or to serve out to customers and receive their sols in return. The steaming pan has frequently made my mouth water, and I give no credit to the fierce and angry look of our stately Turk when startled by his near and unexpected approach. I'd wager a sol did they but encounter in some obscure passage he would himself become a customer to the Giaour's polluted pan.

At the angle formed by the Boulevards du

Temple and St Martin, and opposite to the beautiful Fontaine de Boudi or des Lions, in a snug recess formed by a break in the line of building, may daily be seen a table, covered with a cloth scrupulously white, on which are arranged sundry piles of a peculiarly inviting *gâteau*. This table is constantly surrounded by a certain description of young men, whose bronzed features, mustachioed lips, and confident, insolent stare, denote the *militaire en retraite*, or half-pay officer. Here the presiding goddess is a comely dame of some forty years standing, a little inclined to *embonpoint*, with a bold masculine countenance embrowned by constant exposure, but yet having strong claim to a certain description of beauty, which she understood how to enhance by the tasteful and coquettish arrangement of her blue *cornette* and a studied neatness in every other part of her dress. With her customers this fair dame carries on a conversation animated and somewhat free, if she likes them; but Englishmen are by no means favourites. This portrait will be readily recognised by those to whom the Boulevard St Martin is familiar. The immense number of tables spread with books, as well as little sheds for the sale of the same—and their cheapness, are quite astonishing. I may say the same of engravings, many of them really good. Equally astonishing is the open and barefaced display, in these stalls, &c., of the most licentious works, and pictures of the most indecent kind. Although the best shops are certainly in the Rue Vivienne, &c., yet are there many very splendid ones along the Boulevards, particularly the Boulevard des Italiens. Here are also some good restaurants and cafés; and, amongst other ornamental buildings, the Bains Chinois. Amid all these, however, there is a characteristic eyesore which strikes one as quite incongruous: I allude to the intervention of shabby wooden sheds amongst goodly shops and houses. Besides the book-stalls just spoken of, one sees every here and there a long, low, mean-looking shed, its front almost all window. This is a news-room, where, for a few sols, you may read all the daily journals published in Paris, if you have patience to wait until they be disengaged, for these places are generally full; and I often amuse myself by stopping before the broad windows, always open just now, and contemplating the line of odd figures—some spectacled, others (from the manner of holding the little—after our own — minikin *feuille* at arm's-length) who evidently ought to be; and all absorbed in the meagre nonsense which every one of these papers I have looked into contains : a number of people may commonly be seen in attendance awaiting their turn. The fellows who keep these sheds must make a mint of money. Another feature not confined to the Boulevards, but common to all the public gardens and places of general resort, is the numbers of well-dressed and often dandified loungers on chairs, and the piles of these against the trees. To us at first it was a novelty seeing groups of people seated on chairs in the open street ; but I have now got accustomed to it, and even to appreciate the luxury myself. These chairs, which are of the plainest kind, form the stock-in-trade, and furnish the livelihood, of many a poor old man or woman, who otherwise could do nothing to support themselves; and, *en passant*, I should note the admirable address with which I have seen these people turn the wants of human nature to account. On a rainy day some sally out with a common oil-skin umbrella, which is offered to the first unfortunate wight caught out in a hat or coat likely to suffer. Others, providing themselves with a thick plank, repair to some great thoroughfare where they know there is an insufficient gutter that will overflow—and this may be everywhere. The plank, laid over the rushing stream of black water, is paid for by those who are generous by a sol or two, thus verifying the saying, It is an ill wind that blows nobody good.

The hire of a chair per hour is a mere trifle—a sol or two; and thence it is, I suppose, that a Parisian exquisite seems to think it degrading to occupy only one. Two or three is the common run; but I saw one gentleman this morning who actually occupied five whole chairs. He had chosen an excellent position to be seen, on the Boulevard des Italiens, just by Hardi's, whither I was bound to get some dinner. One chair sustained the main body, another the right leg, a third the left, a fourth afforded a rest for the left arm, whilst the fifth, bearing gloves, *mouchoir*, and *canne à pomme d'or*, stood conveniently by his right. The self-satisfied air with which this exquisite scrutinised with his *lorgnette* the passers-by, was not the least amusing part of this entertaining microcosm. Cogitating on the various means used by mankind to court or win admiration from their fellow-men, I mounted the steps in front of Hardi's, and entered the airy, nicely furnished *salle à manger*. "Garçon! la carte!" I cried, throwing myself into a seat near the window, the table by which appeared unoccupied. There is about as much difference between one of our dark close coffee-

rooms in London and the *salle à manger* of a
Parisian restaurateur (at least Hardis or Very's),
as there is between a tallow - chandler's back
parlour in St Martin's Lane and Lady B.'s beautiful drawing-room in Park Lane. Here are no
closely-shut-up boxes, with their green curtains,
&c.; all is open, airy, and cheerful. Small tables
(just sufficiently large to dine four people)
stand about the room covered with snow-white
table - cloths, napkins, and silver forks; and
instead of the dingy smoked walls of a London
coffee-house, and windows so covered with dust
that the panes of glass, although translucent,
are not transparent, here the walls, covered with
a gay painted paper, have an air of cheerfulness
quite indescribable, especially when connected
with the moving, lively scene without, of which
the constantly open door and windows afford an
uninterrupted view. In looking on the scene
below, the continuous lines of trees give such a
rustic appearance to the whole, that it is difficult
to imagine one's self in the very heart of a great
capital. To me the Boulevard had more the
style of Lewisham or Clapham, or some of those
"*rus in urbe*" sort of places so numerous in the
vicinity of London. It seems bells are not in use
at these places, and calling out or making a noise

is vulgar. Therefore, instead of the constantly reiterated "Waiter! waiter!" a sort of masonic signal has been invented to call the attention of the attendants. I began at my first visit to Hardi's as I would have done in England, and summoned the garçon *viva voce*; but I soon discovered by the glances shot from the tables, and the quick turning of heads, that there was something wrong, at least something unusual. I observed there was no calling, and yet tables were served; and by the occasionally sudden turning and going up to some particular one, I became aware that some other mode of communication must be established. I watched. The garçon was standing near the door looking at an English regiment at that moment passing along the Boulevard. An elderly gentleman, in a sad-coloured suit, who had hitherto been busily employed at the next table discussing his *potage*, stopping suddenly, looked sharply about the room as if in search of some one. His inquisitive glance settled at once on the garçon, and taking up the sharp-pointed knife that lay beside his plate (the knives here are all of one pattern, very common, and apparently made to be used as stilettos instead of for cutting beef or mutton), gently touched with it the side of his wine-glass, producing a slight jingling sound that scarcely reached my ear, close as we were to each other. It proved sufficient though, for the garçon started and was at his side in an instant. "Ma foi!" thought I, "this is a 'wrinkle to my horn.'" I shall be quite an *habitué*. I tried the experiment again and again: —it never failed; and being now up to the thing, I soon observed that everybody used the same signal. It reminds me of the Spanish call, "Hist!" uttered from the tongue alone, without any sound from the chest. Things are uncommonly well cooked at Hardi's, and served in most comfortable and respectable style. The napkins at a public table are quite new to us Englishmen. I had a *potage*, and one or two *petit-plats*, that I selected at random from the *carte*; for amongst the numbers figuring there, I knew not one by name, and most probably as little by nature. One thing I dislike in French cookery is the abominable fashion of disguising vegetables; one cannot even get a potato plain and unsophisticated. *Gâteau de pommes de terre*, or some such mixture of potatoes, butter, &c. &c., is the only way they are eaten here. Having finished my plate of strawberries and a bottle of very excellent *Lafitte*, I set off for the Rue de Malte; but instead of going directly thither down the Rue de Richelieu, I made another little promenade on the Boulevard, and finally down the Passage des Panoramas and Feydeau, Rue Vivienne, Palais Royal, &c. The lamps were already lighted, doors open, sentinels posted, and crowds rushing into the Théâtre des Variétés as I passed. The passages looked brilliant by the light of multitudes of lamps, and the arcades of the Palais Royal, where the illumination was only beginning, already swarmed with depravity, and proposals rung in my ears from my entrance to my sortie from this sink of iniquity. The decreasing light warned me not to loiter; so, mounting Cossack, I made the best of my way over the abominable pavement of the Faubourg St Denis, until, gaining the end of La Chapelle, the road became better adapted for rapid movement. Daylight closed, however, just as I got through St Denis, having just enough to save me from the wheels of the numerous chariots and other vehicles with which its long narrow street is always crowded. Having only open fields to traverse afterwards, I cared less; and trusting myself to Cossack's sagacity, he soon brought me safe home—and thus ends one of the many pleasant days I have passed in this most interesting place. I find Mr Fauigny has been here to-day. He gets hot after his money.

TORMENT OF FLIES.

I doubt, however, if he will ever finger any of it.

August 4*th.*—Beautiful day again. Every pleasure in this life has some drawback—as if this were necessary to prevent our thinking we have already arrived in paradise. That, then, which in a measure neutralises our enjoyment of this fine warm weather, is the incessant torment of swarms of flies (common house-flies) which infest us within and without doors. From these wretches there is no respite, except it be at night, or maybe in a darkened room. The mosquitoes cannot be worse, though they may be as bad. It is not as in England—merely the buzzing about and tickling caused by their alighting on and walking about one. No; here the brutes bite, and so sharply as to bring blood. My greatest suffering from these plagues is in the morning, when I may wish to lie in bed later than usual, which is not often. I am generally up too early for them;* for it is only after the sun acquires strength that they begin to be troublesome: then, unless the room be well darkened, there is no possibility of sleeping; and in my naked house there are not the means

* Early riser as I am, my neighbour here beat me considerably, for I always used to hear him harnessing his horses for work before daylight, which he did with a pretty annoying quantity of noise and chattering.

of doing this—window-shutters, to be sure, but they fit so badly that there is little difference as to light whether they be closed or open. In the village the road is quite black every day in front of our butcher's with the dead flies thrown out. He poisons them with an infusion of quassia sweetened with sugar. In my garden there is abundance of the finest fruit—peaches, nectarines, figs, plums, and splendid grapes, now all quite ripe ; but such swarms of these detestable brutes infest the trees that they spoil everything. It is impossible to eat any of the fruit without first washing it: this spoils it. Half the battle is picking it off the tree and eating it.

What strange things we live to see and hear! I do think that during the period I have been in the world, more strange, wonderful, improbable (and what once would have been deemed impossible) events have occurred than the whole history of the world, since Noah landed on Mount Ararat down to 1789, could furnish altogether. Not the least strange amongst these is the general order just published to the British army by Wellington, calling upon commanding officers to give every assistance required by the French farmers or cultivateurs in getting in the harvest! In consequence, English soldiers and French peasants are seen everywhere side by side, sickle in hand, or binding sheaves, &c—the invader and the invaded alike peaceably occupied, and reciprocating kind offices one with the other. 'Tis a goodly sight, truly. Further good consequences are very perceptible in our village. All mistrust and dislike of each other are at an end; and our people are now quite on an intimate and friendly footing with the peasantry. Many an amicable little knot may be seen of an evening sitting at their doors enjoying at once the cool air, their pipes, and the pleasures of conversation, or rather of trying to understand each other. Some of the villagers have already picked up a little English, and our men a little French. The gayest of the latter occasionally mix in the rustic dance; and although rather rough and bearish in their manner of swinging the girls about, yet are they sought after as partners, the pretty *paysanne* who has for her partner *un canonier* evincing in her look and manner a degree of satisfaction not to be mistaken. Already symptoms of jealousy have made their appearance among the young *paysans*, and I have consulted M. Bonnemain on the subject, expressing my fears lest it might disturb the harmony already subsisting. " A bah ! n'y a pas de danger !—n'importe, n'importe," is always his answer; and accordingly neither I nor my officers have observed anything like a diminution of friendship among the males. These French girls are clever creatures. They have hearts and flattering tongues for all. It is a pleasing sight of an evening to see our people returning frolicking home from the fields, with the loaded carts, the cargoes of which all are busily assisting in stowing away in the *grenier* —soldiers, *paysans*, and *paysannes*.

Generally speaking, these latter (male and female) are very respectable, well-mannered, and well-spoken people in their way. There is, however, one, the most perfect Caliban I ever met with in my life. Bonnemain says he is not an inhabitant of Stain, but comes from some part of Normandy—I forget where. Short, thick-set, and powerfully built; covered with hair—head shaggy as that of a savage; long beard and naked breast, like a bear's; broad squat face and enormous features;—indeed, when standing close to, and trying to converse with him, I feel a sensation as if looking at his face through a powerful magnifier. Of his language (he speaks very fast and very loud) I cannot succeed in catching a single French word, and I observe that the inhabitants themselves seem to have some difficulty in comprehending his meaning. I have christened him Caliban!—beautiful monster!

But it is almost time to go to bed, and as yet I have not mentioned my ride to Paris to-day—I should say *usual*, for few days elapse without my going thither. In general I prefer the road by St Ouen, Clichy, and Monceaux, &c., because it has trees, the scenery is better, the line is not so tediously straight, and by the Barrière de Clichy one enters at once on a decent part of the town, the Rue de Clichy and du Mont Blanc, instead of having to pass through the long blackguard suburbs of La Chapelle and St Denis. To-day, however, I took this road. How unlike the neighbourhood of London, where, for twenty miles (certainly ten) from town, the country is covered with villas, and the roads with carriages, equestrians—indeed, travellers of every kind and in every way! Here we have a long straight road stretching away with an almost imperceptible ascent for about three miles—not a tree nor a bush lends its shade or breaks its painful monotony (if I may so apply the word)—nor house, nor fence. In the middle reigns a horrible pavement, and on each side of this an unpaved road for summer use; after rain these become sloughs, and then, sooner than travel on the pavement, I take to the fields.

These, as I have before said, extend to a considerable distance right and left, naked and cheerless, forming the plain of St Denis. There is another by-road leading off near St Denis, which, keeping about midway between the chaussée just mentioned and that by St Ouen, ascends Montmartre by Clignancour, &c. This may be travelled *in dry weather*. In my progress from St Denis to La Chapelle, as usual, instead of the bustle of a London road, a solitary cabriolet now and then passed me; and from time to time I overtook a long-bodied cart, with what we should call half a load —the horses with their broad painted hames, and the waggoner in his white nightcap (or mayhap a cocked-hat), blue frock and white stockings, *sabots*, &c. These things have now lost their novelty—I am too much at home to be amused by them; so I was pacing along thoughtfully when the wildest thing in the shape of an equipage whisked past in a twinkling. It was Russian— a sort of low clumsily-built barouche, with the head thrown back. In this were seated two officers in full uniform, cocked-hats, and long drooping black or bottle-green plumes; four or five (for I did not exactly ascertain which) little, long-tailed, long-maned, wild-looking horses were driven at a gallop by two boys as wild in their appearance, seated on the off-horses, and using the end of the reins as a whip, in the manner of our hussar bridles. I was delighted; but the thing came up so suddenly, and passed me so rapidly, that I had but half a look at it. *En revanche*, standing at the northern entrance of the Palais Royal, I saw to-day again a regular Russian equipage. This was a low carriage also, but of a peculiar construction, drawn by four little rough horses harnessed with rope. On the driving-box sat one of the most picturesque figures I ever saw in my life. Conceive a head of Jupiter as to features, and the splendid beard that fell in thick masses over his ample chest, eyes shooting thunderbolts, overhung by the brow of majesty itself; the support of this head a neck—such a neck!—such a muscular column!—such a bust altogether! His costume, too, was piquant from its novelty. Nothing European was there except the hat, if one might admit this as such, which differed from anything else of the sort I had ever seen; crown exceedingly low, and about twice the diameter at top as at bottom, encircled by an amazingly broad band; brim very broad, and turned up in a peculiar way at the sides—body wrapped in a kind of caftan with loose sleeves, and girt round the waist by a broad sash. On the off-leader sat one of the most beautiful and wildest urchins it is possible to conceive, wrapped in a caftan of similar colour and make to that of the coachman's, grey forage-cap, and neck quite bare. He was about fourteen this boy, and a more animated, lovely face could scarcely be imagined. In repose it would be lovely; but when lighted up by the quick play of two brilliant eyes, partially overshadowed by long elf-locks, the beauty and wildness of expression almost exceeds belief. Whilst I stood wrapt in admiration of these two figures, a Russian officer in a plain undress came out of the Palais Royal, and stepped into the conveniently low vehicle. The coachman shook his reins, the boy, who had been looking back, turned sharply to the front, uttering a loud, shrill, but musical cry, the little wild horses tossed up their noses with a snort, burst at once into a gallop, and away they went like a whirlwind down the Rue Neuve des Petits Champs. For the rest of this day I have never been able to get them out of my head, and everything Russian has borne with me a double interest. Strange that, going as I do every day to Paris, it should never have fallen to my lot before to see a Russian equipage; and yet every day, at least every time I pass through La Chapelle, I see hundreds of their soldiers (infantry) without bestowing on them the slightest attention. These, smart as they are on the parade, are the dirtiest slovens in the world off it: the usual costume in which one sees them running about La Chapelle is a dirty forage-cap, as dirty a grey greatcoat, generally gathered back by the waist-strap, so as to be out of the way, dirty linen trousers, shoved up at bottom by the projection of the unlaced half-boot. Such is the figure I generally see slipping from house to house, or going across the fields at a sort of Highland trot. Curiosity they have none, or it is restrained by their discipline, for I do not recollect once having met a Russian soldier dressed and walking the streets, as if to see the place. Sometimes, in passing their quarters, I have heard them sing in their squalling, drawling style, in a voice as if mocking some one; there is, however, something wild and plaintive in their ditties. Karl's 'Imitations,' which I always fancied a caricature, is, I find, most excellent. The Prussians, by the by, show themselves as little about the streets as the Russians; but Austrians or Hungarians I meet constantly, generally walking two together—staring into the shop-windows, &c. &c. Tall, heavily-built, boorish-looking fellows, but apparently good-natured and orderly in their behaviour. Happening to go into a shop on the Boulevard a few days ago, one of these came in, and making some observation on my purchase, was surprised at my answering him in German, and immediately became quite friendly. Whether he knew I was an officer or not, it is impossible to say, but he followed me out of the shop, and walked some way along the Boulevard with me, and it was not without difficulty I at last succeeded in shaking him off. They are a heavy people altogether, these Austrians. I frequently pass the hotel where the Emperor lodges, and in this hot weather all the windows being open, see from the Boulevard the whole interior of the waiting-room, where the stiff formality of the Garde du Corps on duty, in their ugly old-fashioned uniforms of grey and silver lace, with ill-shaped cocked-hats stuck square on, is not a little ridiculous. However, they are, as I said before, a good, quiet people.

CHAPTER XXII.

August 5th. — I had intended seeing some of the sights to-day—so accordingly, after breakfast, mounted on Nelly, cigar in mouth, and followed by my smart orderly, Fitzgerald, I paraded slowly through the village, crossed the fields to St Denis, having passed which I had already got over half the dreary road to La Chapelle, when Nelly suddenly fell dead lame. Upon examination we found a great nail which had run into her foot (off hind), between the frog and bars. This put an end to my day. So I returned quietly, put the mule into the stable with Cossack and the brown horse, Nelly into the mule's box, sent to St Denis for Mr Coward, who is veterinary surgeon to our division, made Farrier Price meantime pare her sole almost to the quick, put on a bran poultice, and have at last sat down to amuse myself by scribbling something about Paris—observations, description, or what else it may be. To proceed, then. I shall not soon forget my first ride to Paris from Colombes. Although already noticed in its place, I like to dwell on a subject to me of so much pleasure, and shall ever recall with emotion my feelings on first passing the Barrière de l'Etoile and gaining a *coup d'œil* of the magnificent avenue beyond, terminated by the venerable palace of the French monarch—its noble trees, its crowds of carriages, horsemen and footmen, and all the *et ceteras* of such a scene. Arriving by this side, the head filled with preconceived ideas of filthy narrow streets without *trottoirs*, what was my surprise on passing through the Place Louis Quinze and entering the magnificent Rue Royale. My previous knowledge of Paris, picked up in books of travel, &c., has all proved erroneous. Some travellers are extravagant in its praise; but I think the greater part have dwelt too much on the dark side of the picture, otherwise why these unfavourable impressions that occupied my brain? The natives, on the contrary, are too extravagant in its praise; and knowing their gasconading style, one is slow to believe their highly-coloured descriptions, and particularly their saying, "Qui n'a vû Paris, n'a rien vû"—a sentiment now become a proverb with them. But this same, or

THE ARISTOCRATIC QUARTERS. 235

something very similar, is said of many other cities, if I mistake not—Vienna, Rome, Naples, Florence, Madrid, Lisbon, &c. However, like everything else, this has two sides—both parties are right, both are wrong. In the same manner as any other city, Paris has its clean and its dirty quarters, its St Giles and its Grosvenor Street, its fine and its mean buildings, its poverty and its opulence—in short, its *agrémens* and its *désagrémens*. I can't translate these words. Agreeables and disagreeables won't quite do. Everything depends on the good or bad humour of the traveller, or the reception he meets with in the country he undertakes to describe. It generally, therefore, is either a Pays de Cocagne or a Tierra del Fuego.

Divided into twelve *arrondissements* or *mairies*, and every *arrondissement* into several *quartiers*, one finds such a difference between these divisions—in the manners, habitudes, and physiognomy of their inhabitants—as scarcely to believe they form part of the same community. Thus les Quartiers des Tuileries, des Roule, des Champs Elysées, &c. &c.—in which are situated the court, the hotels of all the *grand seigneurs*, &c., consequently the richest, smartest, and best shops—distinguished for elegance, cheerfulness, and cleanliness. Le Quartier de la Chaussée d'Antin is the residence of the rich bankers, as in like manner that of the Palais Royal is of merchants, brokers, &c. The Marais is inhabited principally by people of moderate incomes, fond of quiet and tranquillity; and among these are to be found the principal remaining specimens of the *bon vieux temps*—good, easy, old-fashioned people. The Pays Latin—as the neighbourhood of the Rues St Jacques, de la Harpe, &c., is called, from containing the College de la Sorbonne, the schools of the University, &c. &c.—is the cradle of science, and the residence of almost all the bookbinders, parchment-makers, &c., of Paris. Here reside professors and students of theology, medicine, law, natural history, &c. &c. All is here quiet gloom, and some small degree of filth. Les Halles present the singular spectacle of a rural population in the heart of a great city. The other parts of Paris, inhabited by various classes of artisans, are not only different from all those already spoken of, but differ even amongst themselves, according to the business pursued in them. Thus the Rue de Clery is one complete magazine of furniture and cabinet-work, &c.; and most of the work in silk, such as curtain-fringe, &c., is done in la Rue de la Feronnerie and Marché des Innocens, &c.—

but of the more distant quarters of this description I only speak from hearsay, the temper of their population being such as to render it dangerous for an Englishman to appear there as an idler; therefore have I never yet seen the Quartier de St Antoine, nor the Place Royale—the very focus of this spirit. It is clear, therefore, that Paris cannot be characterised by a *trait de plûme*—as clean or dirty, grand or mean, &c. Handsome, and what we should call fine, streets there are, and others which, without any pretension to these names, are yet striking from their extent and bustle of business, &c. &c. Of the former are the Rues de la Paix, Royale, de Rivoli, de Mont Blanc, de la Place Vendome, du Faubourg St Honoré, &c. &c. All these are scrupulously clean and very cheerful, full of fine hotels (*not inns*), fine shops, and for the most part have good and spacious *trottoirs*. The first two in particular are very handsome streets. Of the latter description are the Rues de St Denis, de St Martin, de l'Université, du Faubourg St Denis, Neuve des Petits Champs, and many others. These are generally long streets, some of them very wide, but almost all of them without *trottoirs*. Beyond these the streets are generally very narrow, dirty, and dark. This obscurity is caused by the enormous height of the houses in the old parts of the town, and their sombre hue—I was going to say *their being blackened by smoke*, but that can scarcely be possible, since from using so much wood one never sees that thick canopy of smoke hanging over Paris that usually shuts out the feeble rays of the winter's sun from the citizens of our metropolis. The close confined streets, indeed all the older streets of Paris, are redolent at all times of a most disagreeable odour. Evelyn, 160 years ago, said the streets of Paris smelt of sulphur. The innumerable lamps swinging from ropes over the centre of these streets give them, in my eyes, a very mean appearance. I don't know why, but they seem, too, in the way. These ropes lead down the wall on one side of the street in a sort of wooden case, the key of which being kept by the lamplighter, mischievous people are unable to get at the lamps without breaking open these cases—an operation requiring time, and not performed without noise, therefore almost impossible with such a vigilant police. But the greatest ornament of the town, and no doubt that which contributes most to its salubrity, is the great avenue which, under various names, is called generally the Boulevards, from occupying the site of the ancient ramparts of Paris. Since the increase of the faubourgs has placed these in the midst of the town as it were, a second concentric circle, called the New Boulevard, has been formed; but this seems a mere circular road, not much frequented : and along it is the only enclosure Paris now possesses—a simple stone wall, connecting the barriers, and thereby insuring the fiscal duties. Of the old Boulevards I spoke some days ago ; it were needless, therefore, to fill my journal with repetition. They must be acknowledged as a most agreeable and amusing lounge. After the streets, the quays of Paris naturally attract our attention —a feature so ornamental, so commodious, so salubrious, that we wonder our own metropolis should be destitute in this respect. What a noble thing it would be were our fine river bordered by such quays as those de Buonaparte, des Tuileries, de Voltaire, de la Conference, &c., instead of being enclosed as it is between such a set of shabby wooden or brick warehouses !

But if London is inferior to Paris in this respect, how superior she is in public squares! The costly iron railings, the masterly statues that decorate some, and the pleasant shrubberies, smooth, well-kept turf, and well-rolled walks which characterise most of them, are nowhere to be seen in Paris. The Place Louis Quinze is not what we should call a square in London; it is a sort of esplanade, separating the ramparts and gardens of the Tuileries from the Champs Elysées; the third side is closed by the river, and the fourth is the only side having buildings—those of the Garde Meuble. It is an agreeable esplanade, but is no square. The Place Royale is, I believe, the largest square in Paris; but, for the reasons before mentioned, I have as yet never seen it. From all that I have heard, it is surrounded by very lofty, and perhaps once handsome houses, which then were the habitations of the principal *noblesse*, though now of a numerous population of artisans. In the middle of it, I understand, is a fountain, some trees, &c., in the manner of our squares. The Place Vendome is the next in size to the former; it is octagonal, and the houses, all uniformly built, are of a respectable class, but the style of them is heavy and dull: the want of a *trottoir*, the houses standing as they do with their ground-floors unscreened or unprotected from the carriage-way, spite of the splendid column springing from its centre, give this places a mean, *triste* appearance. I could not divest myself of the idea of its being a mews. The Place des Victoires, meant to be circular, is only a small concern, neither handsome nor ornamental, and perhaps only useful as admitting light and air into a very thick and closely-built part of the town. These are, strictly speaking, the only real public squares; for the Parvis Nôtre Dame, Place du Carrousel, &c. &c., are only esplanades in front of the Cathedral and Tuileries. On the whole, however, Paris is a much more cheerful place than London. In this respect there is no comparison between them.

8 P.M.—Rambled up the road to Garges, which is still nearly as deserted as ever; but the rags and tatters, and broken glass, &c., with which the street was strewed, have in a great measure disappeared. After dinner, Cossack being still rather lame, I rode Mula through the vineyards to Pierrefitte. The country is much prettier on that side than with us, being hilly, whereas we are on a dead level. Our waggon-train officers are doing cavalry with a vengeance, and making a great swagger among the natives. Took a round by Villetaneuse—through vineyards, plantations of artichokes, &c.—and passing along the enclosure of a very handsome domain, with a fine house of brick, let Mula find her own road home, which she did very cleverly and very directly. I think (at least on smooth ground) mules are not so sure-footed as is usually believed and asserted — perhaps

amongst rocks and mountains they may be.
6*th.*—Sunday.

7*th.* — To town as usual this morning for sight-seeing. From the Rue de Malte took my course through the court of the Louvre and the Place de Jena, still boarded up, crossed the Pont Neuf, " where it always blows," and accordingly did blow there to-day certainly, more than elsewhere. Henri IV., with his manly countenance and pointed beard, smiled on me as I made my way through the crowd and plunged into the gloomy and shabby streets of the Pays Latin. Stopped at a mean, rather dirty restaurant in the Rue St Jacques, where I got a bad lunch, of course, and a bottle of sour wine; but for this there was no remedy, as I did not know of any better in the neighbourhood, to which I am a stranger. After doubling and threading my way through a number of dirty obscure streets, which no stranger could have done in London, I at last came out on the Quai St Bernard, where suddenly I found myself among hundreds, if not thousands, of pipes of wine ranged in tiers. It is the Marché aux Vins; and whilst seated upon one of these pipes enjoying the busy scene around, I mentally bless the ingenious system of numbering the houses and naming the streets that has enabled me to steer through such a labyrinth as I have just passed, and which might so well and so easily be applied in London. All streets running to the Seine are numbered in *black*; all those parallel, or nearly so, to the river in *red*. Starting from the river, the numbers commence in a double series in these transverse streets; and in the longitudinal streets the series of numbers follow the course of the stream,—equal numbers always on the right, unequal on the left. In the same manner the names at the corners of the streets are of a similar colour to the numbers; and moreover, some remarkable object, giving a designation to the quarter, is painted at the corners. The Jardin des Plantes, or du Roi, is adjoining the Marché aux Vins, and thither I went, walking in amongst other company without let or hindrance of any kind. In this garden, the Menagerie, and the Cabinet d'Histoire Naturelle, I passed nearly the whole afternoon in the most agreeable manner possible. Much as I had heard of this establishment, the reality rather surpassed than fell short of it—and sorry I am to say we can boast of nothing at all equal to it in England; nor, if we did, could our populace be admitted to it with the same freedom as the more volatile yet more considerate *badauds* are to this. Everything would soon be ruined. The men would trample over the beds, the boys would break down the hedges and fences; knives would operate in all directions; even the women would find some means of doing mischief;—in short, it would never do. Here, on the contrary, it was with pleasure that I observed people of all classes of society, even beggars, conducting themselves with a modesty and decency of manner not to be surpassed. The choice of ground has been very judicious, as the plan presents a pleasing undulalation of surface that gives infinite interest to a promenade. The botanical part is flat and even, divided by walks into compartments, each forming a small distinct garden by itself. These are either enclosed by well-kept hedges, or by rails and rustic fences of every possible useful fashion —which may serve as models for those in want of such things.

These little gardens each contains some family of shrubs or plants, and are all arranged according to their respective climates. The dividing walks form most agreeable promenades, as was evinced by the number of people I found lounging in them, many evidently not taking any interest in the botanical treasures around. This flat space is bounded on one side by a magnificent avenue of elms, under the shade of which are numerous *vendeurs de boissons* and *de pâtisserie*, as well as one or two regular restaurateurs. On the other side, the ground, swelling gently into hill and dale as it were, is fitted by enclosures of simple rail or strong stockade, as occasion may require, for the confinement of an elephant or a deer. Here in little paddocks, with room to move about and a house to shelter them, we find a number of animals, who, perhaps, well fed as they are, little regret the loss of liberty. The elephant even has a pond to wallow in, to the great amusement of the *badauds* who constantly throng the stockade. The more savage beasts (*genus Felis*, &c.) are confined as with us, in dens. It was only in looking over the catalogue of the menagerie, and finding the beasts enclosed in the paddocks classed as ruminant and *fauve*, that I remembered we have no term to translate the latter word. This part of the establishment is very entertaining, and I lounged away a great part of my time in wandering about the winding walks between the enclosures, amused by the curiosity and *naïveté* of many of the visitors. The menagerie is separated from the gardens by a rampart and ditch. In the latter are the bears, great favourites with the public, particularly the boys, of whom numbers are always hanging on the wall, watching the heavy animals climbing a high pole set for the purpose. The hothouses contain all sorts of things; but what interested me were the palms —some of these I saw out of doors. Just by the hothouses is a high mount, ascended by a spiral path, bearing a sort of temple on the top, whence there is an extensive and much-vaunted view over the city and neighbourhood; but not half so extensive as, nor in any way comparable to, those from Belleville, Montmartre,* and, above all, from Mont Aurelian. The School of Comparative Anatomy is very interesting: it contains perfect skeletons of almost every species of animal, bird, or fish, from the most diminutive to the largest —from the minnow to the whale, from the shrew-mouse to the mastodon, from the humming-bird to the condor.

Evening was drawing on, and I ran hastily through the two floors of the Cabinet of Natural History, that I might get home before dark. The entrance to the Jardin des Plantes, by a handsome *grille* from the quay opposite the Pont d'Austerlitz, is very good, but I could not stop to admire

* To me the most interesting part of this mound was its history, rising abruptly as it does so much above the surrounding ground. Is it an enormous barrow, like Silbury, or is it a natural accumulation of alluvium?

it; and hurrying along the *quais*, instead of blundering amongst the streets, succeeded again in just getting home in time.

August 8*th*.—It seems as if I were destined always to fall under the Duke's displeasure, and to be the victim of his injustice. When I called on Sir Augustus Frazer this morning at the Hotel du Nord, the first greeting I got on entering the room was, "*Mercer, you are released from arrest!*" At first I thought this a joke, but Sir Augustus assured me seriously that I had not only been in arrest, but *that*, too, ever since our review on the 24th ultimo. He then told me that I had not been the only unfortunate. Himself and Major M'Donald had been supposed under arrest at the same time and for the same *crime;* and what was this?—this very grave crime for which two field officers and a captain had actually been under ignominious punishment for a whole fortnight? In the column of review on the 24th ultimo, my troop was on the extreme left (or rear), except the two brigades of 18-pounders. Our order of marching past was in column of divisions (we have three divisions), and my post for saluting was considerably in front of the leading one, to leave room for the division officers at open order, consequently I was fully a hundred yards distant from my rear division when passing the Duke. Now it so fell out that, at that very moment, a horse of one of the rear-division carriages got his leg over a trace. The limber gunners, with their wonted activity, were off, cleared the leg, remounted, all in sufficient time for the division to pass his Grace steadily and in good order. But this little halt, momentary as it was, checked the 18-pounders; and Ilbert, or whoever commanded them, ignorant of the saluting-point, trotted up to regain his distance, until suddenly, seeing the sovereigns and their suite, he resumed his walk too late, and passed them in confusion. The Duke fell into one of his furious passions, asked how this happened, and (what he did with the foot-artillery I know not) immediately despatched the Adjutant-General to put Sir Augustus Frazer, Major M'Donald, and myself under arrest. The two former, however, had departed; and whilst the Adjutant-General was struggling through the crowd after me, I had cleared the Rue Royale, and setting off at a trot down the Boulevard, had turned down the Rue de Clichy, consequently was out of sight ere he reached the Boulevard, where he gave up the pursuit and said no more about it. Whether the Duke forgot us, or whether he purposely kept us in arrest, we are left to conjecture—certain it is, that we three actually appear by name in the General's orders of yesterday as released from our arrest. *Mens conscia recti*—I snap my fingers at the disgrace.

Leaving Sir Augustus, I accompanied Bell to his pretty lodging in the Rue Mont Blanc. I don't know who the people are, but it is an uncommonly genteel, well-furnished, well-appointed house. A young gentleman there is who visits Bell occasionally, and a young lady who serenades him (if I may so apply the term) continually. She touches the piano well, has a musical voice, and sings with taste. "L'Exile" is the favourite just now, a pretty song, which, from so often hearing there, I shall always henceforward associate with Bell's nicely-furnished apartment, and the little pleasure-ground, of some thirty or forty feet square, with one or two acacias in it. Frazer, too, has very handsome rooms in the Hotel du Nord, richly furnished, with green silk window-curtains, &c. &c. Sir Edward Kerrison and old Platoff also live there. Passed the remainder of this morning lounging about the Boulevard, as much amused as on the first day. All the fun, crowd, &c., I observe, is confined to the right side going up from the Rue Royale; on the left there is comparatively nobody, except, perhaps, at the Porte St Denis and St Martin, through which (or rather by which) a crowd is continually setting, and one is deafened by the importunate clamours of fifty cabriolet-drivers, all calling at once, "Voiture, Monsieur—Voiture?" "St Denis, Monsieur?" "Memorency, Monsieur?" "Garges, Monsieur?" "Arnouville?" &c. &c. These fellows are most active rogues, and their carriages very convenient, and far more agreeable than the fiacres; and that is the opinion of the public in general, I presume, from seeing one fiacre plying for ten cabriolets or coucous, or whatever name they go by. The coachmen of the former are so well aware of this, that they generally are dozing on their boxes, giving themselves no trouble in looking for customers. Perhaps, however, this may arise from their being only servants, whilst the others are themselves the proprietors of the vehicles they drive. Although conscious that these *portes* are in reality triumphal arches, yet I never pass them without experiencing something of the same feeling with which one would view the magnificent bridge built by Philip II. over the dry bed of the Manzanares if ignorant of the impetuous floods to which that river is liable. The Boulevard presented if anything a more busy, noisy scene than usual. The Turk I found with an attentive and apparently much interested audience, whom he was haranguing with vociferations and gesticulations truly astounding. In vain I tried to catch the purport of his harangue—the curious *badauds* were packed so close, and so firmly maintained their ground, that it was impossible to approach one inch into the circle. I lounged on and admired the beautiful Fontaine de Bondy, or de Lions, I know not which it is called, but its sheets of falling water are singular, and I think it a beautiful fountain. What a magnificent air these fountains give to the town! How refreshing and delightful is the splashing of their waters in warm weather! and oh! the contrast presented to them by our conduits, &c.—shapeless masses of masonry or brickwork, with a brass cock stuck in each side, or mayhap the said brass cock protruding from a common wall.

The French are an ingenious people, and contrive a thousand curious, uncommon, and often admirable devices for opening people's purses, instead of sticking to the unvaried, dismal chant of our beggars—although "*Pour l'amour de Dieu*" is not uncommon here. Our wretches drive one away, but the gentlemen of whom I speak grasp, retain, and even squeeze their auditors as one would a lemon. Nor do they always assume the repulsive rags, &c., which our beggars think so essential to obtain their end. An instance of this I frequently meet on the Boulevard St Martin—an elderly man, of a grave physiognomy, well featured, and of rather a genteel appearance, clad in garments somewhat seedy, though fashionably cut. This man I stumbled on to-day at the corner of the Rue du Temple lecturing on moral philosophy. Like the Turk, he had a numerous and attentive audience, but, generally speaking, composed of a better description of people. To a clear, sonorous voice, he added a manner demonstrative without being dogmatic, and persuasive without betraying doubt of his own powers. He defined the motives and rules of human actions, and showed that these rules are immutable — that we cannot violate them with impunity. He then went at some length into the morals of the ancients, touched on the doctrine of expediency, on the desire of distinction, ambition, &c., and very naturally, though cautiously, introduced as an illustration Napoleon. No one could mistake the sensation produced by this magic name—a sensation which, having produced, he proceeded to neutralise by gradually slipping into the connection between religion and morality. I left him explaining the insufficiency of natural religion, &c. Although this man does not beg, there is no doubt he makes a good trade of preaching; numerous were the offerings silently put into his hand and quietly pocketed without once interrupting the thread of his discourse. Another actor of the same description is a man who usually frequents the northern entrance of the Passage Feydeau: an immense power of grimace, and amazing execution on the violin, are the means by which he gains his daily bread. Clad in an old threadbare frock, that once was brown, with a pair of enormous spectacles riding astride on his prominent nose, he takes his stand on the steps at the entrance of the passage. Heels close together, body drawn up at attention, and with his gaze directed upwards at the window of the fourth storey of the opposite house, he appears perfectly unconscious of the presence of the admiring crowd assembled round him, whilst he executes with astonishing justness, feeling, and rapidity, the most difficult passages from some of the favourite composers of the day—distorting his face all the time in a manner so wonderfully ludicrous that his really excellent music is almost drowned by the uncontrollable laughter of the surrounding multitude. These are some of the many means employed in this gay metropolis for extracting coin out of the pockets of their fellow-men. Gay, however, as it is, misery exists here as well as elsewhere, and I shudder even now at the harrowing tale Bell told me this morning of suicide, to which he was witness a day or two ago. Passing through the Place Vendome, he observed several people looking anxiously up at the Column of Austerlitz, and naturally turning his eyes in the same direction, beheld a man in the act of climbing over the rails of the gallery, having effected which, he deliberately lowered himself down until he hung suspended by the arms over the frightful depth below. In this position he remained a few seconds, perhaps as if repenting him of the rash act he was about to perpetrate; but, unable to recover the gallery, he eventually let go his hold, and was dashed to pieces on the pavement at the foot of the column: the very idea is harrowing!

A trait of the times, and a very striking one too, which a person meets with at almost every step in walking about Paris, is the announcement of the change of dynasty—from an empire to a kingdom —exhibited in the titles of shops, *lycées*, and every other establishment; the old word *imperiale* slightly painted over to make way for the more humble *royale—lycée royale*, &c.—which is sometimes painted over it, but more frequently by the side of it, leaving the former word quite legible through the thin daub of paint laid over it. The postilions, too, are changing their imperial green livery for the royal blue; yet this change goes on but slowly, for we still see many of the numerous English equipages daily arriving brought in by postilions in green livery jackets. In the palaces and other public buildings, the letter N was abundantly introduced into all the architectural decorations, besides the armorial bearings of the Emperor: workmen have been some time employed effacing or altering all these. Wherever it is possible, the obnoxious letter is removed altogether; but where that is not the case, which happens frequently, it is changed into an H and the numeral IV. added. These and many other changes incident to the present state give a curious aspect to the nation, and afford much food for speculation and contemplation. Met my old schoolfellow Courtnay Ilbert coming out of town, and we rode together to St Denis, where his 18-pounder brigade is stationed. On reaching home found that M. Fauigny has been here. Poor man! he is not likely to get much from me.

August 9th.—Not quite well this morning, but I went to town to meet Hitchins, and make a sight-seeing day of it. Accordingly we have done pretty well, galloping through the Luxembourg, Les Monumens, and wandering over almost the whole southern part of Paris. I can't say, however, that this has been to me a day of much interest; I prefer a thousand times wandering about the town by myself—observing the habits, manners, &c., of the people—to all the sight-seeing; but I allowed Hitchins to shame me out of the idea of leaving Paris without seeing everything. Much, however, I fear I shall have to blush for, if that be necessary, and amongst others the theatres, not one of which have I ever entered yet. The Luxembourg is a fine palace, and I like its style of architecture much better than that of the Tuileries, though it is vilely situated. The gardens are much the same—parterres, ponds, ramparts—*voilà tout*. The great attractions here are the Chamber of Peers, and the Galleries of Rubens, Vernet, and of the French Raphael Le Sueur. The first I cannot bear, spite of his beautiful colouring and well-managed *chiaro-oscuro*—allegory is my abomination; the pictures of the second are more to my taste; but the blue works of the French Raphael I could not appreciate. Besides

THE CHAMBER OF PEERS. 257

these, we saw a multitude of other masterpieces; and I was particularly pleased at having an opportunity of seeing some by David, of whom I have heard so much. Here disappointment awaited me, and a glance at the " Judgment of Brutus" satisfied me—all yellow and glare, and extravagant attitudes. Surely the human spine would never admit of being doubled in the manner of the fainting female introduced in the foreground of this picture—a perfect parabola. To reach the Chamber of Peers, we passed through a grove of orange-trees in boxes, and then mounted a very fine staircase ornamented with statues of great men, among which two were very spirited— those of Condorcet and of General Dessaix, said to be likenesses; I had no idea the latter was so young. The Chamber itself is a very handsome semicircular hall, having the President's desk in the centre of the chord, and those of the members round the curve. Beyond this is the Salle de la Paix, a very handsome room, the walls of which are covered with paintings by David, representing the victories of Napoleon, weakly enough hid with green baize, and not allowed to be seen.

Of the monuments I have little worth recording. Interesting specimens there are of French sculpture of every age—all preserved by M. Lenoir from revolutionary Vandalism. The only thing, however, that I remember worth noticing, is the tomb of Louis XII. (I think), on which the corpses of himself and queen soon after death are laid out: the countenance of the king is expressive of great suffering. The horrid truth of this sculpture, aided by the colour of the marble—so completely that of a corpse—leads one to believe that it must by some means have been actually copied from nature. In a little yard, about twenty feet square, and surrounded by the high walls of the neighbouring houses, stands the Paraclete. Its situation is a sad drawback to the interest one might otherwise take in this specimen of ancient architecture, for in the history of the Castrato and his love I can take none. In wandering about the town, amongst other places we stumbled upon were the poultry or game market, and that of flowers—two opposite extremes. The first is a very handsome building on the Quai des Grand Augustins, and this being one of the days on which the game, &c., arrives, the quantity was prodigious; but the smell was more than we could stand, and obliged us to a very precipitate retreat; so, crossing to the Cité, we rambled on, and quite by accident found ourselves in the empire of Flora, redolent of mignonette and a thousand other odoriferous plants, and presenting a *coup d'œil* not to be excelled : hortensias and camellias appeared quite common. The Parisian flower-sellers are adepts in making up nosegays, and, I believe, understand using them as the language of love like the Turks. Tired with our walk, we returned to Hardi's, where, having made an excellent dinner, we separated; and here I am half asleep recording the day.

Sunday, 13th.—I have been idle as to writing since Wednesday, but not so otherwise, having been every day in town; in the mean time, domestic transactions require some notice. Our vineyards are blessed this year with a most extraordinary crop of grapes, to secure which from marauders I have acceded to M. Bonnemain's petition in behalf of the villagers, and established a regular patrol of our men—a precaution certainly most necessary, seeing what neighbours we have : at Pierrefitte the waggon-train; on the other side, bivouacking along the chaussée from Garges to St Denis, Joncs's corps of Belgian waggoners, five hundred in number, men totally unacquainted with the restraints of military discipline, with full leisure to meditate mischief, and most persevering foragers for their horses, which are their own private property ; in our rear, at

Garges, &c., are our savage and lawless friends of Nassau, and some Belgians. So surrounded, vigilance becomes absolutely necessary, not only for the sake of our villagers, but also for our own; and nothing has gained their affections, or united us more, than the establishment of this patrol, especially since it has taken some prisoners. The other day the *garde champêtre* detected soldiers stealing along amongst the vines, but not daring to go near them himself, hurried into the village and reported it to the sergeant-major, Oliphant, who lost no time in despatching a corporal and four mounted gunners in pursuit. The fellows were soon taken and brought in triumph to my house, the *garde champêtre* stalking at the head of the procession in his cocked-hat and broad *bandoulière*, prisoners between the escort—M. le Maire and some twenty peasants, making more noise with their *sabots* than the iron hoofs of the horses, bringing up the rear. The unfortunates were Belgians, quite lads, so I held a sort of court-baron in my yard, and upon their expressing great contrition, and begging a thousand pardons, at M. Bonnemain's request I forgave them, but sent the escort to see them home to Garges, whence they came. The effect on the villagers has been very good—they have all become the most kindly obliging creatures possible, and our men are as thick as brothers with them; I trust this harmony may continue. I have likewise another source of amusement, which makes my residence here more agreeable—I have hired a very good violin, and bought some music. The offhanded liberal manner in which Madame Duhan informed me of the hire, and allowed me to take away the instrument, stranger as I was to her, without any security, surprised me much. I rather think none of our musicsellers in London would lend even their worst instrument to a Frenchman in the same manner. On Thursday last I went to see the Bibliothèque Royale, a magnificent establishment, and where I passed a most delightful morning; it is in the Hotel de Colbert, Rue de Richelieu, from which street the main entrance opens into a square court surrounded by the building, and having in its centre a naked statue of Diana in bronze, of fine execution, but in my opinion misplaced here.

The library occupies two entire and part of a third side of the quadrangle (about 300,000 volumes), and is on the most liberal footing. Any well-dressed person is freely admitted, and may range about unobstructed; but he must touch nothing. Chairs, tables, pens, and ink, are there for those who wish to write, and servants, in rich liveries of blue and silver lace, are in attendance to furnish the books required. These people are positively forbidden to accept anything from the visitors; and yet no one can be more obligingly attentive. In the Cabinet des Medailles are many curiosities; amongst the most interesting, I thought, were the iron chair of King Dagobert, and a silver disc found in the Rhone, and supposed to have been the shield of Scipio—I don't know why. Two enormous globes, more than 12 feet in diameter, are mounted on the ground-floor, and circular apertures have been opened in the floor above to admit part of their circumference through it. The fourth side of the quadrangle is a most delightful lounge; it is the Cabinet des Gravures. In this are preserved specimens of the works of every artist of every nation—from the most ancient period down to the present. The collection is immense, and is the constant resort of all the artists of the capital, and a crowd of picture-loving people. I could pass whole days there, so interesting is the collection, and so great the facility of using it. This place occupied my morning so completely that I had barely time to get my *potage à la julienne*, &c., and come home before dark.

Friday.—It sounds oddly to an English ear, smuggling into a town from the country; but the free circulation that exists throughout our country is unknown here. Everything is examined at the *barrière*. What would our farmers and their wives say if they were liable to be stopped at the gate of every principal town, and their loads of hay, or baskets of eggs, &c., submitted to the scrutiny of excisemen? Several loads of hay preceded me this morning as I rode through the Faubourg St Denis. At the *barrière* the column was halted, and as the passage was blocked up, I was obliged to wait patiently and see every load as it passed in succession probed through and through by the officers with long iron skewers, to ascertain that nothing was concealed amongst the hay. The signs exhibited by the various shops in Paris are often quaint and amusing. A description of them would fill a volume. The one which calls forth this remark struck me as I entered the Palais Royal this morning from the Rue Vivienne. I don't well know how to designate the sort of shop which exhibits the sign of the "Gourmand;" they are numerous in this part of the town, and I think more nearly resemble our Italian warehouse than any other. Here is to be procured every dainty that can stimulate the palate—pickles, preserves, hams, tongues, hung-beef, cheese, dried fruits, nuts of all sorts, sauces, dried and cured fish,—in short, everything. The *enseigne* of this shop represents a fat greedy-looking fellow seated at a table, under which his legs are spread out. The table is covered with every kind of dainty, which, whilst discussing a large salmon, he is eagerly devouring with the eyes. If the Boulevard is amusing for the life and movement it exhibits, so is the Palais Royal in a high degree, and to the charms of the former it adds that of an endless variety of rich and beautiful articles of dress, *vertu*, and a number of others, which employ me incessantly at the windows. The display of elegant little toys in Bobon's window is scarcely to be surpassed — such little beauties of watches,[*] not larger than half-a-crown, cases most tastefully chased and set in rich pearls; in other shops rich and elegant shawls, *fichus*, and silks, of the most splendid colours; then jewellery, so much taste combined with costliness; then cutlery and works in steel, &c. &c.; and not the least amusing, the numerous cafés or restaurants. The crowd under the arcades is as varied as it is immense. If,

[*] It must be remembered that in those days these, as well as many other things quite common in England, were novelties to Englishmen.

on entering from Rue Vivienne, one turns to the right, not many paces in that direction will bring him in front of the favourite haunt of Austrian and Prussian officers. It resembles a great conservatory, being all glass, and is in the garden, not in the house, whence every refreshment has to be brought across the piazza. About 2 or 3 every afternoon this is crowded, and it then reminds me of a glass bee-hive, from the busy stir within, and the facility of observing this from without. The celebrated Café aux Milles Colonnes is not far off, up-stairs about half-way down the next branch. I lounged up to it and was disappointed. A decent *salle* enough, which, being everywhere panelled with mirrors, the green marble columns are reflected so repeatedly as to give some colour to the appellation assumed by the establishment. There are several rooms; but whether the place is only frequented at night on certain days, or that something *fâcheux* had occurred, I know not—certain it was not in a state to receive company, wherefore I made no further advance than to the door, and having peeped in, wheeled down-stairs again. Amongst other curiosities of Paris I have often stood and contemplated the air of importance and grave bustle of an establishment unknown to us in London, where the operation in question is performed in a very modest manner in the public streets. This morning I walked into the shop of a fashionable *décrotteur*, that I might see more perfectly all the detail of this most useful business. The *salon*, a large room, was lighted by numerous windows near the ceiling (these, like other artists, affecting a preference for light coming from above : thus I have seen many receiving it through skylights). The handsomest establishment of this kind is in the Passage des Panoramas. A certain degree of taste, too, was visible in the decorations and arrangement of several large mirrors (mirrors are indispensable to a Frenchman). A sort of divan, a few feet broad, extended nearly round the apartment, on which were many gentlemen seated on chairs, gravely reading the daily papers; whilst one foot, raised on a sort of iron resembling the scraper at a door, was being operated on by a journeyman *décrotteur*, who rubbed and polished away with most admirable despatch and dexterity. In the middle of the room stood the master-spirit, superintending the active operations of his myrmidons, receiving the acknowledgment for services performed, ushering the one out of the shop and the other up to the divans, conversing with the newly-arrived aspirants, and doing the amiable everywhere. A good-looking, well-dressed man this master-shoeblack, who might easily be mistaken for a minister.

Disappointment awaits the man who, having read or heard the French account of any place in France or the French dominions, expects to find it realised, or even nearly so. With them all is exaggeration and bombast; even the accounts of their most respectable and veracious writers, in all matters relating to France or the French, must be received *cum grano salis*. Disappointment certainly was mine after reading and hearing so much of the several gardens (as Frascatin, Tivoli, the Jardins Turc and du Prince) when I turned into the latter of these two celebrated places in the Boulevard du Temple. Certes, I took it *en déshabillé*, for the evening and by lamp-light is its hour of triumph, and then I am here always. The guide-book speaks of "un jardin agréable." What did I find? Certainly no garden—a yard (gravelled) divided by hedges (such ones as may be expected in a town) into several compartments, in which are a few boxes; one side bounded by the *salle*, with its usual accompaniments—the others, by gables or back walls of the neighbouring houses; figure irregular, and space very confined. Having nothing fixed for Friday, I made a wandering day of it. Up one gloomy street, down another; at last found myself in the Place des Innocens, in which is held the principal vegetable-market of Paris. The Place is large but gloomy; houses very high, of a dark-coloured stone, and in the usual French style, windows open, and exhibiting all the variety of clothes hanging to dry, flowers, rich curtains and common ones, &c. &c., incident to buildings inhabited by so many diffcrent families. The area presented a varied, characteristic, and moreover an interesting picture. The whole space was covered with large umbrellas, fixed upright over the different tables, &c., the convex surfaces of which, of all the hues of the rainbow (pink predominating), reminded me strongly of the *testudo* of the ancients. Amidst these arose, to the height of some forty or fifty feet, the noble Fontaine des Innocens, with its fine *nappes d'eau*. Not only the Marché itself, but the Rue de la Ferronnerie, and several adjacent ones, seem quite the focus of business, such stir and bustle do they present. The profusion of fruits and vegetables in this market is remarkable, more particularly when it is remembered that not only Paris itself, but also the whole neighbouring country, is occupied by countless hosts of foreigners. The old ladies, seated under their immense umbrellas (formed generally of alternate pink and white breadths), or stumping about in their *sabots*, give a very animated air to this scene, which, however, is rendered less pleasing from the overpowering smell of decayed and decaying vegetable matter profusely strewed over the pavement. It is an amusing place this Marché, and although only now mentioned, I have visited it more than once. Besides this, there are numerous other markets in different parts of the town, the neatest of which, and one that I always have pleasure in passing through, because always clean, is the Marché des Jacobins, off the Rue St Honoré, and not far from the Place Vendome. Speaking of these markets reminds me of the Abattoir de Montmartre, which I frequently pass in my way in or out of town, one of several buildings in different quarters destined for the slaughter of cattle—a most excellent arrangement, since the blood and filth which usually pollute the kennels in the neighbourhood of our slaughter-houses, the disgusting stench arising from them, and the consequent deterioration and unhealthiness of the surrounding atmosphere, are completely obviated.

Yesterday (Saturday) I devoted to another visit to the Louvre and its interesting collections. What crowds of English and other foreigners!

The gallery of pictures exhibits just now a new feature — French and other artists, with their easels, &c., busily employed copying many of the pictures of which they are soon to be deprived. Among them, working with the utmost composure, were two or three women. But women mix themselves up in every transaction in this country— even in war, as has been illustrated in the formation of our Amazonian battalion at Stain. Somehow or another the statues have more attraction for me than the pictures. The *salles* are less crowded than the gallery, consequently one is quieter and more at liberty to contemplate these admirable sculptures at leisure. The naming of these, however, appears to me very gratuitous, and I much doubt whether one half of those in the catalogues are properly designated. Faun is a very vague term. What absorbing reflections arise in the mind whilst wandering amongst this collection of cold marble stones! Even when, as has happened occasionally, I have been the only individual in the vast apartment, it has been hard to fancy myself alone, so surrounded by beauteous forms, amongst which such perfect harmony of expression reigns—not an attitude or gesture amongst them but what is ease and elegance; nothing constrained, nothing proud, forced, or unnatural; in all, passion, emotion, repose and tranquillity, love, anger, joy, sorrow — all, all expressed by these marble stones in language not to be misunderstood. How powerful is the imagination! These forms address themselves peculiarly to it. Some excite a train of thought associated intimately, I might say inseparably, with historical recollections; others, again, are associated with sensations of voluptuousness, which, however repressed, cannot be excluded entirely—beautiful rounded forms associated with our sense of feeling, and conveying to the too ready imagination ideas of softness and elasticity. How much more we should appreciate these splendid specimens of human skill and conception, could we contemplate them separately and alone, instead of thus jumbled together and in public. In the Salle d'Apollon, however, I think this inimitable statue rather favoured by his company, amongst which are several Egyptian statues, the constrained positions of which—knees pressed together, arms hanging straight down by the side, stiff draperies, and angular ornaments—contrast strikingly with the elegant contour and graceful attitude of this masterpiece by an unknown hand. In this same *salle* are two chairs in beautiful *rouge* antique, both of them found in the Roman baths, and said to have been used in the middle ages at the inauguration of the Popes. Pius VI. restored them to the Museum of the Vatican as antiques, and thence they came here.

I cannot admire the coloured walls of these *salles:* there is something in them that does not accord with the severity of statuary, and it struck me that one uniform tint, perhaps maroon, would considerably enhance the *éclat* of these fine statues. Nor do I admire these imitations of nature being perched upon pedestals: were the Venus, for instance, placed on the floor, or on a low platform as the Apollo is, I think it would add considerably to her interest. Every visit to this splendid collection adds to my wonder and admiration, and I returned yesterday evening with my mind full of enthusiasm for the science which could so nobly conceive, and the art which could so skilfully execute, these exquisite productions of the chisel.

CHAPTER XXIII.

I BELIEVE in a former part of this journal I noticed a chateau belonging to an Admiral Rosily. It is situated quite at the extremity, or rather beyond the village, on the road to Garges, and therefore so far out of the way that, except to visit the stables (for we have a detachment in it), I never have paid any attention to it, and suffered the people to do as they please. On my return yesterday evening from Paris I found the following letter :—

"*Ce* 11 *Août* 1815.

"MONSIEUR LE COMMANDANT,—J'apprends que vous faites mettre des chevaux chez moi. Le Duc de Wellington connoit les destructions qu'on a causé dans ma maison, il avoit bien voulu même me donner une sauve garde, qui n'a plus en lieu depuis que le regiment de Lord Portarlington est parti pour Amiens.

"Je vous prie seulement, que les hommes qui ont soin des chevaux n'entrent point dans mon jardin, et respectent ma propriété.—J'ai l'honneur d'être, Monsieur le Commandant, votre serviteur,

"L'AMIRAL COMTE DE ROSILY."

The Admiral has taken a much more efficacious way of preserving his property in thus committing it to my care instead of making a complaint to the Duke, and certainly a more gentlemanly one. I walked down to it this afternoon, and was surprised to find a spacious, well-kept, and most productive garden, enclosed by a high wall, one side of which runs along the side of the road to Garges, and the other along the lane leading up to the village. The house is large, but its exterior not handsome; some fine rooms within, but every scrap of furniture had been removed before our arrival. In the rear, all the offices carefully numbered, and their names and uses painted in large letters on the doors, "*vacherie,*" "*laitérie,*" &c. &c. Our men have behaved well and destroyed nothing, and the produce of the garden has suffered little, the officer of the division having preserved it for himself. I have given

THE DUKE AND THE 5TH DIVISION. 275

directions which no doubt will leave the Admiral no room to repent of the step he has taken, although it is not possible to remove the men and horses.

The Duke, it seems, continues to bear malice. I cantered up this morning to Paris, and called on Sir G. Wood to beg him to forward my application for two months' leave of absence, which he declined doing, as he said it would not be prudent just now "*to remind the Duke of me in any way.*" Rather hard and unjust this!

In the anteroom at the Rue de Richelieu (Sir George's quarter) I met Captain Light (Bull-dog, as he was called at the academy). He is just returning from Egypt, where he has been travelling, and tells me that he ascended the Nile farther than any one yet. All the honour and glory attending his expedition he would have gladly exchanged for that of having served the campaign with us. He much blamed himself for not having done so. Sir George wanted me to stay and dine, but I begged off.

16*th*.—The vengeance of the Duke has at last fallen on the 5th Division, and it must be confessed they deserve it, having ruined one of the prettiest villages and some of the most charming villas in the neighbourhood of Paris. It is said that damages are laid at £5000, and that the Duke has ordered it to be paid. There is, however, no depending on reports, everything is sure to be so much exaggerated. Nothing else to-day, except that I took my usual ride into Paris, where I lounged away the time principally in shopping, &c.

20*th*.—I can hardly tell how, but true it is that my time for writing is wonderfully curtailed, although in reality I have so little to do. The journeys to and from town occupy much time; and now that we are, as it were, settled, people have taken to visiting, so that we have frequently dinner company, which forbids all attempts at nocturnal writing. Sunday is my quietest day in general, although not always. To-day I passed my morning in strolling about the park of the chateau, the village, &c. Our scenery is too flat to be very pretty, although the chaussées on either side of us, with their fine elms, are noble avenues. These are the roads from Pierrefitte and Garges, which unite near St Denis. There are several spots in the park affording interesting peeps in the direction of Paris. Having a clump of picturesque trees in the immediate foreground, the level verdant carpet stretches away until bounded by the rich masses of foliage of elms bordering the chaussée, above which tower the light spires of the Abbey of St Denis; farther on, an opening in the avenue allows the eye to range over the naked plain of St Denis, bounded in the extreme distance by the heights of Montmartre and Belleville, with the dome of St Genevieve rearing itself in the gap between. Except such peeps, our view is everywhere confined by the foliage and the rising ground extending all round our rear from Garges to Pierrefitte. Water, or the want of it rather, is a great drawback on the scenery about the district: true, there are two or three muddy rivulets, such as the Rouillon, La Vieille Mer, Crouy, &c., but they are too insignificant and too much encased to aid in any way the scenery.

Yesterday, when I called at the Hotel du Nord, I was surprised at meeting Lady Frazer, her brother, and two sisters (Dr James and the Misses Lind).

The festival of our patron saint was celebrated last Thursday with much merriment and conviviality, and it was very pleasing to see the familiar and confident manner in which our people mingled in the amusements of the day, and the cordiality with which they were treated by the villagers.

The favourite (indeed, the principal) game played

by the young men was one resembling our trap-ball, with this difference, that instead of a trap, the ball was made to rebound from a large sieve placed on the ground, and propped upon one side so as to present an inclined surface. In the evening a most animated dance was kept up in the park until a comparatively late hour.

Angélique was the distinguished belle of the evening, and by far the best (as she was the stoutest) *danseuse*, although they all dance well. As I saw her swinging through the figure, "Cutty-sark" came forcibly to my recollection, and mentally I exclaimed "weel done," &c. We were at mess when M. Bonnemain called to announce that all was ready, but that he had forbidden the commencing until the sanction of M. le Commandant was obtained.

This is of a piece with his whole conduct now: everything that passes in the village I am made acquainted with; he has even confided to me several important family secrets;—in short, on every affair, even of the slighest moment, M. le Commandant is consulted. Moreover, M. Bonnemain pays me a regular visit at ten every morning to know my pleasure for the day. Several ridiculous petitions to the Duke (all of which he attends to) have been suppressed, and the complainants brought before me. But this is out of fashion; at present nobody thinks of complaining; we are all too good friends for that. Nor is this all: I begin to have hopes that my Fauigny affair has at last obtained a proper hearing, since an officer sent by Sir Edward Barnes came down to inquire how matters stand, and whether I have as yet paid any of the money.

August 21*st*.—Called at Rue de Richelieu this morning to learn from Sir George Wood what is in the wind, but he knew nothing about it.*

August 26*th*.—I find an undoubted communication from Sir George Wood's major of brigade (Captain Baynes, R.A.), informing me that the Fauigny (or lead) affair had assumed a more favourable appearance, and that Sir George desired I would take no further steps in it until I heard again from him. This is established; but

* The rough journal from which I have with much trouble compiled this copy is here so confused and imperfect as to be of little or no use ; and my great auxiliaries—letters to my wife, from which I was enabled to correct or confirm dates, and to make more circumstantial many subjects only mentioned in the journal—I have unwittingly destroyed. During my stay at Stain, too, I wrote by fits and starts. Amongst new scenes of every kind, and new people, the excitement was too great to admit of shutting one's self up for study or writing. Thus, from the period I have now reached, my means are so few, that it is quite impossible to bring my journal (as I wished) down to our final departure from France—as complete as it might have been.

then follow some contradictions which I cannot reconcile, and must therefore note them down as they are, rather than lose them altogether. M. Fauigny, quite elated at the attention paid to his first complaint, had employed an appraiser, or some such person, to draw up a complete estimate of furniture destroyed, and every sort of damage done to the chateau, with which he again waited on the Duke, in the hope that all would be ordered to be paid as before. This time, however, he was unfortunate in arriving just as the Duke dismounted, in a very ill humour, at his residence in the Elysée Bourbon. With true French effrontery, M. Fauigny followed his Grace up the grand staircase. Arrived at the landing, the Duke, probably observing him for the first time, turned sharply, demanding, " What the devil do you want, sir?" Nothing daunted by this rough address, M. Fauigny mentioned his subject in a few words, presenting at the same time his *bill*, instead of taking which, the Duke, turning hastily away, in his usual rough manner, exclaimed to his aide-de-camp, " Pooh! — kick the rascal down-stairs!" Such is the story as I got it— whether exactly true or not is more than I can now decide; but this much is certain, that Sir Edward Barnes immediately communicated to Sir

George Wood M. Fauigny's discomfiture, adding, "Send word of this to your friend Captain Mercer, and let him do as he pleases about the lead."

As I had been anxious for some time to get leave and go to England, I find by the same memorandum that I went that same day to ask Sir George to make an application for me, which, however, he would not do, telling me that the Duke had refused leave (and very angrily) to Captain Cleeve of the German Legion Artillery, though summoned to his father's deathbed. That I eventually escaped paying a heavy sum of money for depredations committed by others, is not attributable to the Duke of Wellington's sense of justice, but to the irritability of his temper. An officer holding a command in his army (particularly of cavalry or artillery) was in constant jeopardy—constantly struggling to reconcile two contradictions: 1st, to conciliate the natives, and thus prevent complaints; and 2d, to keep his men comfortable and horses *fat* (that is the word), which could only be done at the expense of the natives. These, encouraged by the Duke's orders, proclamations, &c., were never backward in complaining—indeed, they soon became insufferably insolent: and whilst affecting to admire and praise the *grand Vellangton*, and draw comparisons between him and Blucher and his Prussian *thieves* (for so they invariably termed them) — " *voleurs Prussiens* "— they in reality laughed at us; whilst even the private soldiers of the Prussian army were (to their face, at least) treated with the most reverential deference. A sad contrast there was between our relative situations. As for gratitude, the wretches have not one grain of it. Many actually imagine that motives of fear have induced the Duke to adopt this (to them) strange line of conduct.

However severe his Grace may be in this respect, he is easy and indulgent in another which materially concerns our comfort—I mean dress. Every one pleases his fancy in the selection of his costume—some wear plain clothes; others, though in uniform (I speak of visiting and walking about Paris), choose to be unencumbered with sword or sash. Many cavalry men, &c., like, in this hot weather, to go with jackets open, with white or fancy waistcoats, &c. Some wear mustaches, others beards; others, again, both beard and mustaches. A neglect of military uniformity so striking, and so much in contrast with the precision and strictness of costume observed by all the other armies, could not but be noticed. Accordingly, it is said, one of the monarchs (Emperor

Alexander, I have heard) made an observation on the subject to the Duke, who, feeling himself called on to do something, gave out a general order on the subject, in which he directed that all officers of the British army appearing in the streets of Paris should be dressed either wholly in plain clothes or in the strict uniform of their corps. No doubt which was chosen. There is another general order of the Duke's quoted, and the cause of it—for which, however, I do not vouch, having never seen it. The story is this: An English officer, walking on the Boulevard, was rudely pushed off the path by a French gentleman, whom the Englishman immediately knocked down. The person so treated happened to be a marshal; and he, without loss of time, complained to the Duke, though unable to identify his man. His Grace in consequence issued a general order commenting on the outrage offered to a person of such high distinction, and winding up with desiring that British officers would in future abstain from beating marshals of France, &c. But I have digressed from the thread of my discourse, to which I must return, and endeavour to render it as connected as my disjointed records, aided by memory, will admit of.

After leaving Sir G. Wood's, I find no notice

AN AFFRAY.

of further transactions until the evening, when, accompanied by Ambrose (our troop surgeon), I set off to ride home by the Rue de St Denis and La Chapelle. Returning through La Chapelle accompanied by Ambrose, a fellow sitting on his cart drove against him. Ambrose's temper is rather peppery, and he repaid the affront by a cut across the shoulders with his horse-whip. The carter, standing up in his cart, fell furiously on Ambrose in return with his whip, and a regular battle ensued, Ambrose trying to mount the cart, the other keeping him down and flogging him. In a twinkling a crowd assembled, and from reviling soon came to active operations; but I rode round the cart and prevented interference. At last they began to throw stones. This was too much. I drew my sword and charged in all directions, everywhere scattering the wretches like chaff, and thus kept the cowardly herd at bay until Ambrose succeeded in mounting the cart and breaking the fellow's whip over his own back, when, the crowd becoming very serious, he jumped on his horse, and we made our retreat, not, however, without showers of stones, none of which touched us, and being obliged two or three times to turn on our persecutors, who followed us some distance. At last we effected our retreat.

31*st.*—Review of the Russian Guards, &c. They were formed as usual along the Neuilly Road, and had the saluting-point in the Place Louis Quinze. A finer body of men can scarcely be imagined; but to me their padded breasts and waspish waists appeared preposterous. The cuirassiers were also very fine men, well mounted, and neatly and serviceably equipped. I was fortunate enough to wedge myself into the very middle of the Imperial *cortège*. The Emperor of Austria received the salutes, and I was immediately behind his Imperial Majesty—on whose right was our Duke with his blue ribbon on, and all round about were princes, marshals, generals — all the mighty and distinguished of Europe. The Emperor of Russia himself gave the word of command, marched past at the head of the column, and saluted. The Prussian monarch took the command of a regiment of which he is colonel, and likewise marched past. When Alexander wheeled round after passing, and joined our group, he saluted Prince Schwartzenberg with a slap on the thigh, his countenance lighted up by his customary good-humoured smile. The proud Austrian bowed in acknowledgment of the honour done him; but as he cast his eye over his shoulder and met mine fixed on him, a frown soon chased away the forced unmeaning smile still lingering round his mouth, and it required no conjuror to see that he did not admire being treated so familiarly. The greatest good-humour and cheerfulness seemed to reign amongst this group of sovereigns, sovereign princes, and renowned chiefs; and that intuitive awe which little people always experience in such company, began to give way to confidence and a feeling of delight at mingling thus intimately, as it were, with those hitherto to me historical characters, on whose faith depend the destinies of Europe. My next neighbour, a man of high rank—general, or what not—might have been a Czernicheff, Wittgenstein, or some other celebrated man; he wore a Russian uniform, and was covered with decorations. As he spoke French fluently (what Russian does not?), and seemed an honest-hearted man, free from vanity, we soon got into conversation, spite of my shabby old pelisse. Never was I more astonished than when, in answer to my question who the smart-looking lancers were who kept the ground, he replied "Cossacks." A very fine set of tall, handsome, genteel-looking young men, faces exhibiting a a delicate pink and white complexion fit for a lady, quite undefiled by beard or mustache; dressed in scarlet jackets without any lace, fitting like stays; large blue-green overalls, with a broad red stripe, and, as usual, the waist drawn into the capacity of a decent grasp; their arms a sabre, brace of pistols stuck in their waist-belt, and a long red-shafted lance without the pennon; small rough horses—not of a piece with the delicate man and the quality of his equipment. The cuirassiers wore black-varnished cuirasses; and one regiment was entirely mounted on beautiful isabels, or cream-coloured horses. But the horse-artillery, as *en régle*, attracted my most particular attention. These, as far as men and horses went, appeared most efficient: the men stout, of active make, and not too tall; their dress smart, though exceedingly plain—dark-green; their equipment, arms, and horse appointments all of the same description—plain, substantially good, and sufficiently neat, without anything superfluous. The gunners' horses were stoutly-made serviceable animals; but the draught-horses (which seemed an anomaly, though they know best) were much smaller—and such little wild-looking beauties as one would be proud to show off in Hyde Park, or down Bond Street. The worst part of the whole were the guns and carriages—the former of very light calibre, and polished like brass candlesticks (not above 3-pounders, I should think); the latter very low, light, and painted bright green, looking more like toys than service articles. To these the horses were harnessed three abreast; the outer one on the off side, more for show than use, prancing along with the neck bent outward in the true classical position, to which it was confined by a side rein. The effect of this, as far as appearance goes, is certainly good. My friend the general, pointing out these pretty horses with an air of triumph that led me to suspect him of being in the corps, assured me that they had been almost incessantly on the march ever since the retreat of the French from Moscow. They were with the pursuing force, took their share of the campaign in Saxony 1813, advanced to Paris in '14. When the Russians retired, these little animals had drawn the guns back again, and had actually arrived on the banks of the Vistula (I think he said), when they were countermanded, and had now arrived a second time in Paris. Is not this quite astonishing? I could well enter into the feeling of satisfaction and complacency with which he begged my opinion as to their appearance, and unhesitatingly gratified him with my unqualified admiration of them. How could it be otherwise! They were round as barrels, sleek-coated, and full of life and spirit—in short, they were so beautiful that the thing looked more like a showy toy than what had for two years been incessantly in the field. The review over, I called on Sir Edward Barnes and asked his intercession with the Duke to obtain my leave, which he readily promised; so I adjourned to No. 36 Rue Mont Blanc, had some chat with Bell, heard his fair young hostess play the "Exile" again, and returned to my dominions.

September 2d.—Care less about Paris than I did, and stay more at home. The parapet of the bridge becomes again my smoking lounge.

7th.—This morning I received the long-wished-for leave of absence for two months; and wishing to start immediately, Ambrose and I rode up to town to take my place in the diligence for Calais. The Bureau des Diligence is in the Cour des Messageries, Rue Nôtre Dame de la Victoire—an establishment of which I had before no conception. The court is very large; there are several offices for different coaches; but what surprised me most was the parade of those heavy dismal-looking machines—I think there must have been fifty drawn up round the court. For Calais there was no room, therefore I have taken my places —one inside for self, one in the cabriolet for William—in the Amiens diligence, which starts to-morrow morning at five o'clock. The seats inside, &c., are not left as with us to the first comer, &c. On paying my fare I received a ticket with the number of my seat on it, which will be respected until I am taken up at St Denis, where they expect to be by six o'clock.

I know not whether the feeling be common to others, but I never leave a place where I have tarried ever so short a time without regret; accordingly my approaching departure has imparted a tinge of melancholy that I cannot shake off. Latterly I have been tolerably comfortable here; have got reconciled to my house; acquainted with the inhabitants; into a certain routine of amusements and occupations. The weather had been generally fine, though hot; and everything had begun to assume a hue *couleur de rose:* no wonder, then, that a slight cloud should interfere to alloy in some degree the joy at returning to all most dear to me.

White Horse Cellar, Piccadilly, September 13*th.*—Here I arrived last night, and having neither time nor inclination to write during my journey, must note down occurrences now as well as I can recollect them before I start for Farringdon; the which done, adieu to pens, ink, and paper—at least for a time.

MY PORTMANTEAU. 291

On the morning of the 8th inst. I was punctually standing on the *trottoir* in front of a villanous *tabagie* in St Denis at six o'clock, William and my portmanteau beside me. The house was full of drunken, and therefore insolent, Flemish waggoners, and I had no inclination to enter. Our Noah's Ark did not keep me long waiting for its arrival, although it tarried sufficiently when it did come.

M. le Conducteur, a little man, but a most important one, wrapped in a brown greatcoat, a silk handkerchief round his throat, and his head covered by one of those grey linen forage-caps, descended from his airy perch on the roof with great gravity, and pulling out his way-bill, demanded of the *cabaretier* where was the English Monsieur who was to be taken up at St Denis. I presented myself. The little man, scrutinising me from head to foot, " Vous avez un portmanteau, monsieur ? " " Oui, monsieur." " Où se trouvé-t-il donc ? " " Le voilà, monsieur." "*Le voilà ?—quoi ceci ?*" " Oui." " Et vous appelez ceci un portmanteau ? Sacre Dieu ! mais c'est une malle que ça ! Elle ne montera pas sur la diligence !" looking up at the insides, who had thrust their heads out of the window on hearing the row. " Sacre Dieu ! cela *un portmanteau !*"

and he began to swagger and fume and pester among the *saboted*, greasy night-capped gentry who stood by, enjoying exceedingly having a John Bull on the horns of a dilemma.

According to our English acceptation of the term, my baggage was literally a large portmanteau; but the passengers within gave me to understand that Monsieur le Conducteur was perfectly right, and that I had better try to conciliate him instead of insisting. I took their advice, and my *malle* became a portmanteau, under which title alone it was admissible on the diligence, according to the laws and ordinances of La Cour des Messageries. I got inside, William mounted the cabriolet, and I bade adieu to St Denis—at all events for two months. I was agreeably surprised at finding the diligence such a comfortable conveyance; well padded and well hung, we rolled along most agreeably, though only at the rate of six miles per hour. My companions inside were —an elderly lady, very taciturn but very amiable; a young one about five-and-twenty, handsome, lively, chatty, and very shrewd—she talked for both; a good, honest, little man, who kept some sort of magazine in Paris; a young lad, clerk in some counting-house; and an officer of our own Rifles. We had not reached Pierrefitte ere

Mademoiselle had managed to introduce us all to each other in such a manner that formality was banished, and we were the best friends possible—laughing, joking, quizzing each other or the *paysans;* nothing could be happier.

At Luzarches, a capital breakfast, and as much time as we pleased to take it in—M. le Conducteur all suavity and amiability. Our lively little friend kept up such an animated conversation that I saw only just enough of the country we were passing through to remark that it became much prettier and more picturesque as we approached Clermont, where the diligence stopped for dinner. M. le Conducteur took the head of the table, and our party was increased by a *soi-disant*, or *soi-pensant*, humorist of the *gendarmerie*, who, seating himself *sans cérémonie*, fell to, tooth and nail, as if he had not touched food for a week. This, however, did not much interrupt the display of wit, which principally was aimed at the cookery and dishes served up. A fricassee of rabbit he vowed he would on no account touch unless Madame produced *les pattes*, since, as he solemnly assured us, they frequently served fricasseed cats instead. Madame did not, however, produce *les pattes*, and although none of us touched it, the dish in a few minutes was cleared of its contents. This fellow reminded me strongly of the parasite in Gil Blas, and, his adulations being entirely addressed to our little vain conducteur, I set him down as the "Antorcha de la Filosofia!"—maybe our hero always dined with the passengers *par ordre et pour l'espionage*. Here, as at Luzarches, no *empressement* was betrayed: the diligence stood passively at the door without horse, without even an hostler visible; the ladies retired to a *chambre;* so the Rifleman and I agreed to walk on, which resolve we communicated to M. le Conducteur, who assented, and off we set. At the end of the town two roads appeared, one running straight along the valley, the other crossing the bridge to the right, then ran rump-fashion up the other side of the valley, divergingly from the former—and this road was our proper one; but, without condescending to ask a question, we very sagaciously chose the other, and had already proceeded some hundred yards along it, when fortunately (no hedges intervened—the valley was all grass, a rivulet running through the middle of it) we saw our lumbering vehicle slowly ascending the opposite hill. The distance that separated us from it was not great, and we shouted to M. le Conducteur to wait for us; but neither he nor the coachman heard us, and,

AT AMIENS. 295

being ignorant of the nature of the rivulet, after a moment's hesitation we decided our most prudent plan was to run back to the bridge, &c. This we immediately did; but although both of us were pretty active runners, we should have been left behind at last had we not luckily met a miller coming down on horseback. Him and his sacks we dismounted *sans cérémonie*, for the diligence, having now arrived at the summit, had commenced its jog-trot. Mounting the animal, I pursued as fast as the end of the halter could persuade my beast to move, and after a long chase succeeded at length in bringing the vehicle to. Our companions, especially the young dame, or demoiselle, had a hearty laugh at our expense, and so had our miller, for he grinned from ear to ear when the silver recompense (never expected) touched his palm, and he was still grinning and bowing when we looked back as the diligence drove on. It was about eleven at night when we reached the *barrière* of Amiens, and I had been some time asleep. A bright light presented to my eyes caused me to start up in surprise, and at first it was difficult to imagine where I was, until I perceived the uniform of a *gendarmerie*, who, after reconnoitring us by holding the lantern to our faces, very quietly demanded something for his trouble. Angry at such a humiliating operation, the Rifleman and I sent him to the devil; but our companions, whilst opening their own purses, made it so clear to us that the fellow had been extremely civil where he might have been extremely troublesome, that we concluded by doing in Rome, &c. &c.; and away we rumbled over the jolting pavement, and through a series of dark narrow streets, until at last we drove into the yard of the Hotel d'Angleterre, as dark and deserted as the streets themselves. Hostlers, however, were soon forthcoming, the horses changed, my *malle* handed down, and William and myself left standing in the middle of the yard wondering what was to become of us. After a little hesitation, one of the hostlers condescended to direct us to the door of the house ere he retired, and after a good deal of knocking at that we succeeded in rousing an old fellow—whose duty I suppose it was to sit up for the diligence—who showed me into a large room, with a bed in one corner; and at my request for supper brought me a couple of cold widgeons, which I soon discussed, and jumped into an excellent bed.

9*th*.—In a dilemma; no conveyance forward but posting. Did not exactly believe this, and therefore inquired from *auberge* to *auberge*, until at last I discovered that a sort of caravan started every morning at nine o'clock from the * * * for Abbeville. This would be getting on, therefore I lost no time in securing my places. Having risen early, I passed the intervening time in visiting some of our people stationed here — younger M'Donald's troop, also 1st Regiment of Dragoons, K.G.L. Him I found in an excellent lodging. Our caravan was a curious machine, very much down by the stern, otherwise resembling a small house on wheels. William and a woman got into the *fond de la voiture*, whilst I occupied the front seat, in company with a neat, dapper, little, big-bellied man, wearing a very smart forage-cap, and speaking a very little English. We travelled very slowly, and made a long halt at Flixcourt (pronounced *Fleeshcour*)—nevertheless, to my great joy, we reached Abbeville by two o'clock. I found here the 13th Light Dragoons and my old troop G; called on Lieutenant Leathes; dined at the Hotel de Londres, a very inferior house. Here I hired a cabriolet to take us forward to Calais for five napoleons. From the first I set my *voiturier* down as a scoundrel, from his physiognomy, and the event proved me a sound judge. The bargain struck, he tried all sorts of shifts and excuses, in the hope, as I discovered, of associating some other traveller with me. As soon as I made the discovery, I insisted on his starting instantly, and after some difficulty at last got him fairly on the road. It proved a very tedious mode of travelling this; he did not choose to hurry his horse, was continually stopping, and more uncivil in his manner than I thought a true Frenchman could be. The motion of the carriage was very disagreeable—sometimes too heavy before, sometimes behind; and at times it became necessary to put a great stone behind to relieve the poor horse of the weight. A sort of commercial traveller (bagman), who overtook us as we slowly crept up hill near Montreuil thus loaded, facetiously remarked, " Ah, monsieur, vous chargez des pierres, donc!" Our driver's villanous countenance became black as thunder, but he answered a dry " Oui;" and the other, seeing it was no joke, passed on.

It was dusk ere we reached Montreuil, and then our poor beast was so completely done up that I was obliged to subscribe to the necessity of halting; and accordingly our friend drew up at the door of a mean-looking *cabaret*, just without the town, and we alighted, expecting but sorry accommodation in such a place. If, however, La Renard continue what it was, I shall have no objection whatever to pass another night there when I return. A pretty little airy parlour, well though plainly furnished, the windows opening on a garden; as neat a little bedroom adjoining, bed the very type of cleanliness; add an excellent supper and a bottle of very fair wine, and it may be imagined that the evening and night passed in the Renard will always be a bright spot in the memory. It must not be concealed, though, that a pair of very brilliant black eyes certainly threw rather a witching light on my apartments. In the morning, whilst Lisette was busy preparing my breakfast, I was taking a stroll up and down the pretty rural garden, when, to my astonishment, the apparition of a true John-Bull farmer stood before me. At first it appeared an illusion, but the voice soon dispelled that—brown frock-coat, breeches and gaiters, with good thick shoes. Out of these, with the real country twang, issued " Marning, zir; queer chaps here, zir; I doant onderstand one word as ony on um says—not I." My friend then proceeded to ask my assistance as his interpreter, and explained his being there. His son, it seems, is the saddler of the 13th Light Dragoons, stationed just now in Abbeville, whither he had been on a visit, and was now making his way back again to Calais, but being short of coin (French — he had plenty of English) and words, found himself here in a dilemma. Sorry I am that I had not time to preserve the history of his adventures and mishaps since arriving in France; they were most amusing and laughable, but I have now forgotten more than odds and ends. As he passed the evening in company with William, probably that worthy may assist me in recollecting somewhat of it.

My bill was extremely moderate for all the comfort I had enjoyed, and I parted best friends imaginable with my attentive hostess and her pretty daughter—*Au revoir!*

It is a curious town Montreuil, with its steep narrow streets and high walls; but I only saw it *en passant*, for we did not stop. Beyond it, after ascending from the valley of the Canch, we traversed a dreary open country for some way, and then came to wood and very pretty ground, which continued until a long descent brought us at length creepingly to Samer, where we stopped to breakfast at the Tête de Bœuf (William Mallet —a Frenchman, spite of the name). A Cockney party of three ladies and two gentlemen had just arrived from Boulogne—evidently the first time any of them had been out of England. They were all flutter and curiosity, quite childishly so—

chattering away bad school French with a regular English enunciation, and giggling when successful in making themselves understood. Had they but guessed that the brown-visaged, mustachioed, befurred hero who stood before them and watched all their movements was English, perhaps they would have been a little more discreet.

One of the gentlemen drew, and had brought a camera lucida, which he adjusted at the door of the Tête de Bœuf, and disposed himself to take a view of Samer, surrounded by some eight or ten gaping clowns in their blue frocks and clumsy *sabots*, too picturesque objects to be missed; and my man stuck two or three of them in positions to enter into his picture—the only feature in it, for the point of view he had chosen was a most unfortunate one. As I leaned from my window, right over the artist's head, and at no great distance above him (for the Tête de Bœuf boasts but a very moderate elevation), many an ogle did I get from the young ladies, who kept running out incessantly in order to persuade our hero that eating his breakfast was better than sketching. But he was stanch to the backbone, and when my *voiturier* summoned me to start, I left him in the same position, indefatigably occupied upon his insipid picture. Before reaching Samer, my rogue had begun expressing doubts of the soundness of one of his wheels; and true enough—for just as we gained sight of Boulogne (beyond which, I believe, he never from the first meant to go), smash it went all to pieces, and down we came gently enough. The vagabond acted his part well—pretended astonishment, *au désespoir*, &c. &c.—but I saw through him. Under the circumstances, only one thing remained to be done, as no assistance was at hand : William shouldered my *malle*, I carried the *et ceteras*, and on we trudged; and after a pretty hot walk we arrived at Boulogne, and entered the first decent-looking house that presented itself, and ordered dinner. Here I learned that a packet was about to sail in the evening for Dover, and decided on cutting connection with my rascally *voiturier*, who managed to bring in his vehicle shortly after us.

Accordingly in the evening we repaired to the pier and embarked at two P.M. My fellow-passengers were—Lord Charles Fitzroy; another officer, his friend; and a very pretty Frenchwoman. We had hardly made any offing, when the breeze falling, left us at the mercy of a long swell—the surface as smooth as a mirror. The rolling was terrible, and the poor Frenchwoman, dreadfully sick, cursing the ship, cursing England, and cursing herself for venturing on the sea. Early* the following morning we reached Dover, where, to the unspeakable horror of our poor friend, she was informed that she could not leave the vessel until her passport had been sent to London to be verified. O England! what naughty things did not she say of you then! A coach, starting within an hour after our landing, was very convenient, and in company of an officer of the 13th Light Dragoons, I took my seat for London, and here I am.

* At three in the morning, when Lord Charles and his companion immediately landed and tried to persuade me to do the same, but I remained on board until daylight.

CHAPTER XXIV.

Two months I rusticated in Berkshire, and then, my leave of absence having nearly expired, set off in the beginning of November, taking with me my wife, whose determination not to be again separated, united to an eager curiosity to see Paris, overcame all the difficulties I threw in the way of such a winter campaign, and rendered her deaf to all my representations of hardships and privations which she would inevitably have to bear and put up with. My journal of this second residence was hurried, meagre, and very irregularly kept. She kept likewise a few memoranda, so that from the two, and what memory and collating will supply, I am enabled to complete this journal to the return of my troop to Canterbury in February 1816.

Sunday, November 5th.—Slept at the York Hotel last night, and embarked this morning on board the packet for Calais—forget her name—Captain Keys. All bustle and confusion when we went on board. Deck encumbered with a carriage and heaps of baggage, amongst which the complete, well-appointed baggage of Hamilton Hamilton, Esq., secretary of legation, or some such thing, was most conspicuous. In time carriage was stowed and baggage sent below, porters, leave-takers, &c., went ashore, and we quitted the pier. Passengers numerous: H. Hamilton does exclusive, and even betrays impatience and vexation at being shut up with such a *canaille;* then an old gentleman, with a broad-brimmed hat, assumes mighty airs of consequence, and even looks a little contemptuously at Hamilton Hamilton himself, who speaks to none but his *own man;* a Scottish gentleman and his spouse, who makes a terrible sputter about her dear little dog Rose, which is somehow or another left behind at Dover; a mean-looking man in a foraging-cap, a melancholy sergeant of dragoons, and his wife; a Russian dressed in forage-cap and green jacket, like a servant's morning one, wearing no gloves, and looking for all the world like a *courrier,* but F. insisting that such a white hand decidedly constitutes him a gentleman; besides a crowd, *gentium minorum,* of whom we make no record. As we left, the guns on Dover Castle announced Guy Faux by a royal salute. A fresh breeze and rather dark day—the one operating on the *physique*, the other on the *morale*, made all the passengers except very few exceedingly sick. More than half-way over, our breeze gradually subsided into a calm, and left us bobbing about at a most tantalising distance from our port. To amuse the tedium of the calm, our Russian (by no means a handsome man), who had been ogling F. from the very beginning, managed to pick up a conversation; and in a very short time from ogling began to make love, which, however, was cut short by her getting squeamish, and being obliged to lie down. He then transferred his attentions to me, and I really found him a most gentlemanly, well-informed man, spite of his exterior. After being tantalised for some time looking at Calais without being able to reach it, at length a breeze sprang up and carried us in. Crowds of Sunday people were on the pier, all anxious to see the arrivals. The usual squabble about baggage and forcing through the surrounding multitude took place, and we went to Quillacq's Hotel without the baggage—which, after all, was detained on board until it could be inspected at the custom-house on Monday morning, a most inconvenient arrangement, as we found ourselves without an article except what we stood in—a great rambling house, with large dreary (at this season of the year) rooms and long corridors. Amused with F.'s surprise at the number of little dishes served up at dinner—all, however, excellent. Obliged to borrow nightcaps of M. and Madame Quillacq.

6th.—Up at seven in the morning, and went to the custom-house for our baggage. *Douaniers*, a set of insolent scoundrels, gave themselves amazing airs, and tumbled everything out on the floor; particularly severe with Ham. Hamilton's baggage, who had sent his servant for it. At last I got mine out of their clutches; hired a cabriolet to take us to Paris, where we give it up to the correspondent. Well stuffed and comfortable, with innumerable little pockets. F. amused again with our set out : started at half-past ten A.M., preceded by the little gentleman in the broad-brimmed hat in one *calèche*, and the two Russians in another. At Marquise we passed them. Nothing extraordinary in our drive except Buonaparte's pillar near Boulogne, and the house he lived in at Pont de Bricq when he visited the army of England. Arrived at M. Mallet, Samer, by half-past four P.M. Found the house comfortable, except that our room smoked somewhat. Girls most merry; gave us an excellent dinner, but so-so wine. Amused ourselves with arrivals and departures. F. looked in vain, however, for her Russian lover—he came not.

But another character of more importance came not: Mr William should have joined us at Dover or Calais; but when at the latter we learned that he remained at Dover waiting for his trunk, which had been left behind in London.

November 7th.—Sophie gave us an excellent breakfast, after which we set off. Our postilion a character, in the imperial green jacket; and from under his leathern hat, instead of the usual thick queue, flowed a mass of locks unrestrained. His beasts were a couple of long-tailed cart-horses, harnessed principally with rope. The long ascent, after leaving Samer, brought us on the plateau occupied by the dreaded forest—dreaded because we had heard reports of banditti and plundering; but we passed through it without interruption, and soon after saw the ramparts of Montreuil crowning the isolated hill, frowning like an acropolis over the lower town — the whole, standing as it does in a country destitute of the smallest feature of the picturesque, presenting a most sombre and forbidding aspect. Nor did the interior belie its exterior aspect, which we entered by a long, squalid, straggling street, and ascended to the upper town by a very steep hill. Whilst the horses were changing we got an omelet. Scotch officer and his wife, who had come on *en voiturier*, we overtook here. As elsewhere, a crowd of beggars assailed us on alighting and re-entering our carriage. In this country they spoil their own trade, for they are too numerous. I hurry over all this, for my notes are very meagre.

Approaching Abbeville by a long descent, its cathedral, proudly elevating its beautiful Gothic front above the other buildings (dingy in colour, and unpicturesque in form)'was the only redeeming point in the view ; but that *was* an interesting one. The town, however, pleased us, though its streets are rather narrow and dirty. Found our old friends the hussars of the Brunswick auxiliaries and my old troop (G) quartered here.

8*th*.—Started at a little after seven A.M. Our postilion was the first one we had had, who astonished F. by wearing jack-boots. Breakfasted at Flixcourt : little slop-basins instead of cups, with large spoons ; as usual, sour bread and soapy butter—for all which the charge was exorbitant. During breakfast the beautiful band of the 1st Hussars, K.G.L., was playing on an open space near the house, where the regiment had its morning parade.

At Pecquigny met a bridal—all in their best; men and boys firing guns, and the bride carrying a little flag. A young rogue who stood by our carriage whilst changing horses begging in a most piteous accent, observing me start when the first gun was fired, just before the procession came in sight, could not resist the desire of amusing himself at my expense, whom he no doubt took for some Cockney, and shouted, in a voice of affected alarm, "C'est l'ennemi, monsieur!" and seeing that his *coup* had *manqué*, burst into laughter.

Beyond Pecquigny came on the valley of the Somme; and the scenery became somewhat interesting. Amiens we found full of Prussians, and only stopped to change horses—Maître de Poste quite a gentlemanly man, riding a managed horse. Fine old town and splendid cathedral. Stopped for the night at Breteuil. Inn an immense old-fashioned house, like an old convent; great rambling wainscoted corridor; and our room large, lofty, and the walls hung with old faded tapestry, and two old-fashioned beds with curtains of yellow damask; sitting-room quite on a par with it. Our attendant Josephine (a very pretty girl) told us our teeth must be bad, because we complained of our fowl being tough; and to our complaint of knives, she said they were too sharp, for that she had just cut her finger with one of them. Apropos of knives, there seems but one pattern all over France, and that a very coarse one, which, however costly the table-service in other respects, appears everywhere to spoil the whole. Its sharp point one sees constantly used as a tooth-pick; and over and over again I have seen it taken from that employment and plunged unhesitatingly into some dish, &c. Soup served in a regular white jorden; however, we find fine Sevres porcelain coffee-services everywhere. Wine here all out of one cask, though Josephine protested that the fifty different kinds she enumerated were literally and truly each from the place named. F. astonished at the immense long loaves. An English family had arrived in a smart barouche, with servants in a cabriolet. Forced to sit in their bedroom, ours being the only *salle*, such as it is.

November 9th.—Early this morning a large detachment of Prussian infantry marched into Breteuil, and the officers, as soon as their parade was over, came tramping *sans cérémonie* through every room in the house. F., whom I had left alone whilst I strolled out to see the place, was terribly frightened by three or four of them walking into the room, and standing there with the door open jabbering for some time, as if no one had been present, one of them ogling most furiously. Spite of our exertions, the family in the barouche got their horses and set off before us, to our great annoyance, as of course they would absorb all the attention and occupy all the accommodation to our exclusion. Josephine gave us a miserable breakfast, no doubt owing to that accursed barouche; and, after all, our bill was most exorbitant. Thought our postilion was mad—for never saw French postilion dash along so recklessly and at such a pace: the cabriolet rolled from side to side, and jerked and jumped so that I expected we should plunge through the windows. Still it was pleasant to get on. At last we overtook the barouche, and the mystery was explained, for our gentleman relapsed at once into the tamest of postilions, sticking himself close up to the other carriage, with his horses' noses under its very dicky. Occupant of this a gentleman's gentleman of the very first water, who sadly annoyed F. by his impudent staring. Urged our hero of the jack-

ARRIVAL AT CLERMONT.

boots and sheep's-skin pelisse to pass ahead, for the heavy barouche, although drawn by four horses, could only get on at a jog-trot pace. Urged long in vain. At last, just as he was about to push on, the gentleman in the dicky dropped his glove, and our most polite postilion actually stopped, dismounted, picked it up, and again driving up in the wake of the barouche, presented it with the utmost deference of manner to the supercilious scoundrel. Got furious now, and commenced such a volley that I at last actually succeeded in driving him ahead of the barouche just as we approached Clermont. Another marriage at St Juste: bride very pretty, and guns fired in abundance as before. Clermont uncommonly prettily situated. Did not alight, but enjoyed some delicious grapes which women and girls brought and sold for a song. Hence to Creil; a great improvement in the scenery, which became rich, diversified, and well wooded, until near that place we descended into the beautiful bottom of the Oise, with its wooded hill and white cliffs. Found here a garrison of Belges. Our postilion still more mad. As we had foreseen, there was some difficulty in getting rooms at the Hotel de Bourbon at Chantilly, and we had scarcely secured them ere the barouche drove up, but could not find accommodation. Visited the chateau of the Prince de Condé. Stables magnificent; an immense lofty hall, as big as a church, with a fine cupola — around are the stalls, &c. — splendid idea! Our dinner even more than usually ridiculous by the number of little *plats*—a regular doll's; liqueurs of sorts, all very bad, in cruet-bottles—aniseed the only one drinkable. In the evening entertained by the singing of the Nassau troops stationed here. Bad news from Paris. In the next room a party of London shop-boys, or some such thing. One of these, pretty drunk, wanted to be called in the morning, and as our doors were open, we had the full benefit and advantage of the fine language propounded to the waiter : " Garçon! mon domestique à cinq heure et demie." Garçon does not comprehend; tries over and over again. "Je ne vous comprends pas, monsieur, se fait entendre toujours." At last impatient, " Well, dammee, 'tis simply this, my man : tell my servant to call me at half-past five o'clock." We went to our bedroom ere the matter was settled. The French seem to think nothing of damp sheets—ours were actually wet.

10th.—Our host gave us a most comfortable breakfast, after which we set off in high spirits for Paris ; the day fine and scenery lovely. Whilst changing horses at Luzarches, some non-commissioned officers of the Belgic or Nassau troops stationed there were exceedingly impertinent to F., but I had no time to obtain redress, so left them.

After passing Pierrefitte, made our postilion turn off the chaussée spite of his objections, and attempt to reach Stain ; but we soon found the cross-road so bad, nearly smashing our wheels, that we were glad to regain the chaussée. Whilst stopping at the post-house at St Denis, Frazer and Ambrose rode up. From them we learned that old Webber had made my house very comfortable ; so determined not to stay in Paris, but to give up our cabriolet, and return forthwith to Stain. This we accordingly did, driving straight to the Remise, Rue Faubourg St Denis, where we hired a fiacre, and reached Stain about dusk. It was a cold gloomy evening. The story of comfort was exaggerated. Webber had hired some little, shabby, old furniture ; but the place looked wretched, and when F. became fully aware of its discomforts, her enthusiasm gave way like snow before the sun ; she burst into tears. The heroics vanished, and she confessed she wished herself again in England. The room had indeed a most forlorn appearance: a handful of fire flickered in the grateless, gaping chimney; the little furniture was of the coarsest kind; the uncarpeted floor of brick;—desolation everywhere! We had had no dinner, and, except some ration-beef, nothing could be procured. Some of this, however, was cooked and despatched; and, as the best thing we could do, we set to work putting to rights, and making the most of it. Nothing could equal the surprise of Madlle. Rose at finding that the smooth-faced bourgeois was indeed the identical mustachioed commandant she had been accustomed to months ago. Next morning found a poultry-yard—rabbits, &c., all provided by the attentions of old Robertson, my quartermaster-sergeant. Things looked better; F. was refreshed, consequently in better spirits. The visits of congratulation and kind attentions of our villagers delighted her; but M. le Maire stood like one thunderstruck when introduced to his old friend with a new face. My cow dead, but another was negotiating for. The history of the defunct was, that she was a commissariat issue to me as so many rations; but, instead of putting her to death, I kept her for her milk.

Here, again, I am without a guide, or nearly so —my diary ends; and, to continue our residence at Stain, I am reduced to a few brief notices preserved in my general journal.

That residence was uncomfortable enough, for the winter set in with a degree of severity unknown in England; and our house, both from its construction and furnishing, was ill calculated, under such circumstances, to afford comfort, or indeed at times to prevent suffering. However, we were in paradise compared to the situation of the little farmers (cultivateurs) and still poorer people amongst whom we were thus domiciliated. With them we found that it was no uncommon practice to live in the stable, &c., among the cattle, for the sake of sparing fuel—the animals helping to keep them warm.

Sometimes I took F. to Paris to see the lions; but it was sad, cold, dirty work. The streets were ankle-deep in mud; even the walks of the Palais Royal, the Passage des Panoramas, &c., were covered with mud, carried in on people's feet. Sometimes I took a walk; but the country, now stripped of its verdure, presented an aspect hideously cheerless. What could be more so than the extensive, dreary, snow-covered plain extending from St Denis to the foot of Montmartre without a redeeming tree? Like other highroads, the one crossing this plain to La Chapelle, we were told, had once been bordered by trees, but they were cut down on the approach of the Allied armies, I think, last year.

Soon after arriving, having published through the commune our want of a female servant, Mademoiselle Rose introduced Angélique. My wife took a liking to her immediately; so, having exchanged written contracts with M. l'Ecuyer (her father), engaging to take care of, and send her back from England free of expense, she was engaged, and forthwith entered on her functions, as cook, lady's-maid, &c. M. l'Ecuyer is (like most of our neighbours) a cultivateur—works his own little bit of land, and is independent, except of poverty; for these little cultivateurs work hard and fare harder, as far as I can learn.

Sometimes our *séjour* was enlivened by visits from our own officers, or from some of those stationed in St Denis, La Vertu, and even from Paris: and occasionally more genial weather allowed F. to ride Cossack; but these rides were necessarily confined to the park. With the villagers we had become as much at home as Frenchmen could be. As for our *ménage*, it got on pretty well; and once we even ventured on giving a dinner to Wells and Ambrose, which went off pretty well; and once we went and

OUTBREAKS OF FIRE.

passed a day with Sir A. Frazer at the Hotel du Nord.

Again, one bitter cold black day, we visited the Abbey of St Denis, and went shivering through its vaults, and were shown the last home prepared by Napoleon for himself. The town was crowded with troops on their march northwards. Once or twice F. was able to ride to Paris; but it was hard work. Amongst other amusements in Stain, we had one not very agreeable, and which kept us in a continual state of excitement. Our men were continually setting fire to their quarters, particularly the chateau of Admiral Rosily. The villagers said this arose from their removing the ashes, and making their fires on the bare hearth, which thus became so hot as to set fire to the beams beneath. They therefore advised the men to leave the ashes and make their new fire on them. This they did; but Admiral Rosily wrote to tell me that no fires ought be lighted up-stairs in his house, as the chimneys were only intended as ventilators, and therefore begged us to confine the fires to the ground-floor. At the stables of the chateau, over which a detachment was lodged, a fire occurred, and continued smouldering in the beams for a fortnight, the centre remaining on fire when we thought it extinguished.

At length the period of our departure drew nigh, and arrangements were made at headquarters which totally disorganised my troop at the moment when a perfect organisation was most necessary. During the campaign, a detachment of the driver-corps had been attached to each troop of horse-artillery, our own establishment being insufficient for the additional carriages. These were now to be withdrawn and sent home; and accordingly, all this rabble from Bull's and other troops still in the neighbourhood of Paris were sent to mine as destined for England. Secondly, all my officers were allowed to desert me. Captain Webber protested he was too weak to undertake such a journey, and obtained leave to remain in Paris; my surgeon (Ambrose) was permitted to remain in charge of him; Lieutenant Bruce neither liked the winter-march nor quitting Paris, where he was doing aide-de-camp to his cousin, Lady Castlereagh; two lieutenants (Maunsell and Wells) remained to march with the troop; but the former had resolved on leaving the service, and the latter had obtained an exchange to a troop forming part of the Army of Occupation, consequently he accompanies us only a part of the way to Calais—and thus no very great zeal could be expected

PREPARATIONS FOR A START. 321

from either of these. Thirdly, we were ordered to give up our white cross-belts to G troop, in exchange for their waist-belts—exhibiting thus our old worn jackets in all their nakedness. Fourthly, our overalls were in rags—new ones had been ordered, and were on the road from Brussels, but we were not allowed to wait for them. Add to all this the casualties of a long winter-march, bad lodging, and worse weather, and the condition of the troop on reaching Calais may be imagined. The defection of Ambrose, however, was counterbalanced by my old friend Hitchins getting leave to accompany us to England. He, too, intended quitting the service.

December 16*th*.—Hitchins joined us at Stain; and as he brought his own bed, I gave him a room in my chateau. The knotty question of how F. and Angélique were to travel was settled between them and Hitchins; and, overruling my scruples, it was arranged that a cabriolet should be hired for Calais, to be drawn by a pair of troop-horses, with the driver for postilion. Accordingly, on the 18th Hitchins went to Paris and procured the vehicle, whilst we continued our preparations.

19*th*.—The troop under Maunsell marched at an early hour for Beaumont, our first halting-place. One would have fancied that the village militia was about to quit home. No one thought of work: the whole population of the commune assembled in the park; endless the leave-takings, and I believe sincere the expressions of friendship and regrets at separation. Many of the cultivateurs, whose carts we had taken for the baggage, cheerfully volunteered accompanying us all the way to Calais.

Our own baggage delayed us so much that it was eleven A.M. before we were under way—F. and Angélique (whose relations to the twentieth degree had thronged our house all the morning) in the *calèche*, Hitchins and myself on horseback, followed by Gunner Fitzgerald, my orderly, and my groom Milward, in uniform and carrying my Waterloo lance. The day was fine, and the country pretty enough for the season; so that, after getting on the chaussée at Pierrefitte, we moved on merrily and agreeably until evening, when the sky clouded over, it became very cold, and soon a heavy fall of snow came on, in the midst of which we arrived at Beaumont, and found our people just forming the park, and those of Major Dyas already snug in their quarters. His battery had been ordered to march with us; but he had also orders not to interfere in any way with me or mine.

Our billet was on an iron merchant, and thither we proceeded, whilst Hitchins went in search of his own. Our house was a respectable-looking one outside; inside it was much like a great foundry, or some such place—almost the whole of it being one vast hall, lighted from above, and full of bar-iron standing against the walls. An open staircase conducted us to a small gallery; up one more step and into a neat little room— but, from the scarcity of furniture and badness of the fire, looking sufficiently cheerless: a table, covered as usual with oil-cloth, two or three plain chairs, a bed without curtains, and windows without shutters;—such was the domicile into which we were ushered by a hideously ugly and most sulky maid-servant. Assistance from the house we soon found we must not expect, and sent out for something to eat; but the answer was *nil*, and we were forced to content ourselves with some bad tea and bread-and-butter. The evening was wretchedly cold, and our fire so insufficient that we were glad to get to bed; but here, again, were *wet* sheets, and we were obliged to get between the blankets. Miserable evening!

20*th.*—Weather improved. Started about eleven, and, traversing a beautiful and fertile country, arrived in the afternoon at the pretty village of Noailles, where we found ourselves billeted on a rich old gentleman, who did not ask us to his table, but in every other respect did his utmost to make us comfortable; and so in reality we were, for our apartment was delightfully so; our fare good; and our host furnished us liberally with good wine and cider. Passed the evening playing dominoes, and wishing we could stay in such nice quarters. Began to find Angélique* very useful in communicating with the people, whose ways she understood better than we. Noailles is but a poor village, although prettily situated; however, there is a manufactory here of those pretty bands which Frenchwomen wear below *the knee.*

21*st.*—A short march to Beauvais, where we arrived early; and whilst I parked the guns and saw my people put up, Hitchins accompanied F. in search of my quarters. My duty finished, I followed to a handsome house, where I understood they were. Whilst making inquiries under the gateway, Madame herself came out and told me rather angrily that I could have no quarters there, as the colonel (my travelling title) and his lady already occupied all she was bound to furnish. I endeavoured to explain that the gentle-

* She cooked for us here.

man up-stairs was my friend, that I was M. le Colonel, and had sent him to escort my wife, &c. &c. At the word *femme*, the *insolente* with a sneer turned from me with, "Ah! soi-disante." A scene occurred; Monsieur himself came out, who I insisted should be responsible for his wife's tongue. At last they begged pardon, and I mounted the staircase according to direction, and found a most comfortable lodging—two well-furnished rooms and a small cabinet. The people sent up soon after to invite us to dinner, they being ordered to feed us; but we would not go, and made them send dinner up to us. Our rooms had only one drawback — they were rather gloomy, the windows opening upon a courtyard. Stayed three days in Beauvais, during which we lived well at the expense of our host; and having bought some cards, Hitchins came every evening to coffee, and we had a game at casino. Our mornings were passed in visiting the beautiful Gothic cathedral and other churches; the manufactory of tapestry, equalling that of the Gobelins, of which this is a branch; in shopping, and in riding about the neighbouring country, which is pretty—somewhat resembling that about Bath. One evening we went to the play—a dark dismal house, and quite a second-rate set of actors.

Don't know what the piece was, but the humour consisted in the *patois* of an old Picard servant, who was continually repeating, "Ya! ya! ya! Munsincur!" There were a good many of us—all the officers of Ross's troop and Dyas's battery, *par excellence*. The pit was full of French soldiers; yet all went off cheerfully, until our people called for "Vive Henri Quatre," which these Napoleonists fiercely opposed, and a row ensued, which terminated at last amicably. The ramparts of Beauvais form a delicious promenade, which I enjoyed; whilst F. and Hitchins were gadding about from shop to shop, buying lace, cambric, &c.

22*d*.—I intended marching forward to-morrow, but Quartermaster Robertson, who was sent on to take up our quarters, returned at midnight with the intelligence that all the villages ahead of us were still full of troops. Relinquished the idea.

Major Dyas came to coffee. When he heard of the insult offered to F. he insisted upon going immediately to pull my host by the nose. "*Bloody D.*" was one of those jewels we received at the Union from the Irish artillery—tall, gaunt, and muscular, with a most truculent physiognomy. His cognomen was received on account of the ferocity he had displayed in the Irish Rebellion. Now he had become a gallant Lothario (not a gay one), and, if report spoke true, had already two wives, and had nearly succeeded in picking up a third in Paris—daughter of a gentleman of very good property, at whose house he had been billeted. Strange how insinuating these Irishmen are. To look at D. one would never suppose that a girl, young enough to be his daughter, handsome, and rich withal, could ever have fallen in love with such a man; and yet those best acquainted with the affair assured me that it was indubitably true.

23d.—Great market or fair—immense quantity of woollen cloth, manufacture of the town and neighbourhood. Preparations making for a grand procession in honour of Jeanne Hachette, who distinguished herself in the defence of the place against the Duc de Bourgogne in 1740. Until I looked into the history, I thought it had been, as some of the people informed me, in honour of Joan of Arc. Beauvais is a gloomy, old-fashioned town; the streets very narrow, and, during our stay, very dirty. What they might be in summer I can't guess, but they look as if they must be then redolent of the same sulphurous odour as those of Paris.

24*th.*—Marched to Grandvilliers; everything looking wretched, for the day was dark and excessively cold: in France, on such occasions, there are no redeeming features. The country is in most cases without enclosures, and the few trees, stripped of their verdure, present most cheerless pictures, unrelieved by any appearance of warmth or comfort about the mean and wretched-looking dwellings of the peasantry. These, when we entered the village, presented rather a better appearance than usual, for all were *en habits de Dimanche*, which was the day. Lodged F. in the post-house (here an inn), and then went round our billets. Village very large, two broad streets crossing each other, but the houses all farms or cottages, most of them of mud, like the Devonshire cobbe, and all thatched; the site of the place a dead flat, but pretty well clothed with trees. At our post-house we procured a tolerably decent though very small parlour, the chimney of which, however, smoked so terribly that, spite of the weather, we were obliged to sit constantly with the door open; up-stairs (this was a sort of addition to the original house projecting into the yard) a bedroom of the same size, in which were two beds; and nothing could exceed the astonishment of our friend the chambermaid at our arrangement of sleeping together. The inhabitants here were ordered by beat of drum to feed us. We now came under the command of Sir Denis Park, who commands at Calais and up the road as far as this place, he having the arrangement of the embarkations.

We lived well at our inn, and remedied the open door by a large screen. Every evening we saw company—*i. e.*, our officers—and, although the weather was very cold, passed our time pleasantly enough. One day an immense market or fair afforded us ample amusement; another, our attention and curiosity were excited by the arrival of a troop of the National Guard, *à cheval*, from Beauvais; but, after staying the whole afternoon and night, they departed the next morning without our being a bit the wiser. One day the Earl of Westmeath arrived, and stopped all night; his lordship was obliged to put up with the rooms we had rejected.

January 1, 1816.—At last the order for our advance having arrived, we marched this morning from Grandvilliers, several *paysannes* of the village following the troop as volunteers for l'Angleterre, betraying the effects of idleness in country quarters. Whilst preparing to set off, our host presented a bill for our living, &c., amounting to nine napoleons, which I was about to pay, when Hitchins and F. interfered, asking the good man whether he would have dared appear before a Prussian officer with such a thing, and telling him after the manner his countrymen had treated all other countries that he ought to think himself well off in being treated so leniently. He did not subscribe to this, and an argument ensued which I was sorry for, but was weak enough to allow my better intentions to be overruled; and at last, when Monsieur begged I would at least certify that he had not been paid, I did so on the bill, stating as reason that the inhabitants had been ordered to feed us. Our march to Poix, the next halting-place, was through a country that never could be very interesting, still less so in its wintry garb, until, from the summit of a high hill, we looked down upon the lovely valley in which that village is situated. On arriving we found all the world *en habit de Dimanche* celebrating the opening of the new year. The principal features in this celebration were the kisses exchanging in all directions, the enormous stiffly-starched caps of the women, and the music that paraded continually through the streets.

The *auberge* we found so noisy, smoky, dirty, and the landlord such an uncivil brute, that we immediately commenced a search for a better billet. For a time success seemed uncertain; the houses of the peasantry were too filthy to be thought of. Not far from the *auberge* we found a good house, but shut-up doors and windows. In vain Hitchins and I knocked and threatened, or asked information of its inhabitants from the neighbours; nobody would answer from within, and nobody would answer without—at least more than "Je n'en sais rien, monsieur." At last we found a respectable sort of old-fashioned farmhouse, the mistress of which (a widow) was factotum to the Prince de Poix, proprietor of the village, and much of the neighbouring country,—and hither we immediately removed, bag and baggage. A labyrinth of dark passages led to a large, gloomy, wainscoted room, in one corner of which was a great old-fashioned bed, with yellow damask curtains, like the one we slept in at Breteuil. Here we established ourselves, and Angélique had a small cabinet hard by, whilst the men were put up in the more distant part of the house occupied by the family. Although there was a large fireplace, in which we kept up capital fires, the place was very cold; but a couple of old screens in some measure remedied this, and at last we thought ourselves tolerably comfortable. Our park was formed on the site of the ancient castle of the princes, now almost entirely gone, except a few mounds marking out the ground-plan. The village of Poix, though covering a great deal of ground, is not large; for, except the few houses standing contiguous to the *auberge*, the others are scattered up and down, widely apart from each other. The situation is extremely pretty in summer, probably beautiful: a deep and rather narrow valley, with a small stream running through it; partly below the village covered with woods, which also ran over and clothed all the surrounding hills—not close thick copse, but composed of trees and thickets of coppice, through which one might ride in all directions on a carpet of turf. On a steep bank, immediately opposite our dwelling, was the little church, unpretending, but having a beautiful Gothic western doorway, over which, as a record of revolutionary folly, was painted in large letters, " *Temple de la Raison;*" these had been either whitewashed or painted over, but insufficiently, for they were still distinctly legible. The weather during our stay at Poix (seven days) was gloomy and very cold, yet we managed to have many interesting rides amongst the woods. Hitchins dined with us always, and came provided with some excellent wine, which he procured from his own hostess. In one of our walks, at the fork of the roads to Amiens and Abbeville, we found a diminutive chapel with a figure of the Virgin in it, and as diminutive a priest, humpbacked. He showed us his chapel, and we put some money into his box, and so parted mutually satisfied. It was at this corner that I met an elderly French veteran trudging towards the village in his *capote* and forage-cap, with the usual goat-skin knapsack : he was *minus* an arm, and upon questioning him I found that he had left it at Waterloo. Something interesting in this interview.

In the village we found a corporal and four privates of the 18th Hussars, stationed here for despatches. The corporal fell in love with Angélique, and proposed for her, but was rejected. Her lover gave us an alert one night to deliver a despatch (these hussars always come in the night!), and I made sure we were off. It was an order to have divine service every Sunday.

8th.—At length on the 7th the order did come, and this day we marched to Airaines through a sufficiently dismal country, and weather very cold and gloomy, still followed by the girls from Grandvilliers. Some part of the country, from its hilliness and numerous orchards, in some measure resembled Devonshire; but as we approached the town these cease, and we saw again only extensive and treeless plains.

Airaines at first sight was not calculated to remove the unpleasant feeling excited by its neighbourhood: rather large for a country town, and lying on a gentle slope; its streets irregular, and buildings mean, dirty, and ruinous-looking; —altogether very gloomy. Our billet was on the *auberge* where the diligences stopped, a house of very inferior description, in which we did not establish ourselves without difficulty, and then wretchedly enough. For ourselves we got a room with two dirty beds in it, and only the coarsest kind of furniture; floor inch-thick in dirt, and having chinks between the planks, so gaping that we could see everything going on below—and being over the gateway, the great lounge of the postilions, *gens-d'armes*, &c., we had not only the advantage of all their conversation, but also of their eternal tobacco-pipes; also the full benefit of a most cooling breeze continually blowing through the gateway. The only room we could procure for Angélique was occupied by a postilion, and he was unwilling to evacuate, so that a little tyranny became necessary to gain possession. We turned him out *vi et armis*. In this wretched place we remained a fortnight, during which the weather, always gloomy, was at times bitterly cold, or heavy rain. As the whole troop could not be lodged here, it was necessary to detach Maunsell with one division to a village at least five miles off; and Wells, pretending there was no lodging to be procured here, asked leave to accompany him—notwithstanding which, our surgeon, Ambrose, who overtook us here, immediately obtained very comfortable quarters. Hitchins also was uncommonly well lodged in the house of an old smuggler. Our park was formed on an open space by the road to Abbeville, just without the town, where, as the weather was too cold for our guard to remain in a tent, I asked the mayor to procure them accommodation in a house hard by. This he refused, until I made preparations to bring our park into the market-place, which alarmed him so much that he immediately complied. The market-place, by the way, was precisely similar to the old buildings one sees in English country towns; and here the two Sundays during our stay I performed divine service. To pass our time here we sometimes rode about the dreary neighbourhood, where we discovered a ruined castle; and in another part a rather pretty village, with a fine manor-house and park; but the people soon drove us away from this last, not only by their abuse, but even pelting us with stones. In bad weather we resorted to a wretched billiard-table opposite our inn, where I taught F. the game, and drank bitter coffee to my cigars. There was nothing extraordinary in her frequenting this table, as it is customary for females to do so; and there were seldom any other people present than our own.

In addition to our other occupations, the diligence afforded a daily and short amusement as it stopped at our inn - door. I can see now the great lumbering machine just drawn up, a clown in a blue smock-frock, linen forage-cap with a huge peak sticking straight out, and a long coach-whip in hand, seated on the near wheeler, guiding by cord-reins the three cart-horses harnessed abreast as leaders; and two tall soldier-like *gens-d'armes*, in their neat blue uniforms and cocked-hats, stepping up to the door, and whilst one examines the way-bill, the other mounts the step of the vehicle and scrutinises the passengers. They were fine fellows these, and we got tolerably intimate with them. Every evening Hitchins came to us and played a rubber of casino. One evening standing at our window, we saw some sheep come down the opposite street; two or three went into the passage of a house, the door of which was instantly closed by an old woman, and we both exclaimed, "Ah, the wretch! she steals the sheep." Our servants who stood by laughed, and explained that the old shepherd (who now appeared sauntering slowly along) was the guardian of the town flock, which he conducted to pasture daily.

Accordingly the next morning the old man again marched under our window towards the fields, blowing his horn, at which sound the door opposite again opened, and out sallied the same sheep following the old man, and forming with others assembling from all quarters a large flock, which we found him with in the fields when we went to ride.

22*d.*—Marched to Abbeville. Billeted on a velvet manufacturer with a pretty wife; excellent house, comfortable living. Visit the cathedral and walk about the town.

Forgot that I tried one of my men by a court-martial at Airaines upon a charge of stealing bacon, brought against him by a peasant of the village where Maunsell was quartered. Sent on to Abbeville for a captain, and Close came over for the purpose. The *patois* of the witnesses was so mixed up with English as to astonish us; one in particular we shrewdly suspected of being an English deserter. It was, however, only the *patois* of Picardy. "Yes" was much oftener used than "oui" by them. On our way here from Airaines, descending to the Somme at Point de Remy, I saw a very large Roman encampment on a neighbouring hill: country about the river pretty as usual. Here most of my horses were put up in the riding-school of the cavalry barrack. Our host's family consisted of himself, a grown-up son, a female cousin, and his pretty wife, who was very civil, and went shopping with F., but disgusted me at breakfast by holding up a beastly pocket-handkerchief and spitting at it.

23*d*.—Much pleased at marching to Montreuil, as we had expected Rue and Nampont would have been our destination. Comfortable inn— the same Sterne was at; and our *salle* the identical room in which La Fleur slept—so said our host. Excellent dinner: Hitchins dined with us, and we drank two bottles of prime champagne. Wells left us here to join my old troop at St Pol. As we were tired, we slept so soundly that we never knew until morning that the house had been set on fire during the night by a drunken officer of infantry.

24th.—Wretched morning, snowing heavily, and very cold. Hitchins suffered much from our ride, and got sulky because F. and Angélique laughed at him. Stopped at Samer to see our friends the Demoiselles Mallet, and get some hot wine.

At Boulogne our billet was on a capital house; but our host, an old officer (I think colonel), extremely sulky and disobliging—obliged to send to a restaurateur's for our dinner. Walked about the town and on the ramparts. No snow here, though the weather was excessively raw and windy. Ramparts pretty; the only trees in the neighbourhood are on them.

At night had gone to bed, expecting to remain a day or two, and were not yet asleep when some one tapped at our window, which opened into a little flagged court. I got up and found a hussar (as usual), who brought me a note, which I could not read until he went and got a light. It was an order to march to-morrow to Guines.

25th.—As our landlord (commandant of the National Guard) had been anything but civil, we set off without taking leave of him. Other cavalry besides ourselves had halted in Boulogne, and we found the road covered with troops, stragglers, and baggage. Amidst these we struggled on as far as Marquise, where we left the chaussée for a villanous cross-road, by which, about noon, we arrived at Guines, a very pretty little town, and the day being fine, a very cheerful-looking one. Our billet (if billet it were) was a capital one—the Chateau de Beauscite; the owner, M. le Baron de Guesclin, with Madame and his daughters, received us most kindly. The family consisted of M. le Baron, a good-natured, but ugly, and not very genteel-looking man, about sixty; Madame la Baronne, a jolly good-looking woman of forty; one very sickly-looking daughter about twenty-two; another a year or so older, hideously marked with small-pox, but extremely obliging and good-natured; and a tall awkward son of about twenty. The house comfortable and well furnished. We were treated quite on the footing of guests, and even welcome ones. Style of living much the same as that of an English country gentleman of easy fortune. After dinner the Baron proposed showing us our room and the house. Passing through his own bedroom, with a knowing wink he gave me to understand that he did not follow modern fashions in sleeping separate from his wife; for, pointing to the ample and handsome bed, he exclaimed loud enough to be heard by all, " M., voila là fabrique des enfans ! " Madame looked archly over her shoulder at me and burst out laughing.

26*th.*—Fine day. Breakfast of tea, &c., got up expressly for us, as when alone they have no such regular meal, but merely take a cup of coffee. Afterwards the son showed me the stables, stud, farm, &c., and then, mounted on a long-tailed Norman horse, with military saddle and bridle, took us to see the obelisk erected on the spot where Blanchard descended after crossing the Channel in his balloon. The country pretty, because well wooded ; and from the hill I once more saw the white cliffs of England, although I will not pretend to have experienced any very great delight in so doing, as the future promised nothing good, and I would rather have remained in France. Reduction, Woolwich duties, and insipidity from the total absence of excitement—such was the prospect before me.

In the afternoon a very handsome young man (an officer in some cavalry corps) came in and dined with us. His father, an old gentleman of good fortune in the neighbourhood, had served many years in the hussars, and was (I believe) Madame's brother. In the evening came in the family confessor—a fat, greasy priest—who made himself quite at home; but they did not seem over well pleased with his company. Servants singing in the kitchen: opened a little trap in the wall of a cupboard which communicated with the kitchen to hear a young girl from St Omer sing "Brulant d'Amour" and "Partant pour la Guerre," which she did with great sweetness. Our hopes of enjoying this pleasant billet for some days disappointed by the order to march to-morrow into Calais, only eight miles off.

27th.—Gloomy cold day. A mass to be celebrated for the soul of Louis XVI. I had promised M. le Baron to allow my men to assist in the procession, but instead was obliged to take leave as they were about to begin. Early in the morning all the front of the chateau was hung with black cloth. Nothing could be kinder or even more affectionate than our leave-taking, and Madame obliged F. to wrap up in a rich *pelerin* of her own, which we were to leave at Quillacq's. The distance being so short, we were not long on the road, which for the most part lay along the canal as far as St Pierre, a great straggling suburb of Calais, in which we were to halt. Nothing could be worse than our accommodations here—horses and men scattered about by twos and threes, far and wide; some of them were sent back almost to Guines—so near at least as to hear distinctly the church-bells. As for us, we were put into a farmhouse, where they gave us a room without a fireplace, insufferable in such a season; therefore, being obliged to go into Calais to report our arrival to Webber Smith, I left F. and Hitchins hunting for another quarter. After some trouble I got a billet from the Quartermaster-General on the Lion d'Argent, in Calais, kept by an impudent English scoundrel named Oakshot, who was not at all well pleased at our being put on him. Rode back to St Pierre, where I found F. and Hitchins in a bedroom they had procured at a dirty smoky *brasserie*; so we all adjourned together to the Silver Lion.

Here we were detained some time, which, however, was of less consequence, as we were lodged well and fed well. In other respects, however, the detention was anything but pleasant. Calais at the best of times must be a dismal stupid hole; at this season of storms, cold, rain, mud, &c. &c. it was scarcely endurable. Great part of my day was passed at or about the pier, whence, from time to time as vessels arrived, we shipped off some of our people.

Nothing can be imagined more harassing and

destructive than this process of embarkation. For example, my people, as before mentioned, were dispersed in all directions round the neighbourhood, even to the distance of six or eight miles, by twos and threes, &c., so that they were under no control whatever. Meantime the guns, ammunition-waggons, &c., all dismounted and ready to put on board, remained exposed to all the weather on the pier. At daylight in the morning, according to orders, men and horses assembled there also, and remained—rain, hail, wind or snow (of all which we had plenty)—until dusk in the evening, when they were permitted to return to their billets for the night. Nothing could be more subversive of discipline and harassing to the men, or more ruinous to the horses; yet, from the system adopted by those who ruled the transport service, it could not well be avoided, since the vessels engaged were all schooners, sloops, &c.; and it was necessary, when any of these returned for a fresh cargo, that the embarkation should be as prompt as possible, not only for the more expeditiously getting the troops across, but because they were obliged to leave the harbour with the same tide, or remain twelve hours. These vessels did not go all to one place; thus my troop was landed by sixes and sevens at

Dover, Sandwich, Deal, Ramsgate, &c., and then assembled at Canterbury. Webber Smith was our immediate commanding officer here ; and Sir Denis Park, who commanded, occasionally rode down to see how things were going on, so that there was no getting out of the way, and our only relief was an occasional stroll about the muddy, dismal streets, lounging in some of the shops, &c. Thus time hung heavily on our hands. Hitchins had left us on the very first evening of our arrival at the Silver Lion, and we sadly missed his kind attentions—especially F., who, whilst I was at the pier, had no one to escort her about, and of course in such a place going alone was out of the question. I found a pleasing companion to while away time at the pier in the harbour-master, an old captain of the French navy, and a well-informed, gentlemanly person, from whom I picked up a good deal of information. I cannot omit noting the fact that a female bookseller here, whose *magazin* we sometimes frequented, one day let out that she implicitly believed every one of the absurd lies respecting England contained in General Pelet's book, and would hardly credit our contradiction of them.

At last our tedious detention came, like all

things else, to a conclusion. Two sloops, capable of containing all the remainder of my troop, came in one evening too late to sail before next morning, and with this last party I decided on embarking. When Angélique heard this she came and begged I would lend her a suit of my plain clothes, as the prefect had prohibited French women going with the English, and had already stopped many. Here was a dilemma. My old Scotch quartermaster, however, got us out of it. I don't know how he passed the gates, but he did manage on the morning of the 25th January 1816 to smuggle Angélique on board before daylight, and conceal her below, without the necessity of changing her female for male attire.

After breakfast we embarked and immediately sailed. Webber Smith went with us, as we were the very last of the Royal Horse-Artillery. The weather was gloomy, cold, and stormy, but the wind was fair, and we were off Dover early in the afternoon. The tide would not admit even our little sloop into this miserable harbour before midnight, and she was hove to almost within speaking distance of the pier-head. Not relishing this position, we were glad to avail ourselves of a pilot-gig that came off and go ashore—although these fellows charged us a guinea a-head for thus carrying us about 200 yards.

After an early dinner at the York Hotel, Smith set off post for Blackheath, where his family was residing.

26th.—To Canterbury. F. and Angélique in a post-chaise, to which I and Milward (carrying his lance) served as an escort, for I had no men to march with.

So ended the memorable campaign of 1815.

THE END.

PRINTED BY WILLIAM BLACKWOOD AND SONS, EDINBURGH.

www.ingramcontent.com/pod-product-compliance
Lightning Source LLC
Chambersburg PA
CBHW071651160426
43195CB00012B/1420